About Island Press

Island Press is the only nonprofit organization in the United States whose principal purpose is the publication of books on environmental issues and natural resource management. We provide solutions-oriented information to professionals, public officials, business and community leaders, and concerned citizens who are shaping responses to environmental problems.

In 2006, Island Press celebrates its twenty-second anniversary as the leading provider of timely and practical books that take a multidisciplinary approach to critical environmental concerns. Our growing list of titles reflects our commitment to bringing the best of an expanding body of literature to the environmental community throughout North America and the world.

Support for Island Press is provided by the Agua Fund, The Geraldine R. Dodge Foundation, Doris Duke Charitable Foundation, The William and Flora Hewlett Foundation, Kendeda Sustainability Fund of the Tides Foundation, Forrest C. Lattner Foundation, The Henry Luce Foundation, The John D. and Catherine T. MacArthur Foundation, The Marisla Foundation, The Andrew W. Mellon Foundation, Gordon and Betty Moore Foundation, The Curtis and Edith Munson Foundation, Oak Foundation, The Overbrook Foundation, The David and Lucile Packard Foundation, The Winslow Foundation, and other generous donors.

The opinions expressed in this book are those of the author(s) and do not necessarily reflect the views of these foundations.

THE ESSENTIAL
Ian McHarg
WRITINGS ON DESIGN AND NATURE

THE ESSENTIAL
Ian McHarg

WRITINGS ON DESIGN AND NATURE

Ian L. McHarg

EDITED BY FREDERICK R. STEINER

ISLANDPRESS

WASHINGTON • COVELO • LONDON

McHarg, Ian L.
  The essential Ian McHarg : writings on design and nature / Ian L. McHarg ; edited by Frederick R. Steiner.
      p. cm.
  Includes bibliographical references and index.
  ISBN-13: 978-1-59726-117-3 (pbk. : alk. paper)
  ISBN-10: 1-59726-117-3 (pbk. : alk. paper)
  1. Landscape architecture. 2. Essays. I. Steiner, Frederick R. II. Title.
  SB472.4.M34 2006
  712.092—dc22

                        2006032460

Printed on recycled, acid-free paper

Manufactured in the United States of America
10 9 8 7 6 5 4 3 2 1

In memory of Ian L. McHarg,
ecological design and planning pioneer

Contents

Chapter 9

Chapter 10

Preface

FREDERICK R. STEINER

Ian McHarg died in March 2001, before the September 11 terrorist attacks, before the Indian Ocean tsunami of December 2004, and before Hurricane Katrina struck the Gulf Coast in August 2005. I believe the September 11 events would have surprised him the most. His optimism grew after the end of the Cold War. He thought we could live in a more peaceful world. We had the opportunity to escape the specter of nuclear war—a threat that, sadly, has returned.

The effects of the tsunami and the hurricane would not have surprised him. After all, McHarg had long preached that we should design with nature. A chapter of his seminal book with that title was devoted to the topic, "Sea and Survival." About hurricanes and their threat to coastal development, McHarg wrote four decades ago, "The evidence is there to be read. The record of cause and effect constitutes the common knowledge of natural scientists. But the status quo ante is being reconstituted without direction or constraint....We hope for the best, but it would be sanguine to expect anything less than disaster." [1]

Ian McHarg opened a new way for us to see the world. His approach for interpreting the play between natural and cultural systems has become the dominant visualization technology of our time, just as Brunelleschi's experiments with linear perspective dominated architectural visualization for 600 years. Ian McHarg provided a roadmap for applying ecological information to how we interpret, plan, and shape our surroundings. This became his quest, his principal contribution. I will summarize McHarg's life, then illustrate how his ideas remain timely.

Nature's Design

Ian Lennox McHarg (1920–2001) experienced the transition between adolescence and manhood as a warrior. He entered World War II as a lanky teenage private. He left military service after the war as a confident major in command of one of Britain's most elite combat units. Before the war, he was a child of the

Great Depression in industrial Glasgow, Scotland. After the war, Ian McHarg, "The Major" as he was called then, marinated in modernism at Harvard.

He left Harvard with the intent to help rebuild his war-ravaged homeland. McHarg worked on housing and new town programs in Scotland and experienced a near-deadly bout with tuberculosis before Dean G. Holmes Perkins enticed him to build a new graduate program in landscape architecture at the University of Pennsylvania. There, McHarg fused his desire to practice with a newfound love for teaching.

His most important contributions derived from this reflective academic practice. At first, this practice was grounded in the modernist principles McHarg had learned at Harvard. Influenced by his mentor, Lewis Mumford, McHarg began to move away from the aesthetic dogma of the international style. He grew highly skeptical of the one-size-fits-all stylistic palette of modernism, instead remaining committed to the *ideals* of modernism. Specifically, he believed knowledge should guide action. Furthermore, this action would result in better housing, more open space, more efficient transportation systems, and, in the end, healthier and safer communities.

He explored these ideals through the design studios at Penn and through his growing practice. For many years the boundaries between the Department of Landscape Architecture, then the Department of Landscape Architecture and Regional Planning, and his consulting practice—Wallace and McHarg Associates, later Wallace, McHarg, Roberts and Todd—blurred. Both the academic department and the firm engaged in action research, advancing several disciplines and professions. This work represented a meaningful dialogue between the academy and professional practice. A synthesis of this dialogue is provided in *Design with Nature*.[2] Although this clarion call presents insightful case studies, it also advances a new theory for design and a new mandate for public policy. What are the origins of his ecologically based theory?

Again, it came both from within the academy and from experience. From the early 1960s on, Ian McHarg became a public personality. He hosted his own high-profile CBS talk show and later narrated a popular PBS documentary. Ian McHarg served on several important commissions and panels, including the influential 1966 White House Commission on Conservation and Natural Beauty. In the process, he befriended Lady Bird Johnson, Stewart Udall, and Laurance Rockefeller, among others.

His early-1960s CBS television show *The House We Live In* emerged from, and then informed, his teaching and, in turn, put forth the theory developed in *Design with Nature*. For twenty-six Sundays in 1960 and 1961, Ian McHarg invited the leading theologians and scientists of the day to discuss our place in the world on network TV. He had initiated this format in his "Man and Environment" course at Penn in 1959. Leading scholars were invited to discuss values and ethics, entropy, the universe, evolution, and plate tectonics in the

classroom and on television. His razor wit, intelligence, and relevance attracted students and TV viewers alike.

Through the 1960s and into the 1970s, "Man and Environment" was the
most popular course on the Penn campus, and it alone changed many lives. I
have a colleague who was a Wharton Business School undergraduate when he
took "Man and Environment." He promptly transferred from finance to
hydrology, eventually earning a Ph.D. and becoming a significant environmental planner. Ian McHarg's growing academic following and environmental activism coalesced during Earth Week in April 1970. McHarg and his students led the events of that week in Philadelphia. Across the nation, other
faculty and students organized similar events. For example, I was the co-chair
of the student-led Earth Day events at the University of Cincinnati. Our activities included a book fair. There were few environmental books then. The one
with the word *Design* on the front cover and the Whole Earth from space on
the back stood out to those of us studying landscape architecture, architecture, planning, and design. Over the next couple of decades, many of us
flocked to Penn. Many more read *Design with Nature.*

Nothing is as practical as a good theory. The dictum "design with nature"
not only changed design and planning but also influenced fields as diverse as
geography and engineering, forestry and environmental ethics, soil science
and ecology. The evidence is ubiquitous: Almost every geographic information system (GIS) presentation begins with a depiction of a layer cake,
although rarely crediting McHarg and often without his eloquence or insight
into how the data should be collected and analyzed. Environmental impact
assessment, new community development, coastal zone management,
brownfield restoration, zoo design, river corridor planning, and ideas about
sustainability and regenerative design all reveal the influence of *Design with
Nature.*

However, Ian McHarg's theoretical and practical contributions extend
beyond this important book. Two other topics occupied much of his energy
in the decades after the initial Earth Day. First, he sought to advance the
understanding of the ecology of our own species. Second, he advocated the
extension of his theoretical framework to the national and global scales.

Humans are as ecological as any other species. We relate with one another
and with our physical and biological environments. Like other organisms, our
species is part of the web of life. The challenge is to see ourselves as part of that
web. According to Alexander Caragonne, "Like the fish that swim in the seas,
we are apparently oblivious to and incapable of describing either the nature or
extent of the medium we inhabit."[3]

Ian McHarg recognized the need for us to understand the medium we
inhabit and how we shape it and it us. He sought support from National Institute of Mental Health (NIMH) to address this topic, writing, "My colleagues

and I had concluded that geomorphology synthesized physical processes and that ecology synthesized both physical and biological processes. How could we extend this model to include people?"[4]

He turned to the science of anthropology for the answer. As he had recruited geologists and ecologists to his landscape architecture department beginning in the 1960s, he added anthropologists and ethnographers in the 1970s. These colleagues taught us that culture is our most important instrument of adaptation. Furthermore, our ability to evolve our culture distinguishes us from other species. Design and planning can then be viewed as adaptive mechanisms, that is, tools for resilience. Adaptation and resilience are related to our health, which has been defined by the World Health Organization as the ability to recover from disease, injury, or insult.

Ian McHarg generated big ideas. As he witnessed the growing application of those ideas through GIS and visualization technologies, he realized that they could be used at the national and even global scales. In the early 1990s, McHarg and several colleagues produced a prototype database for a national ecological inventory. Then–U.S. Environmental Protection Agency (EPA) administrator (and McHarg admirer) Bill Reilly commissioned the study, and the prototype was submitted to EPA in 1992.

McHarg and his team proposed an extensive inventory at three scales—national, regional, and local—including information about the physical oceanography (where applicable), climate, geology, geomorphology, physiography, hydrology, soils, vegetation, limnology, marine biology, wildlife, and land use. They urged that chronology be used as "the unifying rubric." In his autobiography *A Quest for Life*, McHarg states, "We observed that the greatest problem lies not with data, but with integration."[5] A decade later, the greatest problem remains integration.

In the final decade of his life, McHarg advocated this national ecological inventory for the United States and other nations, and he also believed the approach could and should be expanded to the planet. Actually, this global view was deeply rooted in Ian's philosophy. For example, as early as 1968, he wrote, "We must see nature as a process within which man exists, splendidly equipped to become the manager of the biosphere."[6] He called this global responsibility our greatest role. If we agree, then how do we fulfill our greatest role?

Drivers of Landscape Change

Ian McHarg's ideas about ecologically based design, human ecology, and national and global environmental inventories remain crucial for our futures. Let us look at some global drivers of landscape change and the consequences of those changes to illustrate the urgency of McHarg's vision.

Change doesn't just happen. A variety of economic, social, and technological forces drive change. What drivers of change influence landscapes around the world? A few probable drivers are

- Population dynamics and consumption
- Urbanization
- Global and regional environmental processes

Population growth and migration include the factors that will change the demographic structure of the planet. At the beginning of the twentieth century, there were 2 billion people in the world. Now, more than 6 billion people inhabit the planet. The United Nations projects the world's population to plateau at 9.4 billion by the year 2050, then creep up to 10.4 billion by 2100.[7] This translates into some 12.6 billion more people joining us over the next century.[8] We live in the first urban century. For the first time in human history, half of the world's population lives in metropolitan regions. In the future, even more people will live in cities. Global urban populations are expected to double by 2030.[9] By 2050, two thirds of the people in the world will be living in urban regions.

Population growth drives change because everyone needs water, food, shelter, clothing, and energy. However, levels of consumption vary. The United Nations notes that globalization tends to separate the costs from the benefits because "consumers derive goods and services from ecosystems around the world....This tends to hide the environmental costs of increased consumption from those doing the consuming."[10] Our desires to consume the basics and amenities of life affect the level of resources necessary to fulfill those demands, our ecological footprints, and the character of living landscapes that provide the sources and the sinks for those resources.

Population changes—such as growth and migration—and consumption are related to urbanization. The movement of people to cities and metropolitan regions involves the transformation of spaces from rural and natural to urban and suburban, the urbanization of the wild, the abandonment of the rural, and the recovery of the core city and older suburban neighborhoods. Here are some key questions related to both population growth and urbanization:

- Why do people choose to live where they do?
- What policies direct and affect growth and development?
- What are the long-term impacts of these policies?
- What knowledge is necessary to inform interventions designed to mitigate those impacts?

Global environmental processes also drive landscape changes and adaptations. Global warming trends are well known.[11] These changes already influence the life cycles of many species. For example, polar bears in the Arctic normally spend much of the year on the ice bulking up on enough fish to allow them to survive winter hibernation. As the winter seasons shrink and the bears are forced to spend more time on land, they have less time to build their body weight. The health of the species becomes threatened when smaller cubs are born to mothers who have less time to look after their young because of their need for food.

In Costa Rica, the rain forest islands around mountaintops dwindle annually, with less and less cloud cover to support moisture-dependent species. These habitats occur where condensation occurs, which is the top of mountains, where the air cools enough to produce clouds. As the climate warms, the temperature gradient rises up the mountain, diminishing the cloud habitat and effectively trapping the flora and fauna into extinction (such species cannot go down the mountain because it is too warm for them, nor can they "leap" to another, perhaps taller mountain). It is a dead end for them.

Additional environmental drivers of change influencing the global commons and, to varying degrees, specific regions and landscapes include natural disasters (which create more refugees than wars), water quality and quantity, the nitrogen cycle, energy uses, and greenhouse effects. As we learn more about these drivers, we can connect them to change occurring in urban, rural, and wilderness landscapes.

Consequences of Landscape Change

The consequences of landscape change are all around us. A few changes evident in our daily lives include suburban sprawl, the conversion of prime farmlands to other uses, the decline of biodiversity and cultural diversity, social inequity, urban heat island effects, and our health.

Suburban sprawl is dispersed, automobile-dependent development outside compact urban and town centers, along highways, and in the rural countryside. Such development consumes more land, water, and energy than more traditional settlement patterns. Sprawl fragments open space and tends to be homogeneous in appearance.

Sprawl consumes about 365 acres of American countryside every hour. Across the nation, the amount of developed land is growing faster than the population. For example, between 1960 and 1990, metropolitan area population grew by 50 percent while the acreage of developed land increased by 100 percent.[12] The Chicago metropolitan region now covers more than 3,800 square miles. Between 1990 and 2000, the population of the region grew by only 4 percent, but land occupied by housing increased by 46 percent and commercial uses by 74 percent.[13] Meadows and forests are converted to strip malls and subdivisions that serve cars better than people.

Suburban sprawl consumes significant amounts of prime farmland. According to the U.S. Department of Agriculture's National Resources Inventory, an average of 105 acres of farmland was converted to nonagricultural use every hour each year between 1982 and 1992. In California's Central Valley region alone, 15,000 acres of farmland are developed each year. That area produces 10 percent of the value of U.S. farm output on less than 1 percent of the nation's farmland.[14]

Farmlands produce more than food; farms also contribute to our quality of life. Agricultural land uses create diverse landscapes, which are aesthetically pleasing to urban and rural neighbors. They add to the culture and traditions of places that provide character for metropolitan regions. Agriculture creates social opportunities in that farm families have historically provided pools of civic leadership for many communities. Roughly one fifth of the nation's 250 million acres of prime agricultural land can be considered at risk for development because it is within 50 miles of the 100 largest cities in the nation.[15] We depend on that land for much of our food and clothing.

Our current growth patterns also affect other species. Biodiversity is the variety of life and its processes, which includes the abundance of living organisms, their genetic diversity, and the communities and ecosystems in which they live. Ill-planned development, poor land use decisions, and bad land management policies often are incompatible with existing natural habitats.[16] Farm and forest lands, threatened by suburban sprawl, can contribute to biodiversity by providing habitat for a variety of wildlife, including rare and endangered species. Large, unfragmented tracts of farm and forest lands and forest corridors allow interaction and crossbreeding between population groups of the same species, which increase population health and genetic viability.[17]

According to the Environmental Law Institute, the "primary cause of biodiversity loss in the United States is habitat destruction and degradation, followed by competition with or predation by non-native invasive species."[18] Furthermore, the Environmental Law Institute identifies the main causes of habitat destruction and fragmentation as "land conversion for development, road building, water development, outdoor recreation, agriculture, and resource extraction or harvest (e.g., mining and logging)."[19] Intervention in natural processes, such as forest fires and flooding, can negatively influence biodiversity, too. Such activities and processes are best understood through the landscape perspective pioneered by Ian McHarg.

Current patterns of suburban sprawl also exacerbate social inequities in the United States. As growth and prosperity occur at the fringes of metropolitan regions, central cities and inner, older suburbs experience a declining tax base and increasingly concentrated poverty. For example, residents of inner-city neighborhoods are more than twice as likely to live in poverty than their suburban counterparts in the United States.[20] Poverty is especially pronounced in minority communities because African Americans and Latinos have poverty rates nearly three times as high as white Americans.[21]

The group PolicyLink notes, "As critical services such as public schools in older communities erode because of declining tax bases, and employment opportunities, including entry-level jobs, move away from urban centers, low-income residents are increasingly challenged in gaining access. For example, the City of Cleveland contains 80 percent of the metropolitan area's African-American poor while 80 percent of the entry-level jobs are in the suburbs."[22]

As metropolitan regions grow, the local climate changes because of the urban heat island, or heat archipelago, effect. This effect involves the additional heating of the air over urban settlements as a result of the replacement of naturally vegetated surfaces with those composed of asphalt, concrete, rooftops, and other human-made materials. For example, between 1970 and 1990, summer nighttime average temperatures in the Phoenix metropolitan region increased by 2.2°C, and by 6°C between rural desert and inner urban locations.[23] And central Arizona urban and suburban temperatures continue to rise.[24]

Black asphalt is an especially important urban heat island culprit. Albedo is the ratio of light reflectivity to incoming light. We use albedo to assess the absorption and subsequent heating of different surfaces. Thermal admittance is another surface characteristic that determines net heat storage and resultant energy flow over a surface. Surfaces with lower albedos and higher thermal admittances, such as black asphalt, are warmer than those with higher albedos, if not mitigated by other microclimate factors such as evaporation.

As cities and suburbs get hotter, we grow fatter. According to the Centers for Disease Control and Prevention (CDC), some 60 percent of Americans are overweight and at least 18 percent obese. The lack of walking opportunities and the easy access to fast food are two contributing factors. Thus, the design and planning of our surroundings, our landscapes, are a public health issue. Most American cities lack safe and accessible sidewalks, crosswalks, and bike paths. Transportation alternatives are limited, with little pedestrian access to buses and transit systems. Parks and recreation facilities are unsafe, ugly, and not accessible. Shopping and services cannot be accessed without automobiles.[25]

We need to see the connection between obesity and our health in general and the design of our built environments. As Dr. Richard Joseph Jackson, formerly of the CDC, observed in an article titled "What Olmsted Knew,"

Medicine will not be adequate to deal with the health challenges of the 21st century, not even with the help of the sequenced genome and advances in robotic surgery. Even though the United States spends one of every seven dollars on medical care, we will not significantly improve health and the quality of life unless we pay more attention to how we design our living environments. Healthy living environments include not just a clean and heated kitchen, bath, or bedroom, but also the landscape around us. Health for all, especially for the young, aging, poor and disabled, requires that we design healthfulness into our environments as well.[26]

To summarize, we are losing our best farmland, and other species' habitats are disappearing. Meanwhile, the gaps between rich and poor are widening. Urban and suburban places are heating up, and our waistlines are expanding.

Toward a Science and an Art of Landscape Intervention

Each of these consequences can be addressed through design and planning interventions championed by Ian McHarg. In 1967, McHarg initiated a scientific approach for landscape intervention grounded in design after obtaining funding from the Ford Foundation to recruit a faculty of natural scientists into his department at Penn to "integrate their perceptions into a holistic discipline applied to the solution of contemporary problems."[27] As previously noted, he broadened this approach to encompass human ecology because of NIMH support in the 1970s. The notion that one can practice landscape architecture and planning by integrating the views of soil scientists, hydrologists, ecologists, climatologists, ethnographers, and other scientists echoes the multilayered view of geography that McHarg did much to popularize with his *Design with Nature*. This approach has contributed to the creation of many environmental policies and programs.

McHarg grounded his approach to landscape intervention in ecology. He argued that ecology should inform the schemes of designers and planners by helping them to understand interactions between natural phenomena and landscape patterns. His approach is based on collecting data in a chronological order; that is, regional climate helps shape the geology of a place, which in turn affects other abiotic processes such as physiography and hydrology that influence specific soils and microclimates. These abiotic processes come together in combinations that provide niches for plant and animal communities. McHarg suggested that information about these processes can be mapped and overlaid in what he called a layer cake model. The model could be used to determine opportunities and constraints for potential land uses. As a result, the suitability of land uses could be presented to local decision makers.

The multilayered model that McHarg experimented with, initially using transparent overlays, has evolved through GIS technology. GISs and other new technologies give landscape architects, city planners, architects, engineers, and others the ability to intervene in landscapes to address the pressing issues facing communities and regions. For instance, to ameliorate urban heat island effects, the amount of black asphalt should be reduced in streets and parking lots, more shade should be created, and more trees and other plants should be added to urban environments. GISs and visualization programs present tools for planning where such interventions would have the most positive impacts.

Another illustration of how landscape intervention can improve our cities is the creation of more healthful, walkable communities to reduce our weight and to keep us in shape. The executive vice president of the American Society of Landscape Architects, Nancy Somerville, has identified four elements of such communities:

- Safe and accessible sidewalks, crosswalks, and bike paths
- Transportation alternatives, with pedestrian access to buses and transit systems
- Safe, attractive, and convenient parks and recreation facilities
- Shopping and services that can be accessed without automobiles[28]

GISs can enable designers and planners to locate and reconfigure transportation systems accordingly. In addition, visualization technologies help architects, landscape architects, and planners to show how these changes will look in neighborhoods and shopping areas.

We need to focus on the nature of cities, our most significant human ecosystem. Landscapes provide an ideal framework for urban intervention because they represent a synthesis of natural and cultural features. Each landscape is distinguished from others as a result of its unique combination of natural and cultural characteristics.

We know more about our planet than at any time in our history. We can watch hurricanes move through the Caribbean (or troops march across the Iraqi desert) in real time on CNN or al-Jazeera. The National Aeronautics and Space Administration offers its own station with endless Earth views, and we can use Google to find maps and aerial photographs for most places on our planet. We are connected to one another and to vast amounts of information about practically everything through the Internet. Science continues to advance our understanding of land and sea. We have created an informational central nervous system for the planet, but this system lacks a brain. What good is all this information if we don't use it to improve our planet for future generations? The challenges we face require that we pursue and advance the vision Ian McHarg provided.

Through the dual lens of nature and culture, we can begin to use our increased knowledge about our surroundings to take the actions necessary to halt suburban sprawl, to protect prime farmlands and environmentally sensitive areas, to redirect development and investment to existing cities, and to green those cities and reduce the urban heat island in the process. We need to design with nature to heal the earth.

As Ian McHarg observed, "Let us plan to save lives, to protect the environment, to achieve savings from appropriate ecological planning, to improve prediction and placement, and to improve the human condition."[29]

Ian and I enjoyed preparing *To Heal the Earth*, the comprehensive collection of his writings, from which this selection is drawn. For that book I presented possible publications to include, and he approved or suggested alternatives. I wrote introductions for each of Ian's publications and the essays beginning the five parts. We met in Philadelphia and Tempe, Arizona, several times to discuss what I had written. He provided additional insights and suggestions. Island Press and I selected essays from *To Heal the Earth* for *The Essential Ian McHarg*.

Ian died on March 5, 2001, of pulmonary disease. He was 80 years old. From an American Planning Association Conference in New Orleans, I flew to Pennsylvania for the service at a Quaker meeting house in Chester County on March 10. A gigantic oak towers over the entry. He and I visited the meeting house while we were editing *To Heal the Earth*. I mentioned that my mother's family were Quakers and had first immigrated to Chester County before moving to Philadelphia. I wondered aloud whether this was their meeting house. Ian remarked that he hoped it was.

The March landscape of Pennsylvania wages war on itself. Restless life engages this seasonal transition. A sunny day of crocus blooms yields to the undulating dustings of snow. Blistering winds of change rattle the naked branches of our souls. We long for warmth, for days when the songbirds will return from their winter roosts. These March days are unresolved, challenging, yet brimming with optimism.

Ian McHarg resembled such a Pennsylvania March: fighting to change himself, motivating us to change ourselves and everything around us. He hailed from the rocky coast of Scotland, where the city met the countryside, and he spent much of his life in other ecotones.

As he changed from Presbyterian to Quaker, from soldier to scholar, from the Old World to the New, from Harvard to Penn, from site-level concerns to regional and global visions, several characteristics held firm: the irreverence and the generosity, the humor and the leadership, the broad knowledge of science and art, the love of jazz, the ability to spin a yarn and captivate an audience.

Ian McHarg established new territories for his twin disciplines of landscape architecture and planning. He altered their flow: how the fields are perceived by others, how practitioners view themselves. His influence transcends landscape architecture and planning. Architects and ecologists, geologists and foresters, soil conservationists and artists heard his summons and altered their thinking as a result. Ian was a public figure who chatted with talk show hosts and debated the origins of the universe and meaning of life with rabbis and Jesuits on national television broadcasts. He walked with presidents and Hopi elders, with Lady Bird Johnson and Andy Warhol, with physicists and hippies.

In his essay "Walking," Henry David Thoreau observed, "Genius is a light which makes the darkness visible, like the lightning's flash, which perchance shatters the temple of knowledge itself."

Ian McHarg's life's work marked a watershed. Those of us who pursue the same calling cannot return; we can only purl one way or another. We can chart the courses of those streams and establish new directions through the works of our lives. Even so, the tug of nature, of our own human nature, will pull at our feet with the full power of gravity. We can confront nature, our nature, and even conspire with it, but we cannot trump nature's design. Perhaps we can do our best by attempting to be good humans within that design. We should seek to do no harm, to celebrate and advance beauty.

We are linked to something larger, but we are also what we make ourselves to be. We become the shadows of our aspirations. We become who we present ourselves to be. Ian chose a big role. We should all have such courage.

Acknowledgments

This preface is adapted from remarks I first gave on the occasion of an Earth Day tree planting on the U.S. Capitol Grounds honoring Ian McHarg on April 22, 2003. The remarks were expanded for a commentary for *Philosophy & Geography* (Volume 7, Number 1, February 2004, pp. 141–149). Additional portions have been adapted from a remembrance I wrote in *Landscape Journal* (Volume 20, Number 1, 2001, p. vi).

Notes

1. Ian L. McHarg, *Design with Nature.* Garden City, New York: Natural History Press/Doubleday, 1969, p. 17.
2. Ibid.
3. Alexander Caragonne, *The Texas Rangers from an Architectural Underground.* Cambridge, Massachusetts: MIT Press, 1995, p. 150.
4. Ian L. McHarg, *A Quest for Life: An Autobiography.* New York: Wiley, 1996, p. 269.

5. Ibid., p. 363.
6. Ian L. McHarg and Frederick R. Steiner, eds., *To Heal the Earth: Selected Writings of Ian L. McHarg.* Washington, D.C.: Island Press, 1998, 71. Originally published as Ian L. McHarg, "Values, Process and Form", in The Smithsonian Institution, ed., *The Fitness of Man's Environment*, ed., New York: Harper and Row, 1968.
7. Gary W. Barrett and Eugene P. Odum, "The Twenty-First Century: The World at Carrying Capacity," *BioScience*, 50, no. 4 (2000): 363–368, and United Nations, *World Population Prospects: The 1996 Revisions.* New York: The United Nations, 1998.
8. Steward Brand, *The Clock of the Long Now.* New York: Basic Books, 1999.
9. United Nations Development Programme, United Nations Environment Program, World Bank, and World Resources Institute, *World Resources 2001–2002, People and Ecosystems, The Fraying Web of Life.* Amsterdam: Elsevier, 2000.
10. Ibid., p. 23.
11. Paul Harrison and Fred Pearce, *AAA Atlas of Population and Environment.* Berkeley: University of California Press, 2000.
12. U.S. Secretary of Agriculture, *Maintaining Farm and Forest Lands in Rapidly Growing Areas.* Washington, D.C.: U.S. Department of Agriculture, 2001.
13. Ibid.
14. Ibid.
15. Ibid.
16. Environmental Law Institute, *Planning with Nature: Biodiversity Information in Action.* Washington, D.C.: Environmental Law Institute, 2003.
17. U.S. Secretary of Agriculture, *Maintaining Farm and Forest Lands.*
18. Environmental Law Institute, *Planning with Nature*, p. 3.
19. Ibid.
20. PolicyLink, *Promoting Regional Equity.* Miami, Florida: Funders' Network for Smart Growth and Livable Communities, 2002.
21. Institute on Race and Policy, *Racism and Metropolitan Dynamics: The Civil Rights Challenge of the 21st Century.* Minneapolis: Institute on Race and Policy, 2002.
22. PolicyLink, *Promoting Regional Equity*, p. 5.
23. Anthony Brazel, Nancy Selover, Russell Vose, and Gordon Heisler, "The Tale of Two Climates: Baltimore and Phoenix LTER Sites," *Climate Research*, 15 (2000): 123–135.
24. L.1 A. Baker, A. J. Brazel, N. Selover, C. Martin, N. McIntyre, F. R. Steiner, A. Nelson, and L. Musacchio, "Urbanization and Warming of Phoenix (Arizona, USA): Impacts, Feedbacks and Mitigation," *Urban Ecosystems*, 6, no. 3 (2002): 188–203.
25. Howard Frumkin, "Urban Sprawl and Public Health," *Public Health Reports*, 117 (May–June 2002): 201–217.
26. Richard Joseph Jackson, "What Olmsted Knew," *Western City* (March 2001): 1.

27. McHarg, *A Quest for Life*, p. 192.
28. Nancy C. Somerville, "Message from the Executive Vice President," *Land Online* (March 3). Available at http://host.asla.org/land/2002/0308/vp message.html
29. McHarg and Steiner, *To Heal the Earth*, p. 71. Originally published as Ian L. McHarg, "Natural Factors in Planning," *Journal of Soil and Water Conservation*, 52, no. 1 (1997): 13–17.

1

Man and Environment (1963)

Ian McHarg considered the writing of this paper, published in The Urban Condition *edited by Leonard Duhl, as "a threshold in my professional life and . . . the first summation of my perceptions and intentions." It began when McHarg was invited by Duhl to join his Committee on Environmental Variables and Mental Health. Duhl, a medical doctor, was director of research for the National Institute of Mental Health. He selected the members of the committee, which included Herbert Gans, J. B. Jackson, and Melvin Webber.*

For McHarg the paper represented a "tremendous leap in scale." He changed his focus from small-scale urban concerns to a larger regional vision. He wrote "Man and Environment" at the time when he was organizing his The House We Live In *television program for CBS. The influence of the guests from that program is evident in this paper. Not only did the scale of McHarg's concerns change, but also the nature of his audience. Prior to 1962, his lectures outside of Penn had been limited to state associations of garden clubs, where he agreed to devote half his speech to garden design history if he could spend the other half speaking about the environment. This paper is a "coming out," where the half garden designer is shed for the complete environmentalist. It was, according to McHarg, "my most embracing address on the subject of the environment to that point."*

The nature and scale of this enquiry can be simply introduced through an image conceived by Loren Eiseley. Man, far out in space, looks back to the distant earth, a celestial orb, blue-green oceans, green of verdant land, a celestial fruit. Examination discloses blemishes on the fruit, dispersed circles from which extend dynamic tentacles. The man concludes that these cankers are the works of man and asks, "Is man but a planetary disease?"

There are at least two conceptions within this image. Perhaps the most important is the view of a unity of life covering the earth, land and oceans, interacting as a single superorganism, the biosphere. A direct analogy can be found in man, composed of billion upon billion of cells, but all of these operating as a single organism. From this the full relevance of the second conception emerges, the possibility that man is but a dispersed disease in the world-life body.

The conception of all life interacting as a single superorganism is as novel as is the conception of man as a planetary disease. The suggestion of man the destroyer, or rather brain the destroyer, is salutary to society which has traditionally abstracted brain from body, man from nature, and vaunted the rational process. This, too, is a recent view. Yet the problems are only of yesterday. Pre-atomic man was an inconsequential geological, biological, and ecological force; his major power was the threat of power. Now, in an instant, post-atomic man is the agent of evolutionary regression, a species now empowered to destroy all life.

In the history of human development, man has long been puny in the face of overwhelmingly powerful nature. His religions, philosophies, ethics, and acts have tended to reflect a slave mentality, alternately submissive or arrogant toward nature. Judaism, Christianity, Humanism tend to assert outrageously the separateness and dominance of man over nature, while animism and nature worship tend to assert total submission to an arbitrary nature. These attitudes are not urgent when human societies lack the power to make any serious impact on environment. These same attitudes become of first importance when man holds the power to cause evolutionary regressions of unimaginable effect or even to destroy all life.

Modern man is confronted with the awful problem of comprehending the role of man in nature. He must immediately find a *modus vivendi*, he must seek beyond for his role in nature, a role of unlimited potential yet governed by laws which he shares with all physical and organic systems. The primacy of man today is based more upon his power to destroy than to create. He is like an aboriginal, confronted with the necessity of operating a vast and complex machine, whose only tool is a hammer. Can modern man aspire to the role of agent in creation, creative participant in a total, unitary, evolving environment? If the pre-atomic past is dominated by the refinement of concern for man's acts towards man, the inauguration of the atomic age increases the dimension of this ancient concern and now adds the new and urgent necessity of understanding and resolving the interdependence of man and nature.

While the atomic threat overwhelms all other considerations, this is by no means the only specter. The population implosion may well be as cataclysmic as the nuclear explosion. Should both of these threats be averted there remain the lesser processes of destruction which have gathered momentum since the nineteenth century. In this period we have seen the despoliation of continental resources accumulated over aeons of geological time, primeval forests destroyed, ancient resources of soil mined and sped to the sea, marching deserts, great deposits of fossil fuel dissipated into the atmosphere. In the country, man has ravaged nature; in the city, nature has been erased and man assaults man with insalubrity, ugliness, and disorder. In short, man has evolved and proliferated by exploiting historic accumulations of inert and organic resources, historic climaxes of plants and animals. His products are reserved for himself, his mark on the environment is most often despoliation and wreckage.

The Duality of Man and Nature

Conceptions of man and nature range between two wide extremes. The first, central to the Western tradition, is man-oriented. The cosmos is but a pyramid erected to support man on its pinnacle, reality exists only because man can observe it, indeed God is made in the image of man. The opposing view, identified with the Orient, postulates a unitary and all-encompassing nature within which man exists, man in nature.

These opposing views are the central duality, man and nature, West and East, white and black, brains and testicles, Classicism and Romanticism, orthodoxy and transnaturalism in Judaism, St. Thomas and St. Francis, Calvin and Luther, anthropomorphism and naturalism. The Western tradition vaunts the individual and the man-brain, and denigrates nature, animal, non-brain. In the Orient nature is omnipotent, revered, and man is but an aspect of nature. It would be as unwise to deny the affirmative aspects of either view as to diminish their negative effects. Yet today this duality demands urgent attention. The adequacy of the Western view of man and nature deserves to be questioned. Further, one must ask if these two views are mutually exclusive.

The opposition of these attitudes is itself testimony to an underlying unity, the unity of opposites. Do our defining skin and nerve ends divide us from environment or unite us to it? Is the perfectibility of man self-realizable? Is the earth a storeroom awaiting plunder? Is the cosmos a pyramid erected to support man?

The inheritors of the Judaic-Christian-Humanist tradition have received their injunction from Genesis, a man-oriented universe, man exclusively made in the image of God, given dominion over all life and non-life, enjoined to subdue the earth. The naturalist tradition in the West has no comparable identifiable text. It may be described as holding that the cosmos is unitary, that all systems are subject to common physical laws yet having unlimited potential; that in this world man is simply an inhabitant, free to develop his own potential. This view questions anthropocentrism and anthropomorphism; it does not diminish either man's uniqueness or his potential, only his claims to primacy and exclusive divinity. This view assumes that the precursor of man, plant and animal, his co-tenant contemporaries, share a cosmic role and potential.

From its origin in Judaism, extension in Classicism, reinforcement in Christianity, inflation in the Renaissance, and absorption into the nineteenth and twentieth centuries, the anthropomorphic-anthropocentric view has become the tacit view of man versus nature.

Evolution of Power

The primate precursors of man, like their contemporary descendants, support neither a notably constructive, nor a notably destructive role in their ecological community. The primates live within a complex community which has continued to exist; no deleterious changes can be attributed to the primate nor does his existence appear to be essential for the support of his niche and habitat. When the primates abandoned instinct for reason and man emerged, new patterns of behavior emerged and new techniques were developed. Man acquired powers which increased his negative and destructive effect upon environment, but which left unchanged the possibility of a creative role in the environment. Aboriginal peoples survive today: Australian aborigines, Dravidians and Birbory in India, South African Bushmen, Veda in Ceylon, Ainu in Japan, Indians of Tierra del Fuego; none of these play a significantly destructive role in the environment. Hunters, primitive farmers, fishermen—their ecological role has changed little from that of the primate. Yet from aboriginal people there developed several new techniques which gave man a significantly destructive role within his environment. The prime destructive human tool was fire. The consequences of fire, originated by man, upon the ecology of the world cannot be measured, but there is reason to believe that its significance was very great indeed.

Perhaps the next most important device was that of animal husbandry, the domestication of grazing animals. These sheep, goats, and cattle, have been very significant agents historically in modifying the ecology in large areas of the world. This modification is uniformly deleterious to the original environment. Deforestation is perhaps the third human system which has made considerable impact upon the physical environment. Whether involuntary, that is, as an unconscious product of fire, or as a consequence of goat and sheep herding, or as an economic policy, this process of razing forests has wrought great changes upon climate and microclimate, flora and fauna. However, the regenerative powers of nature are great; and while fire, domestic animals, and deforestation have denuded great areas of world surface, this retrogression can often be minimized or reversed by the natural processes of regeneration. Perhaps the next consequential act of man in modifying the natural environment was large-scale agriculture. We know that in many areas of the world agriculture can be sustained for many centuries without depletion of the soil. Man can create a new ecology in which he is the prime agent, in which the original ecological community has been changed, but which is nevertheless self-perpetuating. This condition is the exception. More typically agriculture has been, and is today, an extractive process in which the soil is mined and left depleted. Many areas of the world, once productive, are no longer capable of producing crops. Extractive agriculture has been historically a retrogressive process sustained by man.

The next important agent for modifying the physical environment is the human settlement: hamlet, village, town, city. It is hard to believe that any of the pre-classical, medieval, Renaissance, or even eighteenth-century cities were able to achieve a transformation of the physical environment comparable to the agents mentioned before—fire, animal husbandry, deforestation, or extensive agriculture. But with the emergence of the nineteenth-century industrial city, there arose an agent certainly of comparable consequence, perhaps even of greater consequence, even more destructive of the physical environment and the balances of ecological communities in which man exists, than any of the prior human processes.

The large modern metropolis may be thirty miles in diameter. Much, if not all, of the land which it covers is sterilized. The micro-organisms in the soil no longer exist; the original animal inhabitants have largely been banished. Only a few members of the plant kingdom represent the original members of the initial ecology. The rivers are foul; the atmosphere is polluted; the original configuration of the land is only rarely in evidence; climate and microclimate have retrogressed so that the external microclimate is more violent than was the case before the establishment of the city. Atmospheric pollution may be so severe as to account for 4,000 deaths in a single week of intense "fog," as was the case in London. Floods alternate with drought. Hydrocarbons, lead, carcinogenic agents, carbon dioxide, carbon monoxide concentrations, deteriorating conditions of atmospheric electricity—all of these represent retrogressive processes introduced and supported by man. The epidemiologist speaks of neuroses, lung cancer, heart and renal disease, ulcers, the stress diseases, as the badges of urban conditions. There has also arisen the specter of the effects of density and social pressure upon the incidence of disease and upon reproduction. The modern city contains other life-inhibiting aspects whose effects are present but which are difficult to measure: disorder, squalor, ugliness, noise.

In its effect upon the atmosphere, soil as a living process, the water cycle, climate and micro-climate, the modern city represents a transformation of the original physical environment certainly greater over the area of the city than the changes achieved by earlier man through fire, animal husbandry, deforestation, and extensive agriculture.

Indeed, one can certainly say that the city is at least an ecological regression, although as a human institution it may represent a triumph. Whatever triumphs there are to be seen in the modern city as an institution, it is only with great difficulty that one can see any vestige of triumph in the modern city as a physical environment. One might ask of the modern city that it be humane; that is, capable of supporting human organisms. This might well be a minimum requirement. In order for this term to be fully appropriate—that is, that the city be compassionate and elevating—it should not only be able to support physiological man, but also should give meaning and expression to man as an individual and as a member of an urban society. I contend that far from meeting the full requirements of this criterion, the modern city inhibits life, that it inhibits man as an organism, man as a social being, man as a spiritual being, and that it does not even offer adequate minimum conditions for physiological man; that indeed the modern city offers the least humane physical environment known to history.

Assuredly, the last and most awful agent held by man to modify the physical environment is atomic power. Here we find post-atomic man able to cause evolutionary regressions of unimaginable effect and even able to destroy all life. In this, man holds the ultimate destructive weapon; with this, he can become the agent of destruction in the ecological community, of all communities, of all life. For any ecological community to survive, no single member can support a destructive role. Man's role historically has been destructive; today or tomorrow it can be totally, and for all life existent, irrevocably destructive.

Now, wild nature, save a few exceptions, is not a satisfactory physical environment. Where primitive peoples exist in a wild nature little adapted by man, their susceptibility to disease, life expectancy, vulnerability to climatic vagaries, and to the phenomena of drought and starvation is hardly ideal. Yet the certainty that man must adapt nature and himself does not diminish his dependence upon natural, non-human processes. These two observations set limits upon conceptions of man and nature. Man must adapt through both biological and cultural innovation but these adaptations occur within a context of natural, non-human processes. It is not inevitable that adapting nature to support human congregations must of necessity diminish the quality of the physical environment.

Creation of a physical environment by organisms as individuals and as communities is not exclusively a human skill. The chambered nautilus, the beehive, and the coral formation are all efforts by organisms to take inert materials and dispose them to create a physical environment. In these examples the environments created are complementary to the organisms. They are constructed with great economy of means; they are expressive; they have, in human eyes, great beauty; and they have survived periods of evolutionary time vastly longer than the human span. Can we hope that man will be able to change the physical environment to create a new ecology in which he is primary agent, but which will be a self-perpetuating and not a retrogressive process? We hope that man will be able at least to equal the chambered nautilus, the bee, and the coral—that he will be able to build a physical environment indispensable to life, constructed with economy of means, having lucid expression, and containing great beauty. When man learns this single lesson he will be enabled to create by natural process an environment appropriate for survival—the minimum requirement of a humane environment. When this view is believed, the artist will make it vivid and manifest. Medieval faith, interpreted by artists, made the Gothic cathedral ring with holiness. Here again we confront the paradox of man in nature and man transcendent. The vernacular architecture and urbanism of earlier societies and primitive cultures today, the Italian hill town, medieval village, the Dogon community, express the first view, a human correspondence to the nautilus, the bee, and the coral. Yet this excludes the Parthenon, Hagia Sofia, Beauvais, statements which speak of the uniqueness of man and his aspirations. Neither of these postures is complete, the vernacular speaks too little of the consciousness of man, yet the shrillness of transcendence asks for the muting of other, older voices.

Perhaps when the achievements of the past century are appraised, there will be advanced as the most impressive accomplishment of this period the great extension of social justice. The majority of the population of the Western world moved from an endemic condition of threatening starvation, near desperation, and serfdom, to relative abundance, security, and growing democratic freedoms. Human values utilized the benison of science, technology, and industry, to increase wealth absolutely and to distribute it more equitably. In the process, responsibility and individual freedom increased, brute hunger, bare suppression, and uncontrolled disease were diminished. It is a paradox that in this period of vastly increased wealth, the quality of the physical environment has not only failed to improve commensurately, but has actually retrogressed. If this is true, and I believe that there is more than ample evidence to support this hypothesis, then it represents an extraordinary failure on the part of Western society. The failure is the more inexplicable as the product of a society distinguished by its concern for social justice; for surely the physical environment is an important component of wealth and social justice. The modern city wears the badges which distinguish it as a product of the nineteenth and twentieth centuries. Polluted rivers, polluted atmosphere, squalid industry, vulgarity of commerce, diners, hot dog stands, second-hand car lots, gas stations, sagging wire and billboards, the whole anarchy united by ugliness—at best neutral, at worst offensive and insalubrious. The product of a century's concern for social justice, a century with unequaled wealth and technology, is the least humane physical environment known to history. It is a problem of major importance to understand why the nineteenth and twentieth centuries have failed in the creation of a physical environment; why the physical environment has not been, and is not now, considered as a significant aspect of wealth and social justice.

Renaissance and Eighteenth Century

If we consider all the views in our Western heritage having an anti-environmental content, we find they represent a very impressive list. The first of these is the anthropomorphic view that man exclusively is made in the image of God (widely interpreted to mean that God is made in the image of man). The second assumption is that man has absolute dominion over all life and non-life. The third assumption is that man is licensed to subdue the earth. To this we add the medieval Christian concept of other-worldliness, within which life on earth is only a probation for the life hereafter, so that only the acts of man to man are of consequence to his own soul. To this we add the view of the Reformation that beauty is a vanity; and the Celtic, and perhaps Calvinistic, view that the only beauty is natural beauty, that any intent to create beauty by man is an assumption of God's role, is a vanity, and is sacrilegious. The total of these views represents one which can only destroy and which cannot possibly create. The degree to which there has been retention of great natural beauty, creation of beauty and order, recognition of aspects of natural order, and particularly recognition of these aspects of order as a manifestation of God, would seem to exist independently of the Judaic-Christian view. They may be animist and animitist residues that have originated from many different sources; but it would appear, whether or not they are espoused by Christian and Jew, that they do not have their origins in Judaism or Christianity. It would also appear that they do not have their origins in classical or humanist thought, or even in eighteenth-century rationalist views.

These two opposed views of man's role in the natural world are reflected in two concepts of nature and the imposition of man's idea of order upon nature. The first of these is the Renaissance view most vividly manifest in the gardens of the French Renaissance and the projects of André le Nôtre for Louis XIV. The second is the eighteenth-century English picturesque tradition. The gardens of the Renaissance clearly show the imprint of humanist thought. A rigid symmetrical pattern is imposed relentlessly upon a reluctant landscape. If this pattern was, as is claimed, some image of a perfect paradisiac order, it was a human image which derived nothing from the manifest order and expression of wild nature. It was rather, I suggest, an image of flexed muscles, a cock's crow of power, and an arrogant presumption of human dominance over nature. Le Roi Soleil usurped none of the sun's power by so claiming. Art was perverted to express a superficial pattern while claiming this as an expression of a fundamental order.

If the Renaissance sought to imprint upon nature a human order, the eighteenth-century English tradition sought to idealize wild nature, in order to provide a sense of the sublime. The form of estates in the eighteenth century was of an idealized nature, replacing the symmetrical patterns of the Renaissance. The form of ideal nature had been garnered from the landscape painting of Nicolas Poussin and Salvator Rosa; developed through the senses of the poets and writers, such as Alexander Pope, Abraham Cowley, James Thomson, Joseph Addison, Thomas Gray, the third earl of Shaftesbury, and the Orientalist William Temple—a eulogy of the *campagna* from the painters; a eulogy of the natural countryside and its order from the writers; and from Temple, the occult balance discovered in the Orient. However, the essential distinction between the concept of the Renaissance, with its patterning of the landscape, and that of eighteenth-century England was the sense that the order of nature itself existed and represented a prime determinant, a prime discipline for man in his efforts to modify nature. The search in the eighteenth century was for creation of a natural environment which would evoke a sense of the sublime. The impulse of design in the Renaissance was to demonstrate man's power over nature; man's power to order nature; man's power to make nature in his human image. With so inadequate an understanding of the process of man relating to nature, his designs could not be self-perpetuating. Where the basis for design was only the creation of a superficial order, inevitably the consequence was decoration, decay, sterility, and demise. Within the concepts of eighteenth-century England, in contrast, the motivating idea was to idealize the laws of nature. The interdependence of micro-organisms—plants, insects, and animals, the association of particular ecological groupings with particular areas and particular climates—this was the underlying discipline within which the aristocrat-landscape architect worked. The aim was to create an idealized nature which spoke to man of the tranquillity, contemplation, and calm which nature brought, which spoke of nature as the arena of sublime and religious experience, essentially speaking to man of God. This represents, I believe, one of the most healthy manifestations of the Western attitude toward nature. To this eighteenth-century attitude one must add a succession of men who are aberrants in the Western tradition, but whose views represent an extension of the eighteenth-century view—among them, Wordsworth and Coleridge, Thoreau and Emerson, Jonathan Edwards, Jonathan Marsh, Gerald Manley Hopkins, and many more.

Natural Science and Naturalism

It might be productive to examine the natural scientist's view of the evolution of nature and certain aspects of this order. The astronomer gives us some idea of immensity of scale, a hundred billion galaxies receding from us at the speed of light. Of these hundred billion galaxies is one which is our own, the Milky Way. Eccentric within the immensity of the Milky Way, the inconspicuous solar system exists. Within the immensity of the solar system, revolves the minute planet Earth. The astronomer and geologist together give us some sense of the process during which the whirling, burning gases increased in density, coalesced with cooling, condensed, gave off steam, and finally produced a glassy sphere, the Earth. This sphere with land and oceans had an atmosphere with abundant carbon dioxide, with abundant methane, and little or no free oxygen. A glassy sphere with great climatic ranges in temperature, diurnal and seasonal, comparable to an alternation between Arctic and Equatorial conditions. From the biologist, we learn of the origins of life. The first great miracle of life was this plant-animal in the sea; the emergence of life on land, the succession of fungi, mosses, liverworts, ferns. The miracle beyond life is photosynthesis, the power by which plants, absorbing carbon dioxide, give out oxygen and use the sun's energy to transform light into substance. The substance becomes the source of food and fuel for all other forms of life. There seems to be good reason to believe that the Earth's atmosphere, with abundant oxygen, is a product of the great evolutionary succession of plants. On them we depend for all food and fossil fuels. From the botanist we learn of the slow colonization of the Earth's surface by plants, the degree to which the surface of the Earth was stabilized, and, even more significantly, how plants modified the climatic extremes to support the amphibian, reptilian, and subsequent mammalian evolutionary sequence.

The transcendental view of man's relation to nature implicit in Western philosophies is dependent upon the presumption that man does in fact exist outside of nature, that he is not dependent upon it. In contemporary urban society the sense of absolute dependence and interdependence is not apparent, and it is an extraordinary experience to see a reasonably intelligent man become aware of the fact that his survival is dependent upon natural processes, not the least of which are based upon the continued existence of plants. This relationship can be demonstrated by experiment with three major characters: light, man, and algae. The theater is a cylinder in which is a man, a certain quantity of algae, a given quantity of water, a given quantity of air, and a single input, a source of light corresponding to sunlight (in this case a fluorescent tube). The man breathes the air, utilizes the oxygen, and exhales carbon dioxide. The algae utilize the carbon dioxide and exhale oxygen. There is a closed cycle of carbon dioxide and oxygen. The man consumes water, passes the water, the algae consume the water, the water is transpired, collected. and the man consumes the water. There is a closed water cycle. The man eats the algae, the man passes excrement, the algae consume the excrement, the man consumes the algae. There is a closed cycle of food. The only input is light. In this particular experiment the algae is as dependent upon the man as the man is upon the algae. In nature this is obviously not true. For some two billion years nature did exist without man. There can, however, be absolutely no doubt about the indispensability of the algae or plant photosynthesis to the man. It is the single agent able to utilize radiant energy from the sun and make it available as products to support life. This experiment very clearly shows the absolute dependence of man on nature.

Man has claimed to be unique. Social anthropologists have supported this claim on the ground that he alone has the gift of communication, and again that he alone has values. It might be worthwhile considering this viewpoint. A very famous biologist, David Goddard, said that a single human sperm, weighing one billionth of a gram, contains more information coded into its microscopic size than all of the information contained in all of the libraries of all men in all time. This same statement can be made for the seed of other animals or plants. This is a system of communication which is not rational, but which is extraordinarily delicate, elegant, and powerful, and which is capable of transmitting unimaginable quantities of information in microscopic volume.

This system of communication has enabled all species to survive the evolutionary time span. All forms of extant life share this system of communication; man's participation in it is in no sense exceptional.

Man also claims a uniqueness for himself on the grounds that he alone, of all of the animals, has values from which cultural objectives are derived. It would appear that the same *genetic* system of communication also contains a *value system*. Were this not so, those systems of organic life which do persist today would not have persisted; the genetic information transmitted is the information essential for survival. That information ensures the persistence of the organism within its own ecological community. The genetic value system also contains the essential mutation; that imperfection essential for evolution and survival. This system of communication is elegant, beautiful, and powerful, capable of sifting enormous numbers of conflicting choices. Man participates in and shares this system, but his participation is in no sense exceptional.

Yet another aspect of man's assumption that he is independent of natural processes is the anthropomorphic attitude which implies a finite man who is born, grows, and dies, but who during his life is made of the same unchanging stuff—himself. Not so. If we simply measure that which man ingests, uses, and rejects, we begin to doubt this premise. Hair, nails, skin, and chemical constituents are replaced regularly. He replaces several billion cells daily. The essential stuff of man is changed very regularly indeed. In a much more fundamental way, however, man is a creature of environment. We have learned that he is absolutely dependent upon stimuli—light, shadow, color, sound, texture, gravity; and upon his sense of smell, taste, touch, vision, and hearing. These constantly changing environmental conditions are his references. Without them there would be hallucination, hysteria, perhaps mental disintegration, certainly loss of reality.

The Ecological View

It remains for the biologist and ecologist to point out the interdependence which characterizes all relationships, organic and inorganic, in nature. It is the ecologist who points out that an ecological community is only able to survive as a result of interdependent activity between all of the species which constitute the community. To the basic environment (geology, climate) is added an extraordinary complexity of inert materials, their reactions, and the interaction of the organic members of the community with climate, inert materials, and other organisms. The characteristic of life is interdependence of all of the elements of the community upon each other. Each one of these is a source of stimulus; each performs work; each is part of a pattern, a system, a working cycle; each one is to some lesser or greater degree a participant and contributor in a thermodynamic system. This interdependence common to nature—common to all systems—is in my own view the final refutation of man's assumption of independence. It appears impossible to separate man from this system. It would appear that there is a system, the order of which we partly observe. Where we observe it, we see interdependence, not independence, as a key. This interdependence is in absolute opposition to Western man's presumption of transcendence, his presumption of independence, and, of course, his presumption of superiority, dominion, and license to subdue the earth.

A tirade on the theme of dependence is necessary only to a society which views man as independent. Truly there is in nature no independence. Energy is the basis for all life; further, no organism has, does, or will live without an environment. All systems are depletive. There can be no enduring system occupied by a single organism. The minimum, in a laboratory experiment, requires the presence of at least two complementary organisms. These conceptions of independence and anthropocentrism are baseless.

The view of organisms and environment widely held by natural scientists is that of interdependence—symbiosis. Paul Sears of Yale University has written:

Any species survives by virtue of its niche, the opportunity afforded it by environment. But in occupying this niche, it also assumes a role in relation to its surroundings. For further survival it is necessary that its role at least be not a disruptive one. Thus, one generally finds in nature that each component of a highly organized community serves a constructive, or, at any rate, a stabilizing role. The habitat furnishes the niche, and if any species breaks up the habitat, the niche goes with it. . . . That is, to persist they [ecological communities] must be able to utilize radiant energy not merely to perform work, but to maintain the working system in reasonably good order. This requires the presence of organisms adjusted to the habitat and to each other, so organized as to make the fullest use of the influent radiation and to conserve for use and re-use the materials which the system requires. The degree to which a living community meets these conditions is therefore a test of its efficiency and stability (Sears 1956).

Man, too, must meet this test. Sears states:

Man is clearly the beneficiary of a very special environment which has been a great while in the making. This environment is more than a mere inert stockroom. It is an active system, a pattern and a process as well. Its value can be threatened by disruption no less than by depletion.

The natural scientist states that no species can exist without an environment, no species can exist in an environment of its exclusive creations, no species can survive, save as a non-disruptive member of an ecological community. Every member must adjust to other members of the community and to the environment in order to survive. Man is not excluded from this test.

Man must learn this prime ecological lesson of interdependence. He must see himself linked as a living organism to all living and all preceding life. This sense may impel him to understand his interdependence with the microorganisms of the soil, the diatoms in the sea, the whooping crane, the grizzly bear, sand, rocks, grass, trees, sun, rain, moon, and stars. When man learns this he will have learned that when he destroys he also destroys himself; that when he creates, he also adds to himself. When man learns the single lesson of interdependence he may be enabled to create by natural process an environment appropriate for survival. This is a fundamental precondition for the emergence of man's role as a constructive and creative agent in the evolutionary process. Yet this view of interdependence as a basis for survival, this view of man as a participant species in an ecological community and environment, is quite contrary to the Western view.

I have reminded the reader that the creation of a physical environment by organisms, as individuals and as communities, is not exclusively a human skill; it is shared with the bee, the coral, and the chambered nautilus, which take inert materials and dispose them to create a physical environment, complementary to—indeed, indispensable to—the organism.

When man abandoned instinct for rational thought, he abandoned the powers that permitted him to emulate such organisms; if rationality alone sufficed, man should at least be able to equal these humble organisms. But thereby hangs a parable:

> The nuclear cataclysm is over. The earth is covered with gray dust. In the vast silence no life exists, save for a little colony of algae hidden deep in a leaden cleft long inured to radiation. The algae perceive their isolation; they reflect upon the strivings of all life, so recently ended, and on the strenuous task of evolution to be begun anew. Out of their reflection could emerge a firm conclusion: "Next time, no brains."

Reference

Sears, Paul B. 1956. "The Process of Environmental Change by Man." In W L. Thomas, Jr. ed., *Man's Role in Changing the Face of the Earth*. Chicago: University of Chicago Press.

2

The Place of Nature
in the City of Man (1964)

*In the early 1960s McHarg's interest in values toward nature and the physical envi-
ronment increased. Published in a special issue on urban revival in* The Annals of
the American Academy of Political and Social Science *edited by Robert Mitchell,
this article directs that interest toward the topic of nature in the city. McHarg proposes
a theory for a "simple working method for open space." Essentially, he suggests that environmentally sensitive areas be used as open space. Such areas usually have multiple
benefits. For example, by protecting wetland areas, floods can be controlled and safe
drinking water supplies may be ensured. This theory for a "simple working method
for open space" has had considerable influence since McHarg presented it in 1964.*

Abstract

Unparalleled urban growth is pre-empting a million acres of rural lands each
year and transforming them into the sad emblems of contemporary urbanism. In that anarchy which constitutes urban growth, wherein the major
prevailing values are short-term economic determinism, the image of nature
is attributed little or no value. In existing cities, the instincts of eighteenth-
and nineteenth-century city builders, reflected in the pattern of existing
urban open space, have been superseded by a modern process which disdains
nature and seems motivated by a belief in salvation through stone alone. Yet
there is a need and place for nature in the city of man. An understanding of
natural processes should be reflected in the attribution of value to the constituents of these natural processes. Such an understanding, reflected in city
building, will provide a major structure for urban and metropolitan form, an
environment capable of supporting physiological man, and the basis for an

art of city building, which will enhance life and reflect meaning, order, and purpose.

Introduction

"Before we convert our rocks and rills and templed hills into one spreading mass of low grade urban tissue under the delusion that, because we accomplish this degradation with the aid of bulldozers and atomic piles and electronic computers, we are advancing civilization, we might ask what all this implies in terms of the historic nature of man" (Lewis Mumford 1956, p. 142).

The subject of this essay is an inquiry into the place of nature in the city of man. The inquiry is neither ironic nor facetious but of the utmost urgency and seriousness. Today it is necessary to justify the presence of nature in the city of man; the burden of proof lies with nature, or so it seems. Look at the modern city, that most human of all environments, observe what image of nature exists there—precious little indeed and that beleaguered, succumbing to slow attrition.

William Penn effectively said, Let us build a fair city between two noble rivers; let there be five noble squares, let each house have a fine garden, and let us reserve territories for farming. But that was before rivers were discovered to be convenient repositories for sewage, parks the best locus for expressways, squares the appropriate sites for public monuments, farmland best suited for buildings, and small parks best transformed into asphalted, fenced playgrounds.

Charles Eliot once said, in essence, This is our city, these are our hills, these are our rivers, these our beaches, these our farms and forests. I will make a plan to cherish this beauty and wealth for all those who do or will live here. And the plan was good but largely disdained. So here, as elsewhere, man assaulted nature disinterestedly, man assaulted man with the city; nature in the city remains precariously as residues of accident, rare acts of personal conscience, or rarer testimony to municipal wisdom, the subject of continuous assault and attrition while the countryside recedes before the annular rings of suburbanization, unresponsive to any perception beyond simple economic determinism.

Once upon a time, nature lay outside the city gates a fair prospect from the city walls, but no longer. Climb the highest office tower in the city, when atmospheric pollution is only normal, and nature may be seen as a green rim on the horizon. But this is hardly a common condition and so nature lies outside of workaday experience for most urban people.

Long ago, homes were built in the country and remained rural during the lives of persons and generations. Not so today, when a country house of yesterday is within the rural–urban fringe today, in a suburb tomorrow, and in a renewal area of the not-too-distant future.

When the basis for wealth lay in the heart of the land and the farms upon it, then the valleys were verdant and beautiful, the farmer steward of the landscape, but that was before the American dream of a single house on a quarter acre, the automobile, crop surpluses, and the discovery that a farmer could profit more by selling land than crops.

Once men in simple cabins saw only wild nature, silent, implacable, lonely. They cut down the forests to banish Indians, animals, and shadows. Today, Indians, animals, and forests have gone and wild nature, silence, and loneliness are hard to find.

When a man's experience was limited by his home, village, and environs, he lived with his handiworks. Today, the automobile permits temporary escapes from urban squalor, and suburbanization gives the illusion of permanent escape.

Once upon a time, when primeval forests covered Pennsylvania, its original inhabitants experienced a North Temperate climate, but, when the forests were felled, the climate became, in summer, intemperately hot and humid.

Long ago, floods were described as Acts of God. Today, these are known quite often to be consequences of the acts of man.

As long ago, droughts were thought to be Acts of God, too, but these, it is now known, are exacerbated by the acts of man.

In times past, pure air and clean abundant water were commonplaces. Today, "pollution" is the word most often associated with the word "atmosphere," drinking water is often a dilute soup of dead bacteria in a chlorine solution, and the only peoples who enjoy pure air and clean water are rural societies who do not recognize these for the luxuries they are.

Not more than two hundred years ago, the city existed in a surround of farmland, the sustenance of the city. The farmers tended the lands which were the garden of the city. Now, the finest crops are abject fruits compared to the land values created by the most scabrous housing, and the farms are defenseless.

In days gone by, marshes were lonely and wild, habitat of duck and goose, heron and egret, muskrat and beaver, but that was before marshes became the prime sites for incinerator wastes, rubbish, and garbage—marshes are made to be filled, it is said.

When growth was slow and people spent a lifetime on a single place, the flood plains were known and left unbuilt. But, now, who knows the flood plain? *Caveat emptor.*

Forests and woodlands once had their own justification as sources of timber and game, but second-growth timber has little value today, and the game has long fled. Who will defend forests and woods?

Once upon a time, the shad in hundreds of thousands ran strong up the river to the city. But, today, when they do so, there is no oxygen, and their bodies are cast upon the shores.

The Modern Metropolis

Today, the modern metropolis covers thousands of square miles, much of the land is sterilized and waterproofed, the original animals have long gone, as have primeval plants, rivers are foul, the atmosphere is polluted, climate and microclimate have retrogressed to increased violence, a million acres of land are transformed annually from farmland to suburban housing and shopping centers, asphalt and concrete, parking lots and car cemeteries, yet slums accrue faster than new buildings, which seek to replace them. The epidemiologist can speak of urban epidemics—heart and arterial disease, renal disease, cancer, and, not least, neuroses and psychoses. A serious proposition has been advanced to the effect that the modern city would be in serious jeopardy without the safeguards of modern medicine and social legislation. Lewis Mumford can describe cities as dysgenic. There has arisen the recent specter, described as "pathological togetherness," under which density and social pressure are being linked to the distribution of disease and limitations upon reproduction. We record stress from sensory overload and the response of negative hallucination to urban anarchy. When one considers that New York may well add 1,500 square miles of new "low-grade tissue" to its perimeter in the next twenty years, then one recalls Loren Eiseley's image and sees the cities of man as gray, black, and brown blemishes upon the green earth with dynamic tentacles extending from them and asks: "Are these the evidence of man, the planetary disease?"

Western Views: Man and Nature

Yet how can nature be justified in the city? Does one invoke dappled sunlight filtered through trees of ecosystems, the shad run or water treatment, the garden in the city or negative entropy? Although at first glance an unthinkable necessity, the task of justifying nature in the city of man is, with prevailing values and process, both necessary and difficult. The realities of cities now and the plans for their renewal and extension offer incontrovertible evidence of the absence of nature present and future. Should Philadelphia realize its comprehensive plan, then $20 billion and twenty years later there will be less open space than there is today. (A prediction which, indeed, came to pass, with the single sad exceptions of the numerous "brownfield" sites of abandoned industry as well as deserted and derelict houses and businesses.) Cities are artifacts becoming ever more artificial—as though medieval views prevailed that nature was defiled, that living systems shared original sin with man, that only the artifice was free of sin. The motto for the city of man seems to be: salvation by stone alone.

Within the Western tradition exists a contrary view of man and nature which has a close correspondence to the Oriental attitude of an aspiration to harmony of man in nature, a sense of a unitary and encompassing natural order within which man exists. Among others, the naturalist tradition in the West includes Duns Scotus, Joannes Scotus Erigena, Francis of Assisi, Wordsworth, Goethe, Thoreau, Gerald Manley Hopkins, and the nineteenth- and twentieth-century naturalists. Their insistence upon nature being at least the sensible order within which man exists or a manifestation of God demanding deference and reverence is persuasive to many but not to the city builders.

Are the statements of scientists likely to be more persuasive?

David R. Goddard:

> No organism lives without an environment. As all organisms are depletive, no organism can survive in an environment of its exclusive creation (1960).

F. R. Fosberg:

> An ecosystem is a functioning, interacting system composed of one or more organisms and their effective environment, both physical and biological. All ecosystems are open systems. Ecosystems may be stable or unstable. The stable system is in a steady state. The entropy in an unstable system is more likely to increase than decrease. There is a tendency towards diversity in natural ecosystems. There is a tendency towards uniformity in artificial ecosystems or those strongly influenced by man (1958).

Paul Sears:

> Any species survives by virtue of its niche—the opportunity afforded it by environment. But in occupying this niche, it also assumes a role in relation to its surroundings. For further survival it is necessary that its role at least be not a disruptive one. Thus, one generally finds in nature that each component of highly organized community serves a constructive, or at any rate a stabilizing, role. The habitat furnishes the niche, and, if any species breaks up the habitat, the niche goes with it . . . to

persist [organic systems] must be able to utilize radiant energy
not merely to perform work, but to maintain the working system in reasonably good order. This requires the presence of
organisms adjusted to the habitat and to each other so organized to make the fullest use of the influent radiation and to
conserve for use and reuse the materials which the system
requires (1956, p. 472).

Complex creatures consist of billions of cells, each of which, like any
single-celled creature, is unique, experiences life, metabolism, reproduction,
and death. The complex animal exists through the operation of symbiotic relationships between cells as tissues and organs integrated as a single
organism. Hans Selyé describes this symbiosis as intercellular altruism,
the situation under which the cell concedes some part of its autonomy
towards the operation of the organism and the organism responds to cellular
processes.

Aldo Leopold has been concerned with the ethical content of symbiosis:

Ethics so far studied by philosophers are actually a process in
ecological as well as philosophical terms. They are also a
process in ecological evolution. An ethic, ecologically, is a lim-
itation on freedom of action in the struggle for existence. An
ethic, philosophically, is a differentiation of social from anti-
social conduct. These are two definitions of one thing which
has its origin in the tendency of interdependent individuals
and groups to evolve modes of cooperation. The ecologist calls
these symbioses. There is as yet no ethic dealing with man's
relation to the environment and the animals and plants which
grow upon it. The extension of ethics to include man's relation
to environment is, if I read the evidence correctly, an evolutionary possibility and an ecological necessity. All ethics so far
evolved rest upon a single premise that the individual is a
member of a community of interdependent parts. His instincts
prompt him to compete for his place in the community, but his
ethics prompt him to cooperate, perhaps in order that there
may be a place to compete for (1949).

The most important inference from this body of information is that interdependence, not independence, characterizes natural systems. Thus,
man–nature interdependence presumably holds true for urban man as for his
rural contemporaries. We await the discovery of an appropriate physical and
symbolic form for the urban man–nature relationship.

Natural and Artificial Environments

From the foregoing statements by natural scientists, we can examine certain extreme positions. First, there can be no conception of a completely "natural" environment. Wild nature, save a few exceptions, is not a satisfactory physical environment. Yet the certainty that man must adapt nature and himself does not diminish his dependence upon natural, nonhuman processes. These two observations set limits upon conceptions of man and nature. Man must adapt through both biological and cultural innovation, but these adaptations occur within a context of natural, nonhuman processes. It is not inevitable that adapting nature to support human congregations must of necessity diminish the quality of the physical environment. Indeed, all of preindustrial urbanism was based upon the opposite premise, that only in the city could the best conjunction of social and physical environment be achieved. This major exercise of power to adapt nature for human ends, the city, need not be a diminution of physiological, psychological, and aesthetic experience.

While there can be no completely natural environments inhabited by man, completely artificial environments are equally unlikely. Man in common with all organisms is a persistent configuration of matter through which the environment ebbs and flows continuously. Mechanically, he exchanges his substance at a very rapid rate while, additionally, his conceptions of reality are dependent upon the attribution of meaning to myriads of environmental stimuli which impinge upon him continuously. The materials of his being are natural, as are many of the stimuli which he perceives; his utilization of the materials and of many stimuli is involuntary. Man makes artifices, but galactic and solar energy, gases of hydrosphere and atmosphere, the substance of the lithosphere, and all organic systems remain elusive of human artificers.

Yet the necessity to adapt natural environments to sustain life is common to many organisms other than man. Creation of a physical environment by organisms as individuals and as communities is not exclusively a human skill. The chambered nautilus, the beehive, the coral formation, to select but a few examples, are all efforts by organisms to take inert materials and dispose them to create a physical environment. In these examples, the environments created are complementary to the organisms. They are constructed with great economy of means; they are expressive; they have, in human eyes, great beauty; and they have survived periods of evolutionary time vastly longer than the human span.

Simple organisms utilize inert materials to create physical environments which sustain life. Man also confronts this necessity. Man, too, is natural in that he responds to the same laws as do all physical and biological systems. He is a plant parasite, dependent upon the plant kingdom and its associated microorganisms, insects, birds, and animals for all atmospheric oxygen, all food, all fossil fuel, natural fibers, and cellulose, for the stability of the water cycle and amelioration of climate and microclimate. His dependence upon the plant and photosynthesis establishes his dependence upon the microorganisms of the soil, particularly the decomposers which are essential to the recycling of essential nutrients, the insects, birds, and animals which are in turn linked to survival of plant systems. He is equally dependent upon the natural process of water purification by microorganisms. The operation of these non-human physical and biological processes is essential for human survival.

Having concluded that there can be neither a completely artificial nor a completely natural environment, our attention is directed to some determinants of optimal proportions. Some indication may be inferred from man's evolutionary history. His physiology and some significant part of his psychology derive from the billions of years of his biological history. During the most recent human phase of a million or so years, he has been preponderantly food gatherer, hunter, and, only recently, farmer. His urban experience is very recent indeed. Thus, the overwhelming proportion of his biological history has involved experience in vastly more natural environments than he now experiences. It is to these that he is physiologically adapted.

According to F. R. Fosberg:

> It is entirely possible that man will not survive the changed environment that he is creating, either because of failure of resources, war over their dwindling supply, or failure of his nervous system to evolve as rapidly as the change in environment will require. Or he may only survive in small numbers, suffering the drastic reduction that is periodically the lot of pioneer species, or he may change beyond our recognition. . . . Management and utilization of the environment on a true sustaining yield basis must be achieved. And all this must be accomplished without altering the environment beyond the capacity of the human organism, as we know it, to live in it (1957, p. 160).

Human Ecosystems

There are several examples where ecosystems, dominated by man, have endured for long periods of time; the example of traditional Japanese agriculture is perhaps the most spectacular. Here an agriculture of unequaled intensity and productivity has been sustained for over a thousand years, the land is not impoverished but enriched by human intervention: the ecosystem, wild lands, and farmlands are complex, stable, highly productive, and beautiful. The pervasive effect of this harmony of man–nature is reflected in a language remarkable in its descriptive power of nature, a poetry succinct yet capable of the finest shades of meaning, a superb painting tradition in which nature is the icon, an architecture and town building of astonishing skill and beauty, and, not least, an unparalleled garden art in which nature and the garden are the final metaphysical symbol.

In the Western tradition, farming in Denmark and England has sustained high productivity for two or more centuries, appears stable, and is very beautiful; in the United States, comparable examples exist in Amish, Mennonite, and Pennsylvania Dutch farming.

Understanding of the relationship of man to nature is more pervasive and operative among farmers than any other laymen. The farmer perceives the source of his food in his crops of cereal, vegetables, roots, beef, fish, or game. He understands that, given a soil fertility, his crop is directly related to inputs of organic material, fertilizer, water, and sunlight. If he grows cotton or flax or tends sheep, he is likely to know the source of the fibers of his clothes. He recognizes timber, peat, and hydroelectric power as sources of fuel; he may well know of the organic source of coal and petroleum. Experience has taught him to ensure a functional separation between septic tank and well, to recognize the process of erosion, runoff, flood and drought, the differences of altitude and orientation. As a consequence of this acuity, the farmer has developed a formal expression which reflects an understanding of the major natural processes. Characteristically, high ground and steep slopes are given over to forest and woodland as a source of timber, habitat for game, element in erosion control, and water supply. The more gently sloping meadows below are planted to orchards, above the spring frost line, or in pasture. Here a seep, spring, or well is often the source of water supply. In the valley bottom, where floods have deposited rich alluvium over time, is the area of intensive cultivation. The farm buildings are related to conditions of climate and microclimate, above the flood plain, sheltered and shaded by the farm woodland. The septic tank is located in soils suitable for this purpose and below the elevation of the water source.

Here, at the level of the farm, can be observed the operation of certain simple, empirical rules and a formal expression which derives from them. The land is rich, and we find it beautiful.

Clearly, a comparable set of simple rules is urgently required for the city and the metropolis. The city dweller is commonly unaware of these natural processes, ignorant of his dependence upon them. Yet the problem of the place of nature in the city is more difficult than that of the farmer. Nature, as modified in farming, is intrinsic to the place. The plant community is relatively immobile, sunlight falls upon the site as does water, nutrients are cycled through the system in place. Animals in ecosystems have circumscribed territories, and the conjunction of plants and animals involves a utilization and cycling of energy and materials in quite limited areas. The modern city is, in this respect, profoundly different in that major natural processes which sustain the city, provide food, raw materials for industry, commerce, and construction, resources of water, and pure air are drawn not from the city or even its metropolitan area but from a national and even international hinterland. The major natural processes are not intrinsic to the locus of the city and cannot be.

Nature in the Metropolis

In the process of examining the place of nature in the city of man, it might be fruitful to consider the role of nature in the metropolitan area initially, as here, in the more rural fringes, can still be found analogies to the empiricism of the farmer. Here the operative principle might be that natural processes which perform work or offer protection in their natural form without human effort should have a presumption in their favor. Planning should recognize the values of these processes in decision-making for prospective land uses.

A more complete understanding of natural processes and their interactions must await the development of an ecological model of the metropolis. Such a model would identify the regional inventory of material in atmosphere, hydrosphere, lithosphere, and biosphere, identify inputs and outputs, and both describe and quantify the cycling and recycling of materials in the system. Such a model would facilitate recognition of the vital natural processes and their interdependence which is denied today. Lacking such a model, it is necessary to proceed with available knowledge. On a simpler basis, we can say that the major inputs in biological systems are sunlight, oxygen–carbon dioxide, food (including nutrients), and water. The first three are not limiting in the metropolis; water may well be limiting both as to quantity and quality. In addition, there are many other reasons for isolating and examining water in process. Water is the single most specific determinant of a large number of physical processes and is indispensable to all biological processes. Water, as the agent of erosion and sedimentation, is causal to geological evolution, the realities of physiography. Mountains, hills, valleys, and plains experience a variety of climate and microclimate consequent upon their physiography; the twin combination of physiography and climate determines the incidence and distribution of plants and animals, their niches, and habitats. Thus, using water as the point of departure, we can recognize its impact on the making of mountains and lakes, ridges and plains, forests and deserts, rivers, streams and marshes, the distribution of plants and animals. Lacking an ecological model, we may well select water as the best indicator of natural process. In any watershed, the uplands represent the majority of the watershed area. Assuming equal distribution of precipitation and ground conditions over the watershed, the maximum area will produce the maximum runoff. The profile of watersheds tends to produce the steeper slopes in the uplands with the slope diminishing toward the outlet. The steeper the slope, the greater is the water velocity. This combination of maximum runoff links maximum volume to maximum velocity—the two primary conditions of flood and drought. These two factors in turn exacerbate erosion, with the consequence of depositing silt in stream beds, raising flood plains, and increasing intensity and incidence of floods in piedmont and estuary.

The natural restraints to flooding and drought are mainly the presence and distribution of vegetation, particularly, on the uplands and their steep slopes. Vegetation absorbs and utilizes considerable quantities of water; the surface roots, trunks of trees, stems of shrubs and plants, the litter of forest floor mechanically retard the movement of water, facilitating percolation, increasing evaporation opportunity. A certain amount of water is removed temporarily from the system by absorption into plants, and mechanical retardation facilitates percolation, reduces velocity, and thus diminishes erosion. In fact, vegetation and their soils act as a sponge restraining extreme runoff, releasing water slowly over longer periods, diminishing erosion and sedimentation, in short, diminishing the frequency and intensity of oscillation between flood and drought.

Below the uplands of the watershed are characteristically the more shallow slopes and broad plains of the piedmont. Here is the land most often developed for agriculture. These lands, too, tend to be favored locations for villages, towns, and cities. Here, forests are residues or the products of regeneration on abandoned farms. Steep slopes in the piedmont are associated with streams and rivers. The agricultural piedmont does not control its own defenses. It is defended from flood and drought by the vegetation of the uplands. The vegetation cover and conservation practices in the agricultural piedmont can either exacerbate or diminish flood and drought potential; the piedmont is particularly vulnerable to both.

The incidence of flood and drought is not alone consequent upon the upland sponge but also upon estuarine marshes, particularly where these are tidal. Here at the mouth of the watershed at the confluence of important rivers or of river and sea, the flood component of confluent streams or the tidal component of floods assumes great importance. In the Philadelphia metropolitan area, the ocean and the estuary are of prime importance as factors in flood. A condition of intense precipitation over the region combined with high tides, full estuary, and strong onshore winds combines the elements of potential flood. The relation of environmental factors of the upland component and the agricultural piedmont to flood and drought has been discussed. The estuarine marshes and their vegetation constitute the major defense against the tidal components of floods. These areas act as enormous storage reservoirs absorbing mile-feet of potentially destructive waters, reducing flood potential.

This gross description of water-related processes offers determinism for the place of nature in the metropolis. From this description can be isolated several discrete and critical phases in the process. Surface water as rivers, streams, creeks, lakes, reservoirs, and ponds would be primary; the particular form of surface water in marshes would be another phase; the flood plain as the area temporarily occupied by water would be yet another. Two critical aspects of groundwater, the aquifer and its recharge areas, could be identified. Agricultural land has been seen to be a product of alluvial deposition, while steep slopes and forests play important roles in the process of runoff. If we could identify the proscriptions and permissiveness of these parameters to other land use, we would have an effective device for discriminating the relative importance of different roles of metropolitan lands. Moreover, if the major divisions of upland, piedmont, and estuary and the processes enumerated could be afforded planning recognition and legislative protection, the metropolitan area would derive its form from a recognition of natural process. The place of nature in the metropolis would be reflected in the distribution of water and flood plain, marshes, ridges, forests, and farmland, a matrix of natural lands performing work or offering protection and recreational opportunity distributed throughout the metropolis.

This conception is still too bald; it should be elaborated to include areas of important scenic value, recreational potential, areas of ecological, botanical, geological, or historic interest. Yet, clearly, the conception, analogous to the empiricism of the farmer, offers opportunity for determining the place of nature in the metropolis.

Nature in the City

The conception advocated for the metropolitan area has considerable relevance to the problem of the place of nature in the city of man. Indeed, in several cities, the fairest image of nature exists in these rare occasions where river, flood plain, steep slopes, and woodlands have been retained in their natural condition—the Hudson and Palisades in New York, the Schuylkill and Wissahickon in Philadelphia, the Charles River in Boston and Cambridge. If rivers, flood plains, marshes, steep slopes, and woodlands in the city were accorded protection to remain in their natural condition or were retrieved and returned to such a condition where possible, this single device, as an aspect of water quality, quantity, flood and drought control, would ensure for many cities an immeasurable improvement in the aspect of nature in the city, in addition to the specific benefits of a planned watershed. No other device has such an ameliorative power. Quite obviously, in addition to benefits of flood control and water supply, the benefits of amenity and recreational opportunity would be considerable. As evidence of this, the city of Philadelphia has a twenty-two-mile waterfront on the Delaware River. The most grandiose requirements for port facilities and water-related industries require only eight miles of waterfront. This entire waterfront lies in a flood plain. Levees and other flood protection devices have been dismissed as exorbitant. Should this land be transformed into park, it would represent an amelioration in Philadelphia of incomparable scale.

Should this conception of planning for water and water-related para-meters be effectuated, it would provide the major framework for the role of nature in the city of man. The smaller elements of the face of nature are more difficult to justify. The garden and park, unlike house, shop, or factory, have little "functional" content. They are, indeed, more metaphysical symbol than utilitarian function. As such, they are not amenable to quantification or the attribution of value. Yet it is frequently the aggregation of these gardens and spaces which determines the humanity of a city. Values they do have. This is apparent in the flight to the suburbs for more natural environments— a self-defeating process of which the motives are clear. Equally, the selection of salubrious housing location in cities is closely linked to major open spaces which reflects the same impulse. The image of nature at this level is most important, the cell of the home, the street, and neighborhood. In the city slum, nature exists in the backyard ailanthus, sumac, in lice, cockroach, rat, cat, and mouse; in luxury highrise, there are potted trees over parking garages, poodles, and tropical fish. In the first case, nature reflects "disturbance" to the ecologist; it is somewhat analogous to the scab on a wound, the first step of regeneration towards equilibrium, a sere arrested at the most primitive level. In the case of the luxury highrise, nature is a canary in a cage, surrogate, an artifice, forbidden even the prospect of an arrested sere.

Three considerations seem operative at this level of concern. The first is that the response which nature induces, tranquillity, calm, introspection, openness to order, meaning and purpose, the place of values in the world of facts, is similar to the evocation from works of art. Yet nature is, or was, abun-dant; art and genius are rare.

The second consideration of some importance is that nature in the city is very tender. Woodlands, plants, and animals are very vulnerable to human erosion. Only expansive dimensions will support self-perpetuating and self-cleansing nature. There is a profound change between such a natural scene and a created and maintained landscape.

The final point is related to the preceding. If the dimensions are appro-priate, a landscape will perpetuate itself. Yet, where a site has been sterilized, built upon, buildings demolished, the problem of creating a landscape, quite apart from creating a self-perpetuating one, is very considerable and the costs are high. The problems of sustaining a landscape, once made, are also considerable; the pressure of human erosion on open space in urban housing and the inevitable vandalism ensure that only a small vocabulary of primitive and hardy plants can survive. These factors, with abnormal conditions of groundwater, soil, air, atmospheric pollution, stripping, and girdling, limit nature to a very constricted image.

The Future

Perhaps, in the future, analysis of those factors which contribute to stress disease will induce inquiry into the values of privacy, shade, silence, the positive stimulus of natural materials, and the presence of comprehensible order, indeed natural beauty. When young babies lack fondling and a mother's love, they sometimes succumb to moronity and death. The dramatic reversal of this pattern has followed simple maternal solicitude. Is the absence of nature—its trees, water, rocks and herbs, sun, moon, stars, and changing seasons—a similar type of deprivation? The solicitude of nature, its essence if not its image, may be seen to be vital.

Some day, in the future, we may be able to quantify plant photosynthesis in the city and the oxygen in the atmosphere, the insulation by plants of lead from automobile exhausts, the role of diatoms in water purification, the amelioration of climate and microclimate by city trees and parks, the insurance of negative ionization by fountains, the reservoirs of air which, free of combustion, are necessary to relieve inversion pollution, the nature-space which a biological inheritance still requires, the stages in land regeneration and the plant and animal indicators of such regeneration, indeed, perhaps, even the plant and animal indicators of a healthy environment. We will then be able to quantify the necessities of a minimum environment to support physiological man. Perhaps we may also learn what forms of nature are necessary to satisfy the psychological memory of a biological ancestry.

Today, that place where man and nature are in closest harmony in the city is the cemetery. Can we hope for a city of man, an ecosystem in dynamic equilibrium, stable and complex? Can we hope for a city of man, an ecosystem with man dominant, reflecting natural processes, human and non-human, in which artifice and nature conjoin as art and nature, in a natural urban environment speaking to man as a natural being and nature as the environment of man? When we find the place of nature in the city of man, we may return to that enduring and ancient inquiry—place of man in nature.

References

Fosberg, F. R. 1958. "The Preservation of Man's Environment." In *Proceedings of the Ninth Pacific Science Congress*, 1957, 20.

Goddard, David F. 1960. *The House We Live In.* Transcript of the program broadcast on WCAU-TV (CBS), Channel 10, Philadelphia, Sunday, October 23, hosted and edited by Ian McHarg.

Leopold, Aldo. 1949. *A Sand County Almanac.* Oxford: Oxford University Press.

Mumford, Lewis. 1956. "Prospect." In William L. Thomas, Jr., ed., *Man's Role in Changing the Face of the Earth.* Chicago: The University of Chicago Press, pp. 1132–52.

Sears, Paul B. 1956. "The Processes of Environmental Change by Man." In William L. Thomas, Jr., ed., *Man's Role in Changing the Face of the Earth.* Chicago: The University of Chicago Press, pp. 471–84.

3

Ecological Determinism (1966)

During the 1960s, McHarg directed his own efforts as well as those of his graduate students toward ways ecological principles could be applied to landscape architecture and environmental planning. This paper was presented at a conference convened by The Conservation Foundation in April, 1965, at Airlie House, Warrenton, Virginia. Subsequently it appeared in the book Future Environments of North America *edited by F. Fraser Darling and John P. Milton and published by The Natural History Press (the eventual publisher of Design with Nature). Darling, a distinguished British ecologist, pioneered the study of human ecology in the Scottish highlands. He showed how small technological innovations changed human settlements and landscapes. This paper is an early discussion of McHarg's theory for an ecological planning method.*

Introduction

In the Western world during the past century transformation of natural environments into human habitats has commonly caused a deterioration of the physical environment. However, much improvement to the social environment has been accomplished in these transformations; city slurb and slum are less attractive physical environments than forest, field, and farm that preceded them. In earlier times, because of the slow rate of change, unity of materials, structural method and expression, this was not so. Few among us regret the loss of ancient marshes on which Venice and Amsterdam sit, the loss of even more ancient hills which now seat Athens and Rome. History testifies to human adaptations, accomplished with wisdom and art, which were and are felicitous. Yet the principles which ensured these successes are inadequate for the speed, scale, and nature of change today. In the seventeenth century it required a third of the treasury of France, the mature life of Louis XIV, and the major effort of André Le Nôtre to realize Versailles. Three centuries later greater New York will urbanize at the rate of 50,000 acres and absorb 600,000 people into its perimeter each year without any plan. In the interim the classical city has been superseded by the industrial city, by metropolis, megalopolis, and now, in the opinion of Lewis Mumford, is en route to Necropolis. Paradoxically in this period of change the city plan has remained the Renaissance archetype which motivated Versailles, a poor symbol of man–nature in the seventeenth century, an inexcusable prototype for the twentieth century.

It is clear that the principles which contributed to historic successes in urban form have failed dismally since the industrial revolution. The success of the subsequent city as provider of employment and social services is its best testimony, but as a physical environment it has continually retrogressed. New principles must be developed for human adaptations, for city, metropolis, and megalopolis.

The problem is an enormous one both in extent and speed of change. Three hundred million Americans are expected to populate the United States in the year 2000. If indeed 80 percent of these will live in urban places, then this involves the urbanization of 55 million acres of non-urbanized land. If one extrapolates from the present megalopolis to this future population, then 10 percent of the land area of the United States, 200 million acres, will fall within urban influence, comparable to megalopolis, in a mere 35 years.

Today, the prescriptions for urban location, form, and growth derive almost exclusively from the social sciences. Both analytic and predictive models are based upon economics. The natural sciences have remained aloof from the problem, yet the understanding of physical and biological processes, which reposes in these sciences, is indispensable for good judgment on the problems of human adaptations of environment.

Many central questions can best be answered by natural scientists but at the onset one alone can suffice. What are the implications of natural process upon the location and form of development? The answer to this is vital to administrators, regional and city planners, architects and landscape architects. For the last it is the indispensable basis for their professional role. As the representative of a profession with a historic concern for the relation of man to nature and the single bridge between the natural sciences and the artificers of the urban environment, it is not inappropriate that the spokesperson for this group ask for the formulation of an ecological determinism.

Landscape Architecture

In the Western tradition, with the single exception of the English eighteenth century and its extension, landscape architecture has been identified with garden making, be it Alhambra, Saint Gall, the Villa d'Este, or Versailles. In this tradition decorative and tractable plants are arranged in a simple geometry as a comprehensible metaphysical symbol of a benign and orderly world.

Here the ornamental qualities of plants are paramount; no concepts of community or association becloud the objective. Plants are analogous to domestic pets, dogs, cats, ponies, canaries, and goldfish, tolerant to man and dependent upon him; lawn grasses, hedges, flowering shrubs and trees, tractable and benign, man's cohorts, sharing his domestication.

This is the walled garden, separated from nature, a symbol of beneficence, island of delight, tranquillity, introspection. It is quite consistent that the final symbol of this garden is the flower.

Not only is this a selected nature, decorative and benign, but the order of its array is, unlike the complexity of nature, reduced to a simple and comprehensible geometry. This is then a selected nature, simply ordered to create a symbolic reassurance of a benign and orderly world, an island within the world and separate from it. Yet the knowledge prevails that nature reveals a different form and aspect beyond the wall. Loren Eiseley has said that "the unknown within the self is linked to the wild." The garden symbolizes domesticated nature, the wild is beyond.

The role of garden making remains important. Man seeks a personal paradise on earth, a unity of man and nature. The garden is such a quest for a personal oasis, a paradise garden. In these, man can find peace and in tranquillity discover, in Kenneth Rexroth's words, "the place of value in a world of facts." He can respond to natural materials, water, stone, herbs, trees, sunlight and shadow, rain, ice and snow, the changing seasons, birth, life and death. This is a special microhabitat, a healthy cell in the organism of the city, a most humane expression, yet clearly its relevance, depending upon ornamental horticulture and simple geometry, is inadequate for the leap over the garden wall.

In the eighteenth century in England landscape architects "leap't the wall and discovered all nature to be a garden." The leap did not occur until a new view of nature dispelled the old and a new esthetic was developed consonant with the enlarged arena.

Starting with a denuded landscape, a backward agriculture, and a medieval pattern of attenuated land holdings, this landscape tradition rehabilitated an entire countryside, making that fair image persisting today. It is a testimony to the prescience of William Kent, Lancelot "Capability" Brown, Humphry Repton, and their followers that, lacking a science of ecology, they used native plant materials to create communities which so well reflected natural processes that their creations endured and are self-perpetuating.

The functional objective was a productive, working landscape. Hilltops and hillsides were planted to forest, great meadows occupied the valley bottoms in which lakes were constructed and streams meandered. The product of this new landscape was the extensive meadow supporting cattle, horses, and sheep. The forests provided valuable timber, the lack of which Evelyn had earlier deplored, and supported game, while free-standing copses in the meadows provided shade and shelter for animals.

The planting reflected the necessities of shipbuilding but the preferred trees, oak and beech, were climax species and they were planted *de novo*. On sites where these were inappropriate, northern slopes, thin soils, elevations, pine and birch were planted. Watercourses were graced with willows, alders, osiers, while the meadows supported grasses and meadow flowers. As long as the meadow was grazed, a productive sere was maintained and meanwhile the forests evolved.

The objective, however, was more complex than function alone. Paintings of the *campagna* by Claude Lorrain, Nicolas Poussin, and Salvator Rosa, a eulogy of nature which obsessed poets and writers, had developed the concept of an ideal nature. Yet it clearly did not exist in the raddled landscape of eighteenth-century England. It had to be created. The ruling principle was that "nature is the gardener's best designer," applied ecology of yesteryear. Ornamental horticulture, which had been obtained within garden walls, was disdained and a precursory ecology replaced it. The meadow was the single artifice, the remaining components were natural expressions, their dramatic and experiential qualities exploited, it is true, but deriving in the first place from that observed in nature.

Nature itself produced the esthetic; the simple geometry, not simplicity but simple-mindedness, of the Renaissance was banished. "Nature abhors a straight line" was declaimed. The discovery of an established esthetic in the Orient based upon occult balance, asymmetry, confirmed this view. In the eighteenth century, landscape began the revolution which banished the giant classicism and the imposition of its geometry as a symbol of man–nature.

This tradition is important in many respects. It founded applied ecology as the basis for function and esthetics in the landscape. Indeed before the manifesto of modern architecture had been propounded, "Form follows function," it had been superseded by the eighteenth-century concept wherein form and process were seen to be indivisible facets of a single phenomenon. It is important because of the scale of operation. One recalls that Capability Brown, when asked to undertake a project in Ireland, retorted, "I have not finished England yet." Another reason for its importance lies in the fact that it was a creation. Here the landscape architect, like the empiricist doctor, found a land in ill-health and brought it into good heart and to beauty. Man the artist, understanding nature's laws and forms, accelerated the process of regeneration so well indeed that who today can discern the artifice from the untouched?

It is hard to find fault with this tradition but one must observe that while the principles of ecology and its esthetic are general, the realization of this movement was particular. It reflects in agricultural economy, principally based upon cattle, horses, and sheep. It never confronted the city, which in the eighteenth century remained the Renaissance prototype. Only in the urban square, parks and circuses, in natural plantings, was the eighteenth-century city distinguishable from its antecedents.

The successes of this tradition are manifest. No other movement has accomplished such a physical regeneration and amelioration. Its basis lies in applied ecology. It is necessary that modern ecology become the basis for modern interventions particularly at the scale of city, metropolis, and mega-lopolis, if we are to avert Necropolis.

Ecological Determinism

Processes are expressive; morphology is a superficial expression of the process examined. The creation of a twentieth-century tradition requires an understanding of natural process and the morphology of the artifacts of man as process. Thus, natural processes are deterministic, they respond to laws; they then give form to human adaptations which themselves contain symbolic content.

Beehive huts, igloos, stilt homes on marshes are morphologically determined. We need today an understanding of natural process and its expression and, even more, an understanding of the morphology of man–nature, which, less deterministic, still has its own morphology, the expression of man–nature as process. The eighteenth century developed a morphology for a pastoral landscape in England. What are the prerequisites for discerning the appropriate morphologies for our time?

I believe that there are six elements which are required:

1. Ecosystem inventory
2. Description of natural processes
3. Identification of limiting factors
4. Attribution of value
5. Determination of prohibitions and permissiveness to change
6. Identification of indicators of stability or instability

The final for the artificers is then the perception of the revealed morphology and its realization.

Ecosystem Inventory

The eighteenth-century landscape architects were only fair taxonomists, but, by using collected material, transferring from site to like site and planting in communities, they avoided the errors of caprice, ornamental horticulture, and much traditional forestry. In the intervening years descriptive ecology has developed the concept of community. In the Philadelphia region the identification of open water, reed swamp, sedge meadow, secondary succession, mixed mesophytic forest, and pine barrens has great utility. Recent work which refines these descriptions by identifying gradients adds value to this technique. The conception of range from hydrosere to zerosere is of great value but it is the conception of succession, sere, and climax which adds dynamics to the eighteenth-century view. The first prerequisite for the application of ecology to the planning process is the preparation of ecosystem inventories. This involves the creation of ecological maps at various scales in which communities are identified. The inventory should also include the city. The ailanthus-pigeon-starling "community" is quite as important as the oak-beech-hickory forest. The ecosystem inventory is the basis for planning related to natural processes.

Description of Natural Processes

Inventories and ecological maps have to be supplemented by explanation of natural processes. In particular the stability or instability stage in succession of ecosystems must be described. While this is important for all communities it is particularly necessary for major physiographic regions—coastal plains, piedmont, uplands, etc—and for certain discrete environments—pine barrens, estuarine environment, mixed mesophytic forest, sand dunes, etc. In the city the relation of atmospheric pollution to isolation photosynthesis CO_2 consumption is typical of a human process which affects ecosystems. Transformation of farmland to subdivision and erosion-turbidity-reduced photosynthesis and natural water purification are other examples. Descriptions of natural processes and the degree to which they are affected by man are a vital component of this body of information.

Identification of Limiting Factors

It is important to establish what factors are necessary to ensure the perpetuation of any ecosystem; apart from factors in abundance, which elements are critical—water-plane-table elevation, alkalinity, acidity, fire, first and last frost, etc. This category must be extensive enough to include limiting factors external to the ecosystem under study such as, for example, transformation of a fresh-water into a salt-water marsh through channel deepening and river widening.

Attribution of Value

In eighteenth-century England the land was thought to be the arena for the creation of a metaphysical symbol—all nature is a garden. Nature was attributed a value which transcended any concept of productivity, the landscape was also productive. In the twentieth century, when nature desperately needs a defense in the face of disdain, disinterest, and remorseless despoliation, the first defense is certainly non-economic, the insistence that man is a co-tenant of the universe, sharing the phenomenal world of living and inert processes, an organism in an interacting biosphere. From this some people will conclude that nature is a manifestation of God, others that the cosmos is unitary, all processes subject to physical law yet having infinite potential, that man is an inhabitant free to develop his potential. Each of these views contains an inherent deference, a posture of serious inquiry, and the instinct to exercise care, intelligence, and art in accomplishing human interventions. Such a view characterized eighteenth-century landscape architects, nineteenth-century naturalists, and today is associated with conservationists.

The search for a theology of man–nature–God does not exclude exchanges which involve the coinage of the time and place. This requires that the proponents of nature also attribute values to nature processes so that these may be recognized as parameters in the planning process. Indeed, given ecological inventories, explanation of natural processes, and identification of limiting factors, the next increment of knowledge essential for an applied ecology is precisely the attribution of value to these natural processes.

Four major divisions of value can be discerned: intrinsic value, value as productivity, value as work performed, and, finally, negative value as discouragement to use.

Intrinsic value is thought to exist wherein the landscape neither is "productive" nor "performs work" but simply is. Areas of wilderness, scenic beauty, scientific value, and educational value might fall into this category.

Productivity would include agriculture, forestry, fisheries, extractive minerals, recreation, gamelands, a concept in common usage.

The attribution of value based upon work performed might include water catchment, water purification and storage, flood, drought and erosion control, hydroelectric power generation, "airshed," climate, and microclimate amelioration.

Negative value would include those areas wherein there is a hazard and whence occupancy should be discouraged. No occupancy would avert costs and damages. Thus areas subject to earthquakes, volcanism, hurricanes, avalanches, floods, drought, subsidence, and forest fires should fall into this category.

All of these subdivisions can be subject to the concept of replacement value, a most useful concept which can apply at several scales. For example, in the case of a city park planned for an expressway intersection, the value is not "land value" alone but rather the entire cost of replicating the park including the cost of equally mature trees, shrubs, etc. Where it is intended to fill a marsh, the replacement value would include the cost of equal flood protection, water equalization, and wildlife habitats on another site. In the case of transforming prime agricultural land to housing, replacement value would include the cost of upgrading poorer soils to prime capability. Given attribution of value to natural processes, the concept of replacement value provides an important measuring device for alternative choices. No other device offers a comparable restraint to thoughtless despoliation.

Clearly the concept of value poses many difficulties, the change of value over time is one. Low-grade ores, presently marginal farmland, undistinguished rural areas can increase in value with increased demand and shrunken supply. In addition, value is relative. If, as in the Netherlands, survival is linked to the stability of the dunes, then marram and sedge are valuable. If no such a role exists, then dune grasses are merely decorative. If diatoms are needed for water treatment, then they have value. If water is treated with coagulants, rapid sand filter, and chlorine, then diatoms have, in this local case, no value. Marshes can be seen either as costly obstructions to development or as invaluable defenses against flood; in one case they represent costs, in another they represent values. Another problem arises from the geographic scale of natural process and interdependence. The Mississippi watershed unites suburban Chicago with New Orleans; effects upon water quality will affect values in the entire downstream area. The requirements of clean air unite western and eastern United States. There is no method of accounting which relates snowfall in the Rockies to the value of water in California, no accounting which attributes value to forests of upstream watersheds and flood control in the lower Mississippi. The final difficulty in attribution of value lies in unmeasurable qualities. Who will attribute value to the whooping crane, grizzly bear, or pasque flower? Yet the inability to attribute value to serenity, happiness, and health has not deterred economic determinism. In spite of difficulties, the attribution of value to natural process is a necessary precondition for applied ecology as a basis for determining non-intervention, intervention, and the nature, scale, and location of such intervention.

Determination of Prohibitions and Permissiveness to Change

Given descriptive ecological inventories, supplemented by descriptions of natural process and limiting factors, with a scale of values, the necessary information is available to establish the constraints inherent in natural process which should affect the location and nature of development.

This finally produces the program. No longer is nature an undifferentiated scene, lacking values, defenseless against transformation; it is seen to be a complex interrelated system, in process, having discernible limiting factors, containing values, present or prospective, and, finally, containing both constraints and opportunities. For example, the Arctic and Antarctic; bare mountains, oceans, and perhaps beaches are highly tolerant to human use. Other systems are highly intolerant, wild animals retreat or succumb, natural plant communities are erased and superseded by man's cohorts in the processes of agriculture, industry, and urbanism. Can we select environments, more suitable than these extremely tolerant examples, which, satisfactory for man, are unusually tolerant to him? Can one set limits on transformation of natural habitats implicit in the processes themselves? Thus, how much housing can a forest absorb and still perform an attributed role in the water regimen? How much development can occur on a marsh without destroying its role of water equalization, emergency flood storage, or wildlife habitat? What proportion of an aquifer can be waterproofed by urbanism before its percolation performance is diminished below a required level? The answer to such questions, and many others, is prerequisite to the application of ecology to the planning process.

For the regional planner, landscape architect, city planner, and architect, the development of concepts of prohibition and permissiveness inherent in natural process is the beginning of a modern applied ecology, the gift of natural form, the program for intervention which has relevance to the house and its site, the subdivision, hamlet, village, town, city, metropolis, megalopolis, and the nation.

Identification of Indicators of Stability or Instability

The concept of ecological determinism requires criteria of performance. For pond ecosystems it may be possible to determine stability or instability from the entropy in the system. It seems unlikely that this concept will be capable of dealing with extensive geographic areas or with the problem of the city. Clearly for the moment some simpler devices are necessary by which stability or instability, succession, sere or climax can be discerned; indeed, there is a desperate need for a concept of a "healthy" and "healthful" environment. We need analogies to litmus paper, the canary in the cage, indicators of health and change. Ruth Patrick has developed histograms from which the "state of health" of Pennsylvania streams may be discerned. Luna Leopold has propounded the measure of a "duration curve" against which stability or instability of stream processes can be examined. This writer has advocated the use of the "coefficient of runoff" as a planning determinant for land use relative to the water regimen. "Sky blue" is a measure of the relative presence of atmospheric pollution. The presence of trace metals in the environment is being investigated as an indicator of health. The technique of indicators is established, but it must be extended, not only to "natural" environments, but also to include those dominated by man.

Can we proceed from broad presumptions which have utility while evidence is collected and analyzed? Can one say that where trees cannot live, then man should not try? Can one say that when the most abundant inhabitants, with man, are pigeons, starlings, and rats, a threshold has been crossed and either evacuation or redevelopment is necessary?

It is important that stable and healthy forests, marshes, deserts, rivers, and streams can be defined, that succession and retrogression can be identified, but it is even more necessary to find comparable definitions and indicators for the city. This moves the subject from the orthodoxy of ecology yet those concerned with the environment are the cohorts of medicine. Pathology is the concern of the medical sciences, the environment of health must be the concern of the artificers, but they require from ecologists an identification of healthy and healthful environments.

The role of the ecologists would include the identification of "healthy environments"—that is, for example, a forest wherein trees, shrubs, animals, and fish were conspicuously healthy and a determination of those factors which were contributory to this condition. Healthy natural environments could then be used as criteria against which adjacent urban environments could be compared.

In the city, examination of health or pathology devolves upon the social and medical sciences. It is necessary to determine stressors, the pathology of stress, and the environment of stress. Among stressors the poisons of food, atmosphere and water, density, noise, sensory overload, and sensory deprivation would be included. The pathology of stress—mortality, cancer, heart disease, suicide, alcoholism, crime, neuroses, and psychoses—might be mapped as isobars, and from the incidence and distribution of both stressors and stress disease the environments of stress may be located.

Given identification of healthy "natural" environments and the urban environments of stress pathology, diagnosis of environments becomes possible and therapy can be prescribed. There are environmental variables linked to most urban stressors. In this search for health and pathology in environments, indicators could serve a valuable role in diagnosis. In Philadelphia does the presence of hemlock indicate a tolerable level of particulate matter in the atmosphere? What plant pathology indicates a dangerous level of lead? Are there indicators of sulphur dioxide or nitrogen dioxide at "safe" levels? What creatures can coexist with levels of noise preferred by man? What indicators can be found for the optimum distribution of trace metals? Which reveal optimal concentrations? What can be inferred of human environments when trees degenerate?

This line of inquiry might well be unproductive yet there are now no operative standards of environmental quality, no limits are placed upon density, poisons, noise, no criteria are available as measures of existing environments or as programs for new environments.* It is clear that criteria are needed, and for the empiricist planner, indicators could be a vital tool. The conception of succession or retrogression, stability and instability must be utilized in the examination not only of wild environment, but of those environments dominated by man.

Where does the canary expire, the litmus change color? Where is the disgenic zone, the area of apathetic survival, the environment of full health—and what are the indicators?

The Morphology of Ecological Determinism

Each year a million acres of rural land succumb to hot-dog stands, sagging wires, billboards, diners, gas stations, split-levels, ranches, asphalt, and concrete. Most of this is accomplished without benefit of planning, landscape architecture, or architecture. Where these professionals intervene they utilize some part of available knowledge, the best of them are pressing for better information, yet action must occur even when information is inadequate.

This apologia precedes a description of three experiences in which the writer has been involved, each crude in terms of the available information and the interpretations made, yet, for all of their crudity, so effective in giving form as to justify description. These experiences permit extrapolation on the form of ecological determinism.

New Jersey Shore

From the fifth to the eighth of March 1962 a violent storm lashed the northeast coast from Georgia to Long Island. For three days sixty-mile-per-hour winds whipped high spring tides across 1,000 miles of ocean. Forty-foot waves pounded the shore and vast stretches of barrier islands and bay shore were flooded. In New Jersey alone, 2,400 houses were wrecked, 8,300 partially damaged, and eighty million dollars' worth of direct damages incurred over a three-day period. Almost all of this damage was caused by ignorance of natural process and the resultant destruction of the natural defenses against flood. In this case an ecological inventory existed, natural processes in the beach-bay-shore communities had been described and limiting factors identified, the values involved could be inferred from damages and costs. The requirements requested by this chapter for all ecosystems were satisfied in this one situation.

The theory of dune formation is well understood, as is stabilization by vegetation. The ecological communities from beach dune to bay shore have

---

*Since this essay was written, the Clean Air Acts, the Clean Water Acts, and several other laws have established standards for environmental quality and have placed limits on pollution.

been identified, as have been their limiting factors. In the Netherlands the value of dunes and their stabilizing grasses, and the important role of groundwater are known and attributed value, but not, however, in New Jersey. It is common knowledge that beaches are highly tolerant to human use but that dunes and their grasses are not. Development of the Jersey shore included breaching of dunes for many purposes—home building, beach access, etc. No constraints were placed upon use of dunes so that vegetation died and the dunes became unstable; no effective restraints were placed upon withdrawals of groundwater which inhibited vegetation growth. Considerable areas were waterproofed by buildings, roads, parking areas, which diminished recharge of the aquifers. The consequences were inevitable: With its natural defenses destroyed, the shore was vulnerable and was extensively damaged.

Had development responded to an understanding of natural process, ecological determinism, much if not all of the damage could have been averted. The form of development, however, would have been quite different. The beach, highly tolerant, would have been intensively utilized; the dunes, generally two in number between sea and bay, would have been inviolate, protected, stabilized by marram; access to the beach would have been made possible by bridges over the dunes; woody vegetation would have been protected in the trough; development would have been excluded from dunes and located only in wide areas of trough and on the bay side. Roads and parking would have been constructed of flexible, permeable materials; drainage would have been used for aquifer recharge; buildings would have been of columnar construction; withdrawals of groundwater would have been regulated. The application of this determinism, responsive to natural process, would have located buildings, roads, and drainage systems and determined their form. It would have been the principal determinant of planning, landscape architecture, and architecture. It would indeed produce the morphology of man-dune-bay for the New Jersey shore.

The Green Springs and Worthington Valleys

Seventy square miles of beautiful farmland adjacent to Baltimore were made accessible by the construction of a new expressway. The present population [in 1966] of 17,000 was predicted to rise to 75,000 by 1980, to 110,000 by the year 2000. It became necessary to determine where best this development would be located to ensure the conjunction of optimum development and optimum preservation. The conception of ecological determinism was invoked.

The area is characterized by three major valleys contained by wooded slopes with a large intervening plateau. It transpired that the valley bottoms were coterminous with the major aquifers in the region, that in the valleys were the major surface water systems, flood plains, and extensive soils unsuitable for development using septic tanks. The major source of erosion lay in the slopes defining the valleys. The plateau in contrast contained no major aquifers or minor streams; flood plains were absent, as were soils unsuitable for development using septic tanks.

Ecological determinism suggested prohibition of development in the valleys, prohibitions of development on bare slopes, development limited to one house per three acres on wooded slopes. In contrast, development was concentrated upon the plateau in a hierarchy of country town, villages, and hamlets, related in response to physiography. Development in wooded plateau sites was limited to one house per acre; this standard was waived on promontory sites, where high-rise apartments were recommended.

In this example, ecological analysis revealed the morphology of development; it selected the plateau as most tolerant, the valley bottoms and side slopes as least tolerant. It suggested densities of use appropriate to natural process. When this analysis was carried to a more detailed examination of the plateau, this, too, demonstrated variability in both opportunity and intolerance which suggested a hierarchy of communities, hamlets, villages, and a country town instead of pervasive suburbanization. Here the utilization of a very few determinants—surface water, groundwater, flood plains, alluvial silts, steep slopes, forest cover, and an interpretation of their permissiveness and prohibitions, revealed the morphology of man and the Maryland piedmont.

Metropolitan Open Space from Natural Processes

The Urban Renewal Agency and the states of Pennsylvania and New Jersey supported a research project to establish criteria for the selection of metropolitan open space. The hypothesis advanced was that such criteria can best be discerned by extending the inquiry to examine the operation of the major physical and biological processes in the region. It was suggested that when this is understood, and land-use policies reflect this understanding, not only will the values of natural process be ensured, the place for nature in the metropolis of man, but also there will be discerned a structure of natural process in the metropolitan area, form-giving for metropolitan growth, and the identification of areas for metropolitan open space, recreation, and amenity.

In the country at large and even in metropolitan areas, open space is seen to be absolutely abundant. In the Philadelphia Standard Metropolitan Statistical Area (PSMSA) only 19.1 percent of the area is urbanized; twenty years hence this may reach 30 percent, leaving 2,300 square miles of open space.

The problem of metropolitan open space lies, then, not in absolute area, but in distribution. The commodity concept of open space for amenity or recreation would suggest an interfusion of open space and population. The low attributed value of open space ensures that it is transformed into urban use within the urban area and at the perimeter. Normal process excludes interfusion and consumes peripheral open space.

Yet as the area of a circle follows the square of the radius, large open-space increments can exist within the urban perimeter without major increase in the radius or in the time distance from city center to urban fringe.

The major recommendation of this study was that the aggregate value of land, water, and air resources does justify a land-use policy which reflects both the value and operation of natural processes. Further, that the identification of natural processes, the permissiveness and prohibitions which they exhibit, revealed a system of open space which directs metropolitan growth and offers sites for metropolitan open space.

The characteristics of natural processes were examined; an attempt was made to identify their values, intrinsic value, work performed, and protection afforded. Large-scale functions were identified with the major physiographic divisions of uplands, coastal plain, and piedmont; smaller-scale functions of air-water corridors were identified; and finally, eight discrete parameters were selected for examination. These were: surface water, marshes, flood plains, aquifers, aquifer recharge areas, steep slopes, forests and woodlands, and prime agricultural lands.

For each of the discrete phenomena, and for each successive generalization, approximate permissiveness to other land uses and specific prohibitions were suggested. While all were permissive to a greater or lesser degree, all performed their natural process best in an unspoiled condition. Clearly, if land is abundant and land-use planning can reflect natural process, a fabric of substantially natural land can remain either in low-intensity use or undeveloped, interfused throughout the metropolitan region. It is from this land that metropolitan open space can best be selected.

When this concept was applied to the PSMSA, the uplands were discerned as performing an important role in natural process and offering a specific range of recreational opportunity. The coastal plain was observed to perform an equally important but very different role and offered another range of recreational potential. Uniting uplands and coastal plain to the central city are major air-water corridors, while at the lowest level exist the distribution of the eight parameters selected.

In general, planning for natural process would select uplands, coastal plains, and air-water corridors to remain relatively undeveloped; it would confirm urbanization in the piedmont. It would protect surface water and riparian lands, exempt flood plains from development by land uses other than those unimpaired by flooding or inseparable from waterfront locations, exclude development from marshlands and ensure their role as major water storage areas, limit development on aquifer resources and their recharge areas, protect prime farmland as present and prospective resources of agricultural productivity and scenic beauty, ensure the erosion-control function of forested steep slopes and ridges, and ensure their role, with forests and woodlands, in the water economy, and as a scenic-beauty and recreational potential.

Certain environmentally sensitive lands can be used for some purposes with restrictions. For example, recommended uses for such lands in the Philadelphia metropolitan area are as follows:

Land Type	Recommended Uses
Surface water and riparian lands	Ports, harbors, marinas, water-treatment plants, water-related industry, certain water-using industry, open space for institutions and housing, agriculture, forestry, recreation.
Marshes	Recreation.
Fifty-year flood plain	Ports, harbors, marinas, water-treatment plants, water-related and water-using industry, agriculture, forestry, recreation, institutional open space, open space of housing.
Aquifers	Agriculture, forestry, recreation, industries that do not produce toxic or offensive effluents. All land uses within limits set by percolation.
Aquifer recharge areas	As aquifers.
Prime agricultural lands	Agriculture, forestry, recreation, open space of institutions, housing at one house per twenty-five acres.
Steep lands	Forestry, recreation, housing at maximum density of one house per three acres.
Forests and woodlands	Forestry, recreation, housing at densities not higher than one house per acre, other factors permitting.

This concept, if realized, would ensure a structured system of open space within the metropolitan area within which only limited development would occur. It would produce the "natural" morphology of the metropolis. Due to the small number of parameters examined, this is a coarse-grain study. By increasing the number of phenomena and replacing the descriptive account of natural process by accurate quantitative analysis, the value of this information could be compounded.

The importance of these three examples lies simply in the fact that the commonplaces of natural science, where applied to planning, can be intensely illuminating and provide form in a most dramatic way from the level of the house on the shore to the form of metropolis.

Conclusion

Today, in the face of momentous change in which urbanization is one of the most dramatic phenomena, nature is seen to be defenseless against the positive acts of transformation. The proponents of nature emphasize preservation: a negative position, one of defense, which excludes positive participation in the real and difficult tasks of creating noble and ennobling cities in fair landscapes. Meanwhile, the positive acts of urbanism proceed without perception of natural process, blind to its operation, values, and form-giving rules, scarcely modified by appeals for preservation and protection, remorseless in destruction, and impotent in constructive creation.

The negative view of conservation and the disinterest of natural science in problems of planning and urbanism are disservices to society. The redirection of concern to include not only wild environments, but also those dominated by people is a challenge which the natural sciences and their public arm—conservation—must confront and accept. Understanding of natural process is of central importance to all environmental problems and must be introduced into all considerations of land utilization.

The burden of this chapter is a request to natural scientists, particularly ecologists, to provide the indispensable information which the artificers require—ecological inventories, explanation of natural processes and identification of their limiting factors, the attribution of value, the indicators of healthy and unhealthy environments, and, finally, the degree of permissiveness or prohibition to transformation, implicit in natural processes.

Given this information, those who bring goodwill to the problems of resource planning and urbanism may add knowledge. This information can provide the basis for persuasion in both private and public domains; it can indeed provide the basis for a federal land-use policy based upon natural processes.

Such information can identify roles with geographic locations and attribute values to them. Thus, catastrophe-prone and danger areas would be prohibited to development—earthquake, volcanic, hurricane, avalanche, flood, drought, fire, and subsidence zones; areas having great intrinsic value—wilderness areas, wildlife habitats, areas of great scenic beauty, areas having important scientific and educational value, would be identified and exempted from development; the concept of "work performed" would permit identification of constituent roles—water-catchment areas, dunes, flood, drought-and erosion-control areas, flood plains, airsheds, etc., on which only limited development, responsive to natural process, could occur. Positively this information could select areas suitable for development, tolerant to man. The final component, the indicator, would permit diagnosis and prescription for existing environments.

This ecological information is thus deterministic and might well be called ecological determinism. It reveals the megaform of natural processes at the national level, the mezoform of the region, the microform of the city. From the city down to the level of its parts, ecological determinants become participant parameters in the planning process, but still influential as form-giving.

Precursory ecology made possible the leap over the garden wall in the eighteenth century, but the landscape created was a pastoral one. Modern ecology can enable us to leap more surely into many different environments, reserving some, intervening with deference in others, accomplishing great and wise transformations for human habitats in certain selected locations. When the program is developed and understood, when pervasive, then the artist will make it manifest. His interventions will become metaphysical symbols revealed in art.

The search is then for the place of nature in the city of man and, even more profoundly, for the place of man in nature.

References

McHarg, Ian L., Roger D. Clemence, Ayre M. Dvir, Geoffrey A. Collins, Michael Laurie, William J. Oliphant, and Peter Ker Walker. 1963. *Sea, Storm and Survival, A Study of the New Jersey Shore* (mim.). Philadelphia: Department of Landscape Architecture, University of Pennsylvania.

McHarg, Ian L., David A. Wallace, Ann Louise Strong, William Grigsby, Anthony Tomazinis, Nohad Toulan, William H. Roberts, Donald Phimister, and Frank Shaw. 1963. *Metropolitan Open Space from Natural Processes* (mim.). Philadelphia: Department of Landscape Architecture, University of Pennsylvania.

Wallace, David A., and Ian L. McHarg. 1964. *Plan for the Valleys*. Philadelphia: Wallace-McHarg Associates.

4

Values, Process and Form (1968)

This paper was published while Design with Nature *was being written. McHarg first tested his theoretical concepts on applied ecology in this article, to an audience at the Institute for Advanced Study at Princeton University. He was "absolutely terrified" because of the stature of the audience. McHarg was so gratified by the positive response that he gave the paper again at the Smithsonian Institution, the version that appears here and that was published in* The Fitness of Man's Environment *(Harper and Row). Essentially, McHarg was seeking confirmation for his ideas about ecology and was able to present theories, which he considered risky coming from a landscape architect, to audiences of distinguished scientists at Princeton and the Smithsonian.*

It is my proposition that, to all practical purposes, Western man remains obdurately pre-Copernican, believing that he bestrides the earth round which the sun, the galaxy, and the very cosmos revolve. This delusion has fueled our ignorance in time past and is directly responsible for the prodigal destruction of nature and for the encapsulating burrows that are the dysgenic city.

We must see nature and man as an evolutionary process which responds to laws, which exhibits direction, and which is subject to the final test of survival. We must learn that nature includes an intrinsic value-system in which the currency is energy and the inventory is matter and its cycles—the oceans and the hydrologic cycle, life forms and their roles, the cooperative mechanisms which life has developed, and, not least, their genetic potential. The measure of success in this process, in terms of the biosphere, is the accumulation of negentropy in physical systems and ecosystems, the evolution of apperception or consciousness, and the extension of symbioses—all of which might well be described as creation.

This can be pictured simply in a comparison between the early earth and the present planet. In the intervening billions of years the earth has been transformed and the major change has been in the increase of order. Think of the turbulence and violence of the early earth, racked by earthquakes and vulcanism, as it evolved toward equilibrium, and of the unrestrained movements of water, the dust storms of unstabilized soils, and the extreme alternations of climate unmodified by a green, meliorative vegetative cover. In this early world physical processes operated toward repose, but in the shallow bays there emerged life and a new kind of ordering was initiated. The atmosphere which could sustain life was not the least of the creations of life. Life elaborated in the seas and then colonized the earth, thus increasing the opportunities for life and for evolution. Plants and decomposers created the soils, anchored the surface of the earth, checked the movements of soil particles, modified water processes, meliorated the climate, and ordered the distribution of nutrients. Species evolved to occupy and create more habitats, more niches, each increase requiring new cooperative relationships between organisms—new roles, all of which were beneficial. In the earth's history can be seen the orderings which life has accomplished: the increase to life forms, habitats and roles, symbiotic relationships, and the dynamic equilibrium in the system—the total an increase in order. This is creation.

In the early earth, the sunlight which fell upon the planet equaled the degraded energy which was radiated from it. Since the beginning of plant life, some of the sun's energy has been entrapped by photosynthesis and employed with matter to constitute the ordered beings of plants; thence, to the animals and decomposers, and all of the orderings which they have accomplished. This energy will surely be degraded, but the entrapped energy, with matter, is manifest in all life forms past and present, and in all of the orderings which they have accomplished. Thus, creation equals the energy which has been temporarily entrapped and used with matter to accomplish all of the ordering of physical, biological, and cultural evolution. This, physicists describe as negentropy, in contrast with the inevitable degradation of energy which is described as entropy.

By this we see the world as a creative process involving all matter and all life forms in all time past and in the present. Thus, creation reveals two forms: first, the physical entrapment and ordering which is accomplished primarily by plants and by the simplest animals; and, second, apperception and the resulting ordering for which an increased capacity is observed as species rise in the phylogenetic scale. In this, man is seen to be especially endowed. This view of the world as a creative process involving all of its denizens, including man, in a cooperative enterprise, is foreign to the Western tradition that insists upon the exclusive divinity of man, his independent superiority, dominion, and license to subjugate the earth. It is this man in whose image was God made. This concept of nature as a creative, interacting process in which man is involved with all other life forms is the ecological view. It is, I submit, the best approximation of the world that has been presented to us, and the indispensable approach to determining the role of man in the biosphere. It is indispensable also for investigation, not only of the adaptations which man accomplishes, but of their forms.

The place, the plants, the animals, and man, and the orderings which they have accomplished over time, are revealed in form. To understand this it is necessary to invoke all physical, biological, and cultural evolution. Form and process are indivisible aspects of a single phenomenon: being. Norbert Weiner described the world as consisting of "To Whom It May Concern" messages, but these are clothed in form. Process and fitness (which is the criterion of process) are revealed in form; form contains meaning. The artifact, tool, room, street, building, town or city, garden or region, can be examined in terms of process, manifest in form, which may be unfit, fit, or most fitting. The last of these, when made by man, is art.

The role of man is to understand nature, which is also to say man, and to intervene to enhance its creative processes. He is the prospective steward of the biosphere. The fruits of the anthropocentric view are in the improvement of the social environment, and great indeed are their values, but an encomium on social evolution is not my competence, and I leave the subject with the observation that, while Madison, Jefferson, Hamilton, and Washington might well take pride in many of our institutions, it is likely that they would recoil in horror from the face of the land of the free.

An indictment of the physical environment is too easy, for post-industrial cities are such squalid testimony to the bondage of toil and to the insensitivity of man, that the most casual examination of history reveals the modern city as a travesty of its antecedents and a denial of its role as the proudest testimony to peoples and their cultures. The city is no longer the preferred residence for the polite, the civilized, and the urbane, all of which say "city." They have fled to the illusion of the suburb, escaping the iridescent shills, neon vulgarity of the merchants, usurious slumlords, cynical polluters (household names for great corporations, not yet housebroken), crime, violence, and corruption. Thus, the city is the home of the poor, who are chained to it, and the repository of dirty industry and the commuter's automobile. Give us your poor and oppressed, and we will give them Harlem and the Lower East Side, Bedford-Stuyvesant, the South Side of Chicago, and the North of Philadelphia—or, if they are very lucky, Levittown. Look at one of these habitats through the Cornell Medical School study of Midtown Manhattan, where 20 percent of a sample population was found to be indistinguishable from the patients in mental institutions, and where a further 60 percent evidenced mental disease. Observe the environments of physical, mental, and social pathology. What of the countryside? Well, you may drive from the city and search for the rural landscape, but to do so you will follow the paths of those who preceded you, and many of them stayed to build. But those who did so first are now deeply embedded in the fabric of the city. So as you go you will transect the annular rings of the thwarted and disillusioned who are encapsulated in the city as nature endlessly eludes pursuit. You can tell when you have reached the edge of the rural scene for there are many emblems: the cadavers of old trees, piled in untidy heaps beside the magnificent machines for land despoliation, at the edge of the razed deserts; forests felled; marshes filled; farms obliterated; streams culverted; and the sweet rural scene transformed into the ticky-tacky vulgarity of the merchants' creed and expression. What of the continent? Well, Lake Erie is on the verge of becoming septic, New York suffers from water shortages as the Hudson flows foully past, and the Delaware is threatened by salt water intrusion. Smog, forest fires, and mud slides have become a way of life for Los Angeles. In San Francisco, the Bay is being filled and men build upon unconsolidated sediments, the most perilous foundations in this earthquake-prone area. DDT is in Arctic ice and ocean deeps, radioactive wastes rest on the Continental Shelf, the Mississippi is engorged with five cubic miles of topsoil each year, the primeval forests are all but gone, flood and drought become increasingly common, the once-deep prairie soils are thinner now and we might as well recognize that itinerant investment farming is just another extractive industry.

This is the face of our Western inheritance—Judaism, Christianity, Humanism, and the Materialism which is better named "Economic Determinism." The countryside, the last great cornucopia of the world's bounty, ravaged; and the city of man (God's Junkyard, or call it Bedlam) a vast demonstration of man's inhumanity to man, where existence, sustained by modern medicine and social legislation, is possible in spite of the physical environment. Yet we are the inheritors of enormous beauty, wealth, and variety. Our world is aching for the glorious cities of civilized and urbane men. Land and resources are abundant. We could build a thousand new cities in the most wonderful locations—on mountains and plains, on rocky ocean promontories, on desert and delta, by rivers and lakes, on islands and plateaus. It is within our compass to select the widest range of the most desirable lands and promulgate policies and regulations to ensure the realization of these cities, each in response to the nature of its site. We can manage the land for its health, productivity, and beauty. All of these things are within the capacity of this people now. It is necessary to resolve to fulfill the American Revolution and to create the fair image that can be the land of the free and the home of the brave. But to resolve is not enough; it is also necessary that society at large understand nature as a process, having values, limiting factors, opportunities, and constraints; that creation and destruction are real; that there are criteria by which we can discern the direction and tests of evolution; and, finally, that there are formal implications revealed in the environment which affect the nature and form of human adaptations.

What inherited values have produced this plight, from which we must be released if the revolution is to be completed? Surely it is the very core of our tradition, the Judeo-Christian-Humanist view which is so unknowing of nature and of man, which has bred and sustained his simple-minded anthropocentrism and anthropomorphism. It is this obsolete view of man and nature which is the greatest impediment to our emancipation as managers of the countryside, city builders, and artists. If it requires little effort to mobilize a sweeping indictment of the physical environment which is man's creation, it takes little more to identify the source of the value system which is the culprit. Whatever the origins, the text is quite clear in Judaism, was absorbed all but unchanged into Christianity, and was inflated in Humanism to become the implicit attitude of Western man to nature and the environment. Western man is exclusively divine, all other creatures and things occupy lower and generally inconsequential status; man is given dominion over all creatures and things; he is enjoined to subdue the earth. Here is the best of all possible texts for him who would contemplate biocide, carelessly extirpate great realms of life, create Panama Canals, or dig Alaskan harbors with atomic demolition. Here is the appropriate injunction for the land rapist, the befouler of air and water, the uglifier, and the gratified bulldozer. Dominion and subjugation, or better call it conquest, are their creeds. It matters little that theologians point to the same source for a different text, and choose rather the image of man the steward who should dress the garden and keep it. It matters little that Buber and Heschel, Teilhard de Chardin, Weigel and Tillich retreat from the literality of the dominion and subjugation text, and insist that this is allegory. It remains the literal injunction which has been so warmly welcomed and enshrined at the core of the Western view. This environment was created by the man who believes that the cosmos is a pyramid erected to support man on its pinnacle, that reality exists only because man can perceive it, that God is made in the image of man, and that the world consists solely of a dialog between men. Surely this is an infantilism which is unendurable. It is a residue from a past of inconsequence when a few puny men cried of their supremacy to an unhearing and uncaring world. One longs for a psychiatrist who can assure man that his deep-seated cultural inferiority is no longer necessary or appropriate. He can now stand erect among the creatures and reveal his emancipation. His ancient vengeance and strident cries are a product of an earlier insignificance and are now obsolete. It is not really necessary to destroy nature in order to obtain God's favor or even his undivided attention. To this ancient view the past two centuries have added only materialism—an economic determinism which has merely sustained earlier views.

The face of the city and the land are the best testimony to the concept of conquest and exploitation—the merchants' creed. The Gross National Product is the proof of its success, money is its measure, convenience is its cohort, the short term is its span, and the devil take the hindmost is its morality. The economists, with some conspicuous exceptions, have become the spokesmen for the merchants' creed and in concert they ask with the most barefaced effrontery that we accommodate our values to theirs. Neither love nor compassion, health nor beauty, dignity nor freedom, grace nor delight are true unless they can be priced. If not, they are described as nonprice benefits and relegated to inconsequence, and the economic model proceeds towards its self-fulfillment—which is to say more despoliation. The major criticism of this model is not that it is partial (which is conceded by its strongest advocates), but more that the features which are excluded are among the most important human values, and also the requirements for survival. If the ethics of society insist that it is man's bounden duty to subdue the earth, then it is likely that he will obtain the tools with which to accomplish this. If there is established a value system based upon exploitation of the earth, then the essential components for survival, health, and evolution are likely to be discounted, as they are. It can then come as no surprise to us that the most scabrous slum is more highly valued than the most beautiful landscape, that the most loathsome roadside stand is more highly valued than the richest farmland, and that this society should more highly prize tomato stakes than the primeval redwoods whence they come.

It is, in part, understandable why our economic value system is completely blind to the realities of the biophysical world—why it excludes from consideration, not only the most important human aspirations, but even those processes which are indispensable for survival. The origins of society and exchange began in an early world where man was a trifling inconsequence in the face of an overwhelming nature. He knew little of its operation. He bartered his surpluses of food and hides, cattle, sheep and goats; and valued such scarcities as gold, silver, myrrh, and frankincense. In the intervening millennia the valuations attributed to commodities have increased in range and precision and the understanding of the operation of this limited sphere has increased dramatically. Yet, we are still unable to identify and evaluate the processes which are indispensable for survival. When you give money to a broker to invest you do so on the understanding that this man understands a process well enough to make the investment a productive one. Who are the men to whom you entrust the responsibility for ensuring a productive return on the world's investment? Surely, those who understand physical and biological processes realize that these are creative. The man who views plants as the basis of negentropy in the world and the base of the food chain, as the source of atmospheric oxygen, fossil fuels and fibers, is a different man from one who values only economic plants, or that man who considers them as decorative but irrelevant aspects of life. The man who sees the sun as the source of life and the hydrologic cycle as its greatest work, is a different man from one who values sunlight in terms of a recreation industry, a portion of agricultural income, or from that man who can obscure sky and sunlight with air pollution, or who carelessly befouls water. The man who knows that the great recycling of matter, the return stroke in the world's cycles, is performed by the decomposer bacteria, views soils and water differently from the man who values a few bacteria in antibiotics, or he who is so unknowing of bacteria that he can blithely sterilize soils or make streams septic. That man who has no sense of the time which it has taken for the elaboration of life and symbiotic arrangements which have evolved, can carelessly extirpate creatures. That man who knows nothing of the value of the genetic pool, the greatest resource which we bring to the future, is not likely to fear radiation hazard or to value life. Clearly, it is illusory to expect the formulation of a precise value system which can include the relative value of sun, moon, stars, the changing seasons, physical processes, life forms, their roles, their symbiotic relationships, or the genetic pool. Yet, without precise evaluation, it is apparent that there will be a profound difference in attitude—indeed, a profoundly different value system—between those who understand the history of evolution and the interacting processes of the biosphere, and those who do not.

The simpler people who were our ancestors (like primitive peoples today) did not subscribe to anthropocentric views, nor did the eighteenth-century English landscape tradition which is the finest accomplishment of Western art in the environment, and which derives from a different hypothesis. The vernacular architecture in the Western tradition and the attitudes of the good farmer come from yet another source, one which has more consonance with the Orient than the West. But the views which ensured successes for the hunter and gatherer, for the vernacular farmer, and for the creation of a rich and beautiful pastoral landscape are inadequate to deal with twentieth-century problems of an inordinate population growth, accelerating technology, and transformation from a rural to an urban world. We need a general theory which encompasses physical, biological, and cultural evolution; which contains an intrinsic value system; which includes criteria of creativity and destruction and, not least, principles by which we can measure adaptations and their form. Surely, the minimum requirement for an attitude to nature and to man is that it approximate reality. Clearly, our traditional view does not. If one would know of these things, where else should one turn but to science. If one wishes to know of the phenomenal world, where better to ask than the natural sciences; if one would know of the interactions between organism and environment, then turn to the ecologist, for this is his competence. From the ecological view, one can conclude that by living one is united physically to the origins of life. If life originated from matter, then by living one is united with the primeval hydrogen. The earth has been the one home for all of its evolving processes and for all of its inhabitants; from hydrogen to man, it is only the bathing sunlight which changes. The planet contains our origins, our history, our milieu—it is our home. It is in this sense that ecology, derived from *oikos,* is the science of the home. Can we review physical and biological evolution to discern the character of these processes, their direction, the laws which obtain, the criteria for survival and success? If this can be done, there will also be revealed an intrinsic value system and the basis for form. This is the essential ingredient of an adequate view of the world: a value system which corresponds to the creative processes of the world, and both a diagnostic and constructive view of human adaptations and their form.

The evolution of the world reveals movement from more to less random, from less to more structured, from simplicity to diversity, from few to many life forms—in a word, toward greater negentropy. This can be seen in the evolution of the elements, the compounds, and life. It is accomplished by physical processes, as in the early earth when matter liquefied and coalesced, forming the concentric cores of the planet. Vulcanism revealed the turbulence of early adaptations toward equilibrium. So, too, did the creation of the oceans. Evaporation and precipitation initiated the processes of erosion and sedimentation in which matter was physically sorted and ordered. When, from the aluminosilicate clays in the shallow bays, there emerged that novel organization, life, there developed a new agency for accomplishing ordering. The chloroplast of the plant was enabled to transmute sunlight into a higher ordering, sustaining all life. The atmosphere, originally hostile to life, was adapted by life to sustain and protect it, another form of ordering. The emergence of the decomposers, bacteria and fungi, permitted the wastes of life forms—and their substance after death—to be recycled and utilized by the living, the return stroke in the cycle of matter in the biosphere. The increasing number of organisms in the oceans and on land represent negentropy in their beings and in the ordering which they accomplish. We can now see the earth as a process by which the falling sunlight is destined for entropy, but is arrested and entrapped by physical processes and creatures, and reconstituted into higher and higher levels of order as evolution proceeds. Entropy is the law and demands its price, but while all energy is destined to become degraded, physical and biological systems move to higher order—from instability towards steady-state—in sum, to more negentropy. Evolution is thus a creative process in which all physical processes and life forms participate. Creation involves the raising of matter and energy from lower to higher levels of order. Retrogression and destruction consist of reduction from the higher levels of order to entropy.

As life can only be transmitted by life, then the spore, seed, egg, and sperm contain a record of the entire history of life. The journey was shared with the worms, the coelenterates, the sponges, and, later, with the cartilaginous and bony fishes. The reptilian line is ours, the common ancestor that we share with the birds. We left this path to assume mammalian form, live births, the placenta, and suckling of the young; the long period of infantile dependence marks us. From this branching line the monotremes, marsupials, edentates, and pangolins followed their paths, and we proceeded on the primate way. Tree shrew, lemur, tarsier, and anthropoid, are our lineage. We are the line of man—the raised ape, the enlarged brain, the toolmaker—he of speech and symbols, conscious of the world and of himself. It is all written on the sperm and on the egg although the brain knows little of this journey. We have been through these stages in time past and the imprint of the journey is upon us. We can look at the world and see our kin; for we are united, by living, with all life, and are from the same origins. Life has proceeded from simple to complex, although the simplest forms have not been superseded, only augmented. It has proceeded from uniform to diverse, from few to many species. Life has revealed evolution as a progression from greater to lesser entropy. In the beginning was the atom of hydrogen with one electron. Matter evolved in the cosmic cauldrons, adding electron after electron, and terminating in the heaviest and most ephemeral of elements. Simple elements conjoined as compounds, thus reaching the most complex of these as amino acids, which is to say life. Life reached unicellular form and proceeded through tissue and organ to complex organisms. There were few species in the beginning and now they are myriad; there were few roles and now they are legion. There were once large populations of few species; now there is a biosphere consisting of multitudes of communities composed of innumerable interacting species. Evolution has revealed a progression from simple to complex, from uniform to diverse, from unicellular to multicelled, from few to many species, from few to many ecosystems, and the relations between these processes have also evolved toward increased complexity.

What holds the electrons to the nucleus? The molecules in rocks, air, and water may have ten atoms, but the organic molecule may have a thousand. Where is the catalytic enzyme which locks and unlocks the molecules? The single cell is very complex indeed; what orchestrates the cytoplasm and nucleus, nucleolus, mitochondria, chromosomes, centrosomes, Golgi elements, plastids, chromoplasts, leucoplasts, and, not least, chloroplasts? The lichen shows an early symbiosis at the level of the organism as the alga and the fungus unit. The plant and the decomposer enter into symbiosis to utilize energy and matter, to employ the first and recycle the latter. The animal enters the cycle, consuming the plant, to be consumed by the decomposer and thence by the plant. Each creature must adapt to the others in that concession of autonomy toward the end of survival that is symbiosis. Thus parasite and host, predator and prey, and those creatures of mutual benefit develop symbioses to ensure survival. The world works through cooperative mechanisms in which the autonomy of the individual, be it cell, organ, organism, species, or community is qualified toward the survival and evolution of higher levels of order culminating in the biosphere. Now these symbiotic relationships are beneficial to the sum of organisms although clearly many of them are detrimental to individuals and species. While the prey is not pleased with the predator or the host far from enamored of the parasite or the pathogen, these are regulators of populations and the agents of death—that essential return phase in the cycle of matter, which fuels new life and evolution. Only in this sense can the predator, parasite, and pathogen be seen as important symbiotic agents, essential to the creative processes of life and evolution. If evolution has proceeded from simple to complex, this was accomplished through symbiosis. As the number of species increased, so then did the number of roles and the symbiotic arrangements between species. If stability increases as evolution proceeds, then this is the proof of increased symbiosis. If conservation of energy is essential to the diminution of entropy, then symbioses are essential to accomplish this. Perhaps it is symbiosis or, better, altruism that is the arrow of evolution.

This view of the world, creation, and evolution reveals as the principal actors: the sun, elements and compounds, the hydrologic cycle, the plant, decomposers, and the animals. Further, if the measure of creation is negentropy, then it is the smallest marine plants which perform the bulk of the world's work, which produce the oxygen of the atmosphere, the basis of the great food chains. On land it is the smallest herbs. Among the animals the same is true; it is the smallest of marine animals and the terrestrial herbivores which accomplish the greatest creative effort of raising the substance of plants to higher orders. Man has little creative role in this realm although his destructive potential is considerable. However, energy can as well be considered as information. The light which heats the body can inform the perceptive creature. When energy is so considered, then the apperception of information as meaning, and response to it, is also seen as ordering, as antientropic. Noise to the unperceptive organism, through perception becomes information from which is derived meaning. In an appraisal of the world's work of apperception, it is seen that the simpler organisms, which create the maximum negentropy, are low on the scale of apperception which increases as one rises on the evolutionary scale. Man, who had no perceptible role as a creator of negentropy, becomes prominent as a perceptive and conscious being. We have seen that the evolution from the unicellular to the multicellular organism involved symbiotic relationships. Hans Selyé has described intercellular altruism as the cooperative mechanism which makes 30 billion human cells into a single integrated organism. He also has described interpersonal altruism. Surely one must conclude that the entire biosphere exhibits altruism. In this sense, the life forms which now exist on earth, and the symbiotic roles which they have developed, constitute the highest ordering which life forms have yet been able to achieve. The human organism exists as a result of the symbiotic relationships in which cells assume different roles as blood, tissues, and organs, integrated as a single organism. So, too, can the biosphere be considered as a single superorganism in which the oceans and the atmosphere, all creatures, and communities play roles analogous to cells, tissues, and organs. That which integrates either the cell in the organism or the organism in the biosphere is a symbiotic relationship. In sum, these are beneficial. This then is the third measure, the third element, after order and complexity, of the value system: the concession of some part of the autonomy of the individual in a cooperative arrangement with other organisms which have equally qualified their individual freedom toward the end of survival and evolution. We can see this in the alga and fungus composing the lichen, in the complex relationships in the forest, and in the sea. Symbiosis is the indispensable value in the survival of life forms, ecosystems, and the entire biosphere. Man is superbly endowed to be that conscious creature who can perceive the phenomenal world, its operation, its direction, the roles of the creatures, and physical processes. Through his apperception, he is enabled to accomplish adaptations which are the symbioses of man–nature. This is the promise of his apperception and consciousness. This examination of evolution reveals direction in retrospect— that the earth and its denizens are involved in a creative process of which negentropy is the measure. It shows that creation does have attributes which include evolution toward complexity, diversity, stability (steady-state), increase in the number of species, and increase in symbiosis. Survival is the first test, creation is the next; and this may be accomplished by arresting energy, by apperception, or by symbiosis. This reveals an intrinsic value system with a currency: energy; an inventory which includes matter and its cycles, life forms and their roles, and cooperative mechanisms.

All of the processes which have been discussed reveal form; indeed, form and process are indivisible aspects of a single phenomenon. That which can be seen reveals process. Much of this need not be superficially visible; it may lie beneath the skin, below the level of vision, or only in invisible paths which bespeak the interactions of organisms. Yet, the place, the plants, animals, men, and their works, are revealed in form.

All of the criteria used to measure evolutionary success apply to form. Simplicity and uniformity reveal a primitive stage, while complexity and diversity are evidence of higher evolutionary forms: few elements or species as opposed to many, few interactions rather than the multitude of advanced systems. Yet, there is need for a synoptic term which can include the presence or absence of these attributes in form. For this, we can use "fitness" both in the sense that Henderson employs it, and also in Darwinian terms. Thus, the environment is fit, and can be made more fitting; the organism adapts to fit the environment. Lawrence Henderson speaks of the fitness of the environment for life in the preface to his book, *The Fitness of the Environment.*

> Darwinian fitness is compounded of a mutual relationship between the organism and the environment. Of this, fitness of environment is quite as essential a component of the fitness which arises in the process of organic evolution; and in fundamental characteristics the actual environment is the fittest possible abode for life.

Henderson supports his proposition by elaborating on the characteristics of carbon, hydrogen, oxygen, water, and carbolic acid, saying that "No other environment consisting of primary constituents, made up of other known elements, or lacking water and carbolic acid, could possess a like number of fit characteristics, or in any manner such great fitness to promote complexity, durability, and the active metabolism and the organic mechanism we call life."

The environment is fit for life and all of the manifestations which it has taken, and does take. Conversely, the surviving and successful organism is fitted to the environment. Thus, we can use fitness as a criterion of the environment, organisms and their adaptations, as revealed in form. Form can reveal past processes and help to explain present realities. Mountains show their age and composition in their form; rivers demonstrate their age and reflect the physiography of their passage; the distribution and characteristics of soils are comprehensible in terms of historical geology, and climate and hydrology. The pattern and distribution of plants respond to environmental variables represented in the foregoing considerations, while animals respond to these and to the nature of the plant communities.

Man is as responsive, but he is selective; the pattern and distribution of man is likely to be comprehensible in these same terms. The term "fitness" has a higher utility than art for the simple reason that it encompasses all things—inert and living, nonhuman and those made by man—while art is limited to the last. Moreover, it offers a longer view and more evidence. Nature has been in the business of form since the beginning, and man is only one of its products. The fact that things and creatures exist is proof of their evolutionary fitness at the time, although among them there will be those more or less fit. There will be those which are unfit and will not persist, those are the misfits; then, those which are fit; and finally, the most fitting—all revealed in form. Form is also meaningful form. Through it, process and roles are revealed, but the revelation is limited by the capacity of the observer to perceive. Arctic differs from rain forest, tundra from ocean, forest from desert, plateau from delta; each is itself because. The platypus is different from seaweed, diatom from whale, monkey from man . . . because. Africans differ from Asians, Eskimo from Caucasoid, Mongoloid from Australoid . . . because; and all of these are manifest in form.

When process is understood, differentiation and form become comprehensible. Processes are dynamic, and so coastlines advance and recede as do ice sheets, lakes are in the process of filling while others form, mountains succumb to erosion and others rise. The lake becomes marsh, the estuary a delta, the prairie becomes desert, the scrub turns into forest, a volcano creates an island, while continents sink. The observation of process, through form and the response, represents the evolution of information to meaning. If evolutionary success is revealed by the existence of creatures, then their fitness will be revealed in form; visible in organs, in organisms, and in communities of these. If this is so, then natural communities of plants and animals represent the most fitting adaptation to available environments. They are most fitting and will reveal this in form. Indeed, in the absence of man, these would be the inevitable expression. Thus, there is not only an appropriate ecosystem for any environment, and successional stages toward it, but such communities will reveal their fitness in their expression. This is a conclusion of enormous magnitude to those who are concerned with the land and its aspect: that there is a natural association of creatures for every environment. This could be called the intrinsic identity of the given form.

If this is so, then there will be organs, organisms, and communities of special fitness, and these will, of course, be revealed in form. This might well be described as the ideal. The creation of adaptations which seek to be metaphysical symbols is, in essence, the concern with representing the ideal. Adaptation of the environment is accomplished by all physical processes and by all life. Yet, certain of these transformations are more visible than others, and some are analogous to those accomplished by man. Throughout the natural world, many creatures are engaged in the business of using inert material to create adaptive environments. These reveal the individual, a society, or a population. Can the criteria of fitness be applied then to the artifact? We can accept that the stilt's legs, the flamingo's beak, and the mouth of the baleen whale are all splendid adaptations, and visibly so. It is no great leap to see the tennis serve, the left hook, and the jumping catch, as of the same realm as the impala's bound, the diving cormorant, or the leopard's lunge. Why then should we distinguish between the athletic gesture and the artifacts which are employed with them: the golf club, bat, glove, or tennis racquet? The instrument is only an extension of the limb.

If this is so, then we can equally decide if the hammer and saw are fit, or the knife, fork, and spoon. We can conclude that the tail-powered jet is more fit for the air than the clawing propellers. If we can examine tools, then we can as well examine the environments for activities: the dining room for dining, the bedroom for sleeping or for loving, the house, street, village, town, or city. Are they unfit, misfit, fit, or most fitting? It appears that any natural environment will have an appropriate expression of physical processes, revealed in physiography, hydrology, soils, plants, and animals.

There should then be an appropriate morphology for man-site, and this should vary with environments. There will then be a fitting-for-man environment. One would expect that as the plants and animals vary profoundly from environment to environment, this should also apply to man. One would then expect to find distinct morphologies for man–nature in each of the major physiographic regions. The house, village, town, and city should vary from desert to delta, from mountain to plain. One would expect to find certain generic unity within these regions, but marked differentiation between them.

If fitness is a synoptic measure of evolutionary success, what criteria can we use to measure it? We have seen that it must meet the simplicity-complexity, uniformity-diversity, instability-stability, independence-interdependence tests. Yet, in the view of Ruth Patrick, as demonstrated by her study of aquatic systems, these may all be subsumed under two terms: ill-health and health. A movement towards simplicity, uniformity, instability, and a low number of species characterizes disease. The opposites are evidence of health. This corresponds to common usage: ill-health is unfit; fitness and health are synonymous. Thus, if we would examine the works of man and his adaptations to the countryside, perhaps the most synoptic criteria are disease and health. We can conclude that which sustains health represents a fitting between man and the environment. We would expect that this fitness be revealed in form. This criterion might well be the most useful to examine the city of man: wherein does pathology reside? What are its corollaries in the physical and social environment? What characterizes an environment of health? What are its institutions? What is its form? Know this, and we may be able to diagnose and prescribe with an assurance which is absent today.

What conclusions can one reach from this investigation? The first is that the greatest failure of Western society, and of the post-industrial period in particular, is the despoliation of the natural world and the inhibition of life which is represented by modern cities. It is apparent that this is the inevitable consequence of the values that have been our inheritance. It is clear, to me if to no one else, that these values have little correspondence to reality and perpetrate an enormous delusion as to the world, its work, the importance of the roles that are performed, and, not least, the potential role of man. In this delusion the economic model is conspicuously inadequate, excluding as it does the most important human aspirations and the realities of the biophysical world. The remedy requires that the understanding of this world which now reposes in the natural sciences be absorbed into the conscious value system of society, and that we learn of the evolutionary past and the roles played by physical processes and life forms. We must learn of the criteria for creation and destruction, and of the attributes of both. We need to formulate an encompassing value system which corresponds to reality and which uses the absolute values of energy, matter, life forms, cycles, roles, and symbioses.

We can observe that there seem to be three creative roles. The first is the arresting of energy in the form of negentropy, which offers little opportunity to man. Second is apperception and the ordering which can be accomplished through consciousness and understanding. Third is the creation of symbiotic arrangement, for which man is superbly endowed. It can be seen that form is only a particular mode for examining process and the adaptations to the environment accomplished by process. Form can be the test used to determine processes as primitive or advanced, to ascertain if they are evolving or retrogressing. Fitness appears to have a great utility for measuring form: unfit, fit, or most fitting. When one considers the adaptations accomplished by man, they are seen to be amenable to this same criterion but, also, synoptically measurable in terms of health. Identify the environment of pathology; it is unfit, and will reveal this in form. Where is the environment of health— physical, mental, and social? This, too, should reveal its fitness in form. How can this knowledge be used to affect the quality of the environment? The first requirement is an ecological inventory in which physical processes and life forms are identified and located within ecosystems, which consist of discrete but interacting natural processes. These data should then be interpreted as a value system with intrinsic values, offering both opportunities and constraints to human use, and implications for management and the forms of human adaptations.

The city should be subject to the same inventory and its physical, biological, and cultural processes should be measured in terms of fitness and unfitness, health and pathology. This should become the basis for the morphology of man–nature and man–city. We must abandon the self-mutilation which has been our way, reject the title of planetary disease which is so richly deserved, and abandon the value system of our inheritance which has so grossly misled us. We must see nature as a process within which man exists, splendidly equipped to become the manager of the biosphere; and give form to that symbiosis which is his greatest role, man the world's steward.

5

Open Space from
Natural Processes (1970)

This essay resulted from a study of metropolitan open space sponsored by the U.S. Department of Housing and Urban Development (HUD) and the states of New Jersey and Pennsylvania. McHarg's partner and colleague, David Wallace, edited the book Metropolitan Open Space and Natural Process *(published by the University of Pennsylvania Press), which was based on the HUD study. Contributors to the study and the book included McHarg and Wallace's Penn colleagues: Ann Strong, William Grigsby, William Roberts, and Nohad Toulan.*

McHarg's very specific study for open space in the Philadelphia metropolitan region became the model for other open space studies. Essentially, the study was based on the "simple working method for open space" that he had been exploring for a decade (see, for example, chapter 2 of this book, "The Place of Nature in the City of Man"). McHarg's concept of protecting environmentally sensitive areas (marshes, swamps, flood plains, steep slopes, and prime habitats) was followed in many subsequent regional open space plans. For example, the 1995 Desert Open Spaces plan for the Phoenix region undertaken by Design Workshop for the Maricopa Association of Governments has many similarities to McHarg's efforts three decades earlier. The concept also influenced environmental planning rule making, as for example, the elevated position wetlands (in 1970 called marshes and swamps) eventually received in environmental policy. Although the open space plan for Philadelphia was not implemented, McHarg later collaborated on a similar effort for Tulsa, Oklahoma, which was followed.

There is need for an objective and systematic method of identifying and evaluating land most suitable for metropolitan open space based on the natural roles that it performs. These roles can best be understood by examining the degree to which natural processes perform work for man without his intervention, and by studying the protection which is afforded and values which are derived when certain of these lands are undisturbed.

Introduction

A million acres of land each year are lost from prime farmland and forest to less sustainable and uglier land uses. There is little effective metropolitan planning and still less implementation of what is planned. Development occurs without reference to natural phenomena. Flood plains, marshes, steep slopes, woods, forests, and farmland are destroyed with little if any remorse; streams are culverted, groundwater, surface water, and atmosphere polluted, floods and droughts exacerbated, and beauty superseded by vulgarity and ugliness. Yet the instinct for suburbia which has resulted in this enormous despoliation of nature is based upon a pervasive and profoundly felt need for a more natural environment.

The paradox and tragedy of metropolitan growth and suburbanization is that it destroys many of its own objectives. The open countryside is subject to uncontrolled, sporadic, uncoordinated, unplanned development, representing the sum of isolated short-term private decisions of little taste or skill. Nature recedes under this careless assault, to be replaced usually by growing islands of developments. These quickly coalesce into a mass of low-grade urban tissue, which eliminate all natural beauty and diminish excellence, both historic and modern. The opportunity for realizing an important part of the "American dream" continually recedes to a more distant area and a future generation. For this is the characteristic pattern of metropolitan growth. Those who escape from the city to the country are often encased with their disillusions in the enveloping suburb.

The Hypothesis

This pattern of indiscriminate metropolitan urbanization dramatizes the need for an objective and systematic way of identifying and preserving land most suitable for open space, diverting growth from it, and directing development to land more suitable for urbanization. The assumption is that not all land in an urban area needs to be, or even ever is, all developed. Therefore choice is possible. The discrimination which is sought would select lands for open space which perform important work in their natural condition, are relatively unsuitable for development, are self-maintaining in the ecological sense, and occur in a desirable pattern of interfusion with the urban fabric.

The optimum result would be a system of two intertwining webs, one composed of developed land and the second consisting of open space in a natural or near natural state.

Heretofore, urbanization has been a positive act of transformation. Open space has played a passive role. Little if any value has been attributed to the natural processes often because of the failure to understand their roles and values. This is all the more remarkable when we consider the high land values associated with urban open space—Central Park in New York, Rittenhouse Square in Philadelphia being obvious examples. This lack of understanding has militated against the preservation or creation of metropolitan open space systems complementary to metropolitan growth. In this situation, governmental restraints are necessary to protect the public from the damaging consequences of private acts which incur both costs and losses to the public, when these acts violate and interrupt natural processes and diminish social values. There is an urgent need for land-use regulations related to natural processes, based upon their intrinsic value and their permissiveness and limitations to development. This in turn requires general agreement as to the social values of natural process.

Planning that understands and properly values natural processes must start with the identification of the processes at work in nature. It must then determine the value of subprocesses to man, both in the parts and in the aggregate, and finally establish principles of development and nondevelopment based on the tolerance and intolerance of the natural processes to various aspects of urbanization. It is presumed that when the operation of these processes is understood, and land-use policies reflect this understanding, it will be evidence that the processes can often be perpetuated at little cost.

The arguments for providing open space in the metropolitan region, usually dependent on amenity alone, can be substantially reinforced if policymakers understand and appreciate the operation of the major physical and biological processes at work. A structure for metropolitan growth can be combined with a network of open spaces that not only protects natural processes but also is of inestimable value for amenity and recreation.

In brief, it is hypothesized that the criteria for metropolitan open space should derive from an understanding of natural processes, their value to people, their permissiveness, and their prohibition to development. The method of physiographic analysis outlined here can lead to principles of land development and preservation for any metropolitan area. When applied as a part of the planning process, it can be a defensible basis for an open space system which goes far toward preserving the balance of natural processes and toward making our cities livable and beautiful.

Normal Metropolitan Growth Does Not Provide Open Space, Although Land Is Abundant

Without the use of such a method as described earlier, open space is infinitely vulnerable. An examination of the growth in this century of the major metropolitan areas of the United States demonstrates that urbanization develops primarily on open land rather than through redevelopment. The open space interspersed in areas of low-density development within the urban fabric is filled by more intensive uses and open space standards are lowered. Urban growth consumes open space both at the perimeter and within the urban fabric. The result is a scarcity of open space where population and demand are greatest. This phenomenon has aroused wide public concern as the growth of the cities, by accretion, has produced unattractive and unrelieved physical environments. Amenity, breathing space, recreational areas, and the opportunity for contact with nature for an expanding population are diminished. As important, it often exacerbates flood, drought, erosion, and humidity and it diminishes recreational opportunity, scenic, historic, and wildlife resources. Further, the absence of understanding of natural processes often leads to development in locations which are not propitious. When natural processes are interrupted, there are often resultant costs to society.

Demand for urban space is not only relatively but absolutely small. The 37 million inhabitants of megalopolis, constituting 24 percent of the U.S. population, occupied 1.8 percent of the land area of the continental United States (Gottman 1996, p. 26). Only 5 percent of the United States is urbanized today; it is projected that less than 10 percent will be so utilized by the year 2000. Space is abundant. Even in metropolitan regions, where large urban populations exist in a semi-rural hinterland, the proportion of urban to rural land does not basically contradict the assertion of open space abundance. For example, in the Philadelphia Standard Metropolitan Statistical Area (PSMSA), with 3,500 square miles or 2,250,000 acres, only 19.1 percent was urbanized in 1960. Here an increase in population from 4 million to 6,000,000 is anticipated by 1980. Should this growth continue and occur at an average gross density of three families per acre, only 30 percent of the land area would be in urban land use at that time. Some 2,300 square miles or 1,500,000 acres would still remain in open space.

The difficulty in planning lies in the relationship of this open space to urban uses. The market mechanism which raises the unit price of land for urban use tends to inhibit interfusion of open space in the urban fabric. Open space becomes normally a marginal or transitional use, remaining open only while land is awaiting development. The key question then is, if land is absolutely abundant, how can growth be guided in such a way as to exploit this abundance for the maximum good?

Exceptions to the General Experience

While generally metropolitan growth has been unsympathetic to natural processes, there are exceptions. In the late nineteenth- and early twentieth-century park planning, water courses were an important basis for site selection. The Capper Cromptin Act selected river corridors in Washington, D.C. The Cook County Park System around Chicago consists of corridors of forests preponderantly based upon river valleys. The first metropolitan open space plan, developed for Boston by Charles Eliot in 1893, emphasized not only rivers, but also coastal islands, beaches, and forested hills as site selection criteria. In 1928 Benton MacKaye, the originator of the Appalachian Trail, proposed using open space to control metropolitan growth in America but did not base his open space on natural process.

Patrick Abercrombie's Greater London Plan pays implicit attention to natural process in the location for the satellite towns, in the insistence on open space breaks between nucleated growth, in the recommendation that prime agricultural land should not be urbanized, and in specifying that river courses should constitute a basis for the open space system.

In recent studies conducted by Philip Lewis on a state-wide basis for Illinois and Wisconsin (e.g., State of Wisconsin 1962) physiographic determinants of land utilization have been carried beyond these earlier examples. Corridors have been identified which contain watercourses and their flood plains, steep slopes, forests, wildlife habitats, and historic areas. These characteristics are of value to a wide range of potential supporters—conservationists, historians, and the like—and the studies demonstrate the coincidence of their interests in the corridors. The expectation is that these groups will coordinate their efforts and combine their influence to retain the corridors as open space. Resource development and preservation is advocated for them. In another recent study, ecological principles were developed and tested as part of a planning process for the Green Spring and Worthington valleys, northwest of Baltimore Maryland.[1] Here the design process later described was evolved. Two more elaborate ecological studies, the first for Staten Island (McHarg 1969, pp. 103–15) and the second for the Twin Cities Metropolitan Region in Minnesota (Wallace, McHarg, Roberts, and Todd 1969), have undertaken to analyze natural processes to reveal intrinsic suitabilities for all prospective land uses. These are shown as unitary, complementary, or in competition.

The present study of metropolitan Philadelphia open space is more general in its objective. It seeks to find the major structure of open space in the PSMSA based upon the intrinsic values of certain selected natural processes to set the stage for further investigations.

Need for the Ecological Approach

There are, of course, several possible approaches. The first of these, beloved of the economist, views land as a commodity and allocates acres of land per thousand persons. In this view nature is seen as a generally uniform commodity, appraised in terms of time-distance from consumers and the costs of acquisition and development. A second approach also falls within the orthodoxy of planning, and may be described as the geometrical method. Made popular by Patrick Abercrombie, the distinguished British planner, this consists of circumscribing a city with a green ring wherein green activities, agriculture, recreation, and the like, are preserved or introduced.

The ecological approach, however, would suggest quite a different method. Beginning from the proposition that nature is process and represents values, relative values would be ascribed to certain discernible processes. Then, operating upon the presumption that nature performs services for man without his intervention or effort, certain service-processes would be identified as social values. Yet further, recognizing that some natural processes are inhospitable to human use—floods, earthquakes, hurricanes—we would seem to discover intrinsic constraints or even prohibitions to man's use or to certain kinds of use.

Objective discussion between the ecologist and the economist would quickly reveal the fallacy of the commodity approach. Nature is by definition not a uniform commodity. In contrast, each and every area varies as a function of historical geology, climate, physiography, the water regimen, the pattern and distribution of soils, plants, and animals. Each area will vary as process, as value and in the opportunities and constraints which it proffers or withholds from human use.

In a similiar discussion between ecologist and green belt advocate, the question which most embarrasses the latter is whether nature is uniform within the belt and different beyond it. The next question is unlikely to receive an affirmative answer, "Does nature perform particular roles within the belt to permit its definition?" Clearly the ecologist emerges a victor in these small skirmishes, but now the burden is upon him. What is the ecological approach to the selections of metropolitan open space?

The Value of Natural Process in the Ecosystem

There is, at present, no existing ecological model for a city or metropolitan region; it is necessary, therefore, to embark upon a theoretical analysis of natural process without the aid of such a model.[2]

Plant and animal communities require solar energy, food, nutrients, water, protection from climate extremes, and shelter. These conditions must be substantially regular in their provision. In order to ensure these optimal conditions, non-human or primitive-human systems have adapted to the natural environment and its constituent organisms to ensure a complex process of energy utilization, based upon photosynthesis, descending through many food chains to final decomposition and nutrient recirculation. In response to the problem of climatic extremes these communities do modify the microclimate. Such natural systems have mechanisms whereby water movement is modified to perform the maximum work. The aggregate of these processes is a stable, complex ecosystem in which entropy is low and energy is conserved (Odum 1959, ch. 3).

The net result is a system with high energy utilization and production, continuous soil formation, natural defenses against epidemic disease, microclimatic extremes diminished, minimal oscillation between flood and drought, minor erosion, and natural water purification. There obviously are many advantages which accrue to civilized man from this condition—a viable agriculture and forestry, abundant fish and wildlife, natural water purification, stability in the water system, defense against flood and drought, diminished erosion, sedimentation and silting, and a self-cleaning environment with high recreational potential and amenity.

The values of the natural processes far exceed the values which usually are attributed to them. Agriculture, forestry, and fisheries are taken into consideration in the evaluation of regional assets, but atmospheric oxygen, amelioration of climate and microclimate, water evaporation, precipitation, drainage, or the creation of soils tend to be disregarded. Yet the composite picture of the region's resources must include all natural processes. Beginning with the values of agriculture, forestry, and fisheries, the value of minerals and the value of the land for education, recreation, and amenity may be added. Agricultural land has an amenity which is not generally attributed, since it is also a landscape which is maintained as a byproduct. Forests equally have an amenity value and are self-cleaning environments, requiring little or no maintenance.

Water has values which transcend those related to certain discrete aspects of the hydrologic cycle. In this latter category are many important processes—water in agriculture, industry, commerce, recreation, education and amenity, consumption, cooling, hydroelectric generation, navigation, water transport and dilution, waste reduction, fisheries, and water recreation.

Value is seldom attributed to the atmosphere; yet the protection from lethal cosmic rays, insolation, the abundance of oxygen for animal metabolism and the carbon dioxide for plant metabolism which it affords, all demonstrate an indispensability equal to land and water. In terms of positive attributed value the atmosphere has been accorded virtually none. Only when atmosphere has become polluted are the cost and necessity of ensuring clean air recognized.

Even in the exceptional condition when natural processes are attributed value as in agriculture and forestry, these are generally held in such low esteem that they cannot endure in the face of competition from urban or industrial uses. It is impossible to construct a value system which includes the vast processes described. It is, however, quite possible to recognize the fundamental value of these processes, their characteristics, and their relationship to industrial and urban processes. This understanding should lead to a presumption in favor of nature rather than the prevailing disdain.

Working toward the goal of developing working principles for land-use planning in general and the selection of metropolitan open space in particular, it is advantageous to examine the degree to which natural processes perform work for man without his intervention and the protection achieved by leaving certain sub-processes in their natural state without development. While this cannot yet be demonstrated quantitatively, it can be described.

Natural processes which perform work for man include water purification, atmospheric pollution dispersal, microclimate amelioration, water storage and equalization, flood control, erosion control, topsoil accumulation, and the ensurance of wildlife populations.

Areas which are subject to volcanic action, earthquakes, tidal waves, tornadoes, hurricanes, floods, drought, forest fires, avalanches, mud slides, and subsidence, should be left undeveloped in order to avoid loss of life and property. In addition, there are other areas which are particularly vulnerable to human intervention; this category includes beach dunes, major animal habitats, breeding grounds, spawning grounds, and water catchment areas. There are also areas of unusual scenic, geological, biological, ecological, and historic importance. In each of these cases, it is apparent that wise land-use planning should recognize natural processes and respond to them. As many of these processes are water related, it would seem that water may be a useful indicator of these major physical and biological processes described as natural processes.

Water and Natural Processes

Water, as the agent of erosion and sedimentation, is linked with geological evolution to the realities of physiography. The mountains, hills, valleys, and plains which result, experience a variety of climate and microclimate consequent upon their physiography. The combination of physiography and climate determines the incidence and distribution of plants and animals, their niches and habitats.

The use of water as a unifying concept links marsh and forest, rivers and clouds, ground and surface water, all as interdependent aspects of a single process. It permits us to see that the marsh filled in the estuary and the upland forest felled are comparable in their effect, that pollution to surface water may affect distant groundwater, that building of an outlying suburb may affect the flood height in the city. Although we lack an ecological model, a gross perception of natural process may be revealed through the selection of water as a unifying process. This may suggest land-use policies reflecting the permissiveness and prohibitions of the constituent phases of water in process. By this useful method the constituent roles of open space may be seen and the optimal distribution of open space in the metropolitan region may be discerned.

Water is not the best indicator or theoretical tool for ecological planning. The physiographic region is perhaps the best unit for ecological studies since there tends to be a marked consistency within each physiographic region and distinct variations between them.

Water and the Roles of Major Physiographic Regions

In the Philadelphia metropolitan area study, the roles of the physiographic regions have been simplified to three components: the first, the uplands of the piedmont, second, the remainder of that region with the final category being the coastal plain. The area to be studied is the PSMSA three and one-half thousand square miles which constitute the metropolitan region and straddle coastal plain and piedmont, a situation typical of many cities on the eastern seaboard.

The Uplands

The uplands are the hills of the watershed, the highest elevations, wherein many streams begin, their watercourses narrow, steep, and rocky. The soils tend to be thin and infertile from long-term erosion. In the Philadelphia metropolis, the uplands consist of a broad band of low hills, 12 to 20 miles wide, bending northeast-southwest obliquely through the area. As a result of the absence of glaciation in this area the rivers and streams lack natural impoundments and are, therefore, particularly susceptible to seasonal fluctuations.

The natural restraints to flooding and drought, contributing to equilibrium, are mainly the presence and distribution of vegetation, principally forests and their soils, particularly on the uplands and their steep slopes. Vegetation absorbs and utilizes considerable quantities of water. In fact, vegetation and their soils act as a sponge restraining extreme runoff, releasing water slowly over longer periods, diminishing erosion and sedimentation—in short, diminishing the frequency and intensity of oscillation between flood and drought and operating toward equilibrium.

In the uplands, land-use policies should protect and enhance forests and other vegetative cover to diminish runoff, oscillation between flood and drought, and the insurance of natural water purification. On steep slopes, land-use management would notably include forestation programs. Land uses should then be related to permissiveness and prohibitions inherent in such a region related to the primary role of the upland sponge in the water economy.

The Piedmont

The piedmont is also non-glaciated in the study area, and consists of the gentler slope below the uplands. It sustains fertile soils which, in limestone areas, are equal in fertility to the richest in the entire United States. In the three divisions it is in the piedmont alone that fertile soils abound. Unglaciated, the piedmont, like the uplands, lacks natural impoundment and is flood prone.

Here is the land most often developed for agriculture. These lands, too, tend to be favored locations for villages, towns, and cities. Here, forests are often residues or the products of regeneration on abandoned farms. Steep slopes in the piedmont are associated with the dissected banks of streams and rivers.

The agricultural piedmont does not control its own defenses. It is either affected by or defended from flood and drought by the conditions in the uplands and coastal plain. When cropland is ploughed and lacks vegetation, when building sites are bared, they are subject to erosion and contribute to sediment yield. Even when covered with growing crops, the average runoff here exceeds the forest. Nonetheless, the vegetative cover, configuration, and conservation practices in the agricultural piedmont can either increase or diminish flood and drought. The piedmont is particularly vulnerable to both. The presence of forests and woodlands will act as ameliorative agents as they do in the uplands and the presence of vegetation will diminish runoff by absorption, friction, and through increased percolation.

The fine capillary streams of the uplands become the larger streams and rivers of the piedmont, and their volume increases proportionately, as does their flood potential and their oscillation to low flow.

In the piedmont, fertile soils should be perpetuated as an irreplaceable resource. Both agriculture and urbanization are primary contributors to erosion and sedimentation; they are also the major contributors to water pollution from pesticides, fertilizers, domestic and industrial wastes.

Planning should relate water pollution to specific stream capacities; withdrawals of water to specific capacities of surface water and groundwater; conservation practices to erosion control for farmland and construction sites.

The Coastal Plain

The coastal plain has been, through much of geologic time, a vast depository of sediments eroded from the uplands. The soils are shallow and acid, overlaying sedimentary material. These are naturally infertile although in New Jersey such sandy soils with abundant fertilizer and water, support extensive truck farming.

The major physiographic characteristics of the coastal plain are its flatness, the poverty of its soils, the abundant marshes, bays, estuaries, the unique flora of the pine barrens, and finally, the great resources of groundwater in aquifers.

The incidence of flood and drought in the piedmont and coastal plains is not only consequent upon the upland sponge, but also upon estuarine marshes, particularly where these are tidal. Here, at the mouth of the watershed, at the confluence of important rivers or river and sea, the flood components of confluent streams or the tidal components of flood assume great importance. In the Philadelphia metropolitan area, the estuary and the ocean are of prime importance as factors in flood.

A condition of intense precipitation over the region combined with high tides, full estuary, and strong on-shore winds brings together the elements that portend floods. The estuarine marshes and their vegetation constitute the major defense against this threat. These areas act as enormous storage reservoirs, absorbing mile-feet of potentially destructive waters, thus reducing flood potential. This function may be described as the estuarine sponge, in contrast to the upland sponge. The water resources of these aquifers represent a significant economic value.

In the coastal plain, the susceptibility to flood of these areas and the invaluable role of marshlands as flood storage reservoirs should also be reflected in land-use policies which could ensure the perpetuation of their natural role in the water economy. The value of groundwater in aquifers should be reflected in land-use policy.

Finally, the extensive forests of the pine barrens and their unique flora depend upon fire, which is an inevitable and recurrent threat. Here extensive urbanization makes such a threat actuality: pine barrens are not suitable sites for development.

These three major divisions are clearly different in their permissiveness and prohibition, and in their roles in the water regimen: the uplands should be viewed and planned as the upstream control area for water processes, flood, drought, water quality, erosion control, and an area of high recreational potential. This region is not normally selected for extensive urbanization and can be easily protected from it. But it performs its role best when extensively forested.

The coastal plain performs a primary flood control, water supply, and water-related recreation function, and is not suited to extensive urbanization. The entire region, characterized by rivers, marshes, bays, and estuaries is critical to wildlife. Properly used, it offers a great recreational potential. In contrast, the piedmont, with the exception of prime agricultural areas, is tolerant to urbanization. Although the prime farmland of this region is an irreplaceable resource, a scenic value, and requires defense against urbanization, the piedmont should be the region for major urban growth in the future.

Planning for natural processes at this scale would regulate urban development in uplands and coastal plains, concentrate it in the piedmont, on non-prime agricultural land. Connecting these regions would be an undeveloped fabric of streams, rivers, marshes, bays, and estuaries, the steep slopes of dissected watercourses, as water corridors permeate the entire metropolis.

Significant Physiographic Phenomena and Their Roles

The major physiographic divisions reveal the principal roles in the water regimen and should constitute an important generalized basis for identification of natural processes and planning. Yet it is necessary to have a greater specificity as to the constituent roles of natural process. Toward this end, eight components have been selected for identification and examination. It is clear that they are to some extent identifiable and perform discrete roles. These eight constituent phenomena are:

1. Surface water
2. Marshes
3. Flood plains
4. Aquifers
5. Aquifer recharge areas
6. Prime agricultural lands
7. Steep lands
8. Forests and woodlands

The first five have a direct relationship to water; the remaining three are water-related in that they either have been determined by, or are determinants of water-in-process.

This group of water-related parameters is selected as containing the most useful indicators of natural process for a majority of metropolitan regions in the United States. They appear to be the most productive for the project area under study, but the underlying hypothesis of natural process would take precedence in these areas where other parameters prove to be more illuminating. That is, the selection of criteria for a system of metropolitan open space can best be developed from an understanding of the major physical and biological process *of the region itself*. The interconnected phenomena should be integrated into a unified system to which the planning process responds.

Varying Permissiveness to Urban Uses

Having identified certain sub-processes, it is necessary to describe their intrinsic function and value and then to determine the degree to which the performance of natural process is prohibitive or permissive to other land uses.

The terms prohibitive and permissive are used relatively. In no case does natural process absolutely prohibit development. Yet in a condition of land abundance, there is available a choice as to location of development. This being so, areas of importance to natural process should not be selected where alternative locations of lesser importance are available. Further, development of natural process areas should occur only where supervening benefits result from such development, in excess of those provided by natural process. Still further, the tolerances of natural processes to development by type, amount, and location are an important constituent of land-use policy.

Surface Water (5,671 linear miles)

In a situation of land abundance, restraints should be exercised on the development of surface water and riparian land. In principle, only those land uses which are inseparable from waterfront locations should occupy riparian lands; land uses thereon should be limited to those which do not diminish the present or prospective value of surface water or stream banks for water supply, amenity, or recreation.

In the category of consonant land uses would fall port and harbor facilities, marinas, water treatment plants, sewage treatment plants, water-related industry, and in certain instances, water-using industries.[3]

In the category of land uses which need not diminish existing or prospective value of surface water would fall agriculture, forestry, institutional open space, recreational facilities, and, under certain conditions, open space for housing.

In the category of land uses which would be specifically excluded would be industries producing toxic or noxious liquid effluents, waste dumps, non-water-related industry or commerce.

The presumption is then that surface water as a resource best performs its function in a natural state and that land uses which do not affect this state may occupy riparian land, but other functions be permitted according to the degree which their function is indivisibly water-related.

Marshes (133,984 acres; 7.44 percent)

In principle, land-use policy for marshes should reflect the roles of flood and water storage, wildlife habitat, and fish spawning grounds. Land uses which do not diminish the operation of the primary roles are compatible. Thus, hunting, fishing, sailing, recreation, in general, would be permissible. Certain types of agriculture, notably cranberry bogs, would also be compatible. Isolated urban development might also be permitted if the water storage role of marshes was not diminished by the filling and accelerated runoff that such development would entail.

Flood Plains (339,760 acres; 18.86 percent)

The flood-plain parameter must be attributed a particular importance because of its relation to loss of life and property damage. The best records seem to indicate that the incidence and intensity of flooding in metropolitan areas is on the increase (Witala 1961). The presumption is that this results from the reduction of forest and agricultural land, erosion and sedimentation, and the urbanization of watersheds. This being so, there is every reason to formulate a land utilization policy for flood plains related to safeguarding life and property.[4]

The incidence of floods may be described as recorded maxima. For the Delaware River, the maximum recorded floods are those of 1950 and 1955. The alternate method of flood description relates levels of inundation to cyclical storms and describes these as flood levels of anticipated frequency or probability.

There is, then, a conflict of use for this land between water and other types of occupancy. This conflict is most severe in areas of frequent flooding which, however, occupy the smallest flood plain. The conflict diminishes in frequency with the more severe floods, which occupy the largest flood plain. It would seem possible to relate the utilization of the flood plain to the incidence and severity of cyclical flooding.[5]

Increasingly, the 50-year or two percent probability flood plain is being accepted as that area from which all development should be excluded save those functions which are either benefited or unharmed by flooding or those land uses which are inseparable from flood plains.

Thus, in principle, only such land uses which are either improved or unharmed by flooding should be permitted to occupy the 50-year flood plain. In the former category fall agriculture,[6] forestry, recreation, institutional open space, and open space for housing. In the category of land uses inseparable from flood plains are ports and harbors, marinas, water-related industry, and under certain circumstances, water-using industry.

Aquifers (149,455 acres; 8.3 percent)

The definition of an aquifer as a water-bearing stratum of rock, gravel, or sand is so general that enormous areas of land could be so described. For any region the value of an aquifer will relate to the abundance or poverty of water resources. In the Philadelphia area the great deposits of porous material parallel to the Delaware River are immediately distinguishable from all other aquifers in the region by their extent and capacity.

Aquifers may vary from groundwater resources of small quantity to enormous underground resources. They are normally measured by yields of wells or by the height of the water table. The aquifer in New Jersey parallel to the Delaware River has been estimated by the Soil Conservation Service [currently called the Natural Resources Conservation Service] to have a potential capacity of one billion gallons per day. This valuable resource requires restraints upon development of the surface to ensure the quality and quantity of aquifer resources. Consequently, development using septic tanks and industries disposing toxic or noxious effluents should be regulated. Injection wells should be expressly prohibited. The matter of surface percolation is also important, and as percolation will be greatest from permeable surfaces there are good reasons for maximizing development at the extremes of density— either sewered high density development or very low density free standing houses. Land-use policy for aquifers is less amenable to generalized recommendation than the remaining categories, as aquifers vary with respect to capacity, yield, and susceptibility. Consequently, there will be ranges of permissiveness attributable to specific aquifers as a function of their role and character.

In principle, no land uses should be permitted above an aquifer which inhibit the primary role as water supply and reservoir regulating oscillations between flood and drought.

Agriculture, forestry, and recreation clearly do not imperil aquifers. Industries, commercial activities, and housing, served by sewers, are permissible up to limits set by percolation requirements. Sources of pollutants or toxic material, and extensive land uses which reduce soil permeability, should be restricted or prohibited.

Aquifer Recharge Areas (83,085 acres; 4.61 percent)

Such areas are defined as points of interchange between surface water and groundwater. In any water system certain points of interchange will be critical; in the Philadelphia metropolitan area the interchange between the Delaware River, its tributaries and the parallel aquifer, represents the recharge area which is most important and which can be clearly isolated. Percolation is likely to be an important aspect of recharge. Thus, two considerations arise: the location of surface-to-groundwater interchange below the ground, and percolation of surface to groundwater.

By careful separation of polluted river water from the aquifer and by the impounding of streams transecting the major aquifer recharge areas, the aquifer can be managed and artificially recharged. Groundwater resources can be impaired by extensive development which waterproofs the surfaces, by development which occupies desirable impoundments valuable for aquifer management, and by pollution.

In principle, all proposed development on aquifer recharge areas should be measured against the likely effect upon recharge. Injection wells and disposal of toxic or offensive materials should be forbidden; channel widening, deepening, and dredging should be examined for their effect upon recharge as should deep excavations for trunk sewers. Surface development and sewage disposal on such an area should be limited by considerations of percolation.

Prime Agricultural Land (248,816 acres; 11.7 percent)

Prime agricultural soils represent the highest level of agricultural productivity; they are uniquely suitable for intensive cultivation with no conservation hazards. It is extremely difficult to defend agricultural lands when their cash value can be multiplied tenfold by employment for relatively cheap housing. Yet, the farm is the basic factory, the farmer is the country's best landscape gardener and maintenance work force, the custodian of much scenic beauty. Utilization of farmland by urbanization is often justifiable as the highest and best use of land at current land values, yet the range of market values of farmlands does not reflect the long-term value or the irreplaceable nature of these living soils. An omnibus protection of all farmland is indefensible; protection of the best soils in a metropolitan area would appear not only defensible, but also clearly desirable.

Jean Gottman has recommended that "the very good soils are not extensive enough in Megalopolis to be wastefully abandoned to nonagricultural uses" (1961, p. 95). The soils so identified are identical to the prime agricultural soils in the metropolitan area.

While farmland is extremely suitable for development and such lands can appreciate in value by utilization for housing, it is seldom considered that there is a cost involved in the development of new farmland. The farmer, displaced from excellent soils by urbanization, often moves to another site on inferior soils. Excellent soils lost to agriculture for building can finally only be replaced by bringing inferior soils into production. This requires capital investment. Land that is not considered cropland today will become cropland tomorrow, but at the price of much investment.

In the PSMSA by 1980 only 30 percent of the land area will be urbanized; 70 percent will remain open. Prime agricultural lands represent only 11.7 percent of the area. Therefore, given a choice, prime soils should not be developed.

In principle, U.S. Department of Agriculture (USDA) Land Capability System Type 1 soils are recommended to be exempted from development (save by those functions which do not diminish their present or prospective productive potential). This would suggest retirement of prime soils into forest, utilization as open space for institutions, for recreation, or in development for housing at densities no higher than one house per 25 acres.

Steep Lands (262,064 acres; 14.55 percent)

Steep lands and the ridges which they constitute are central to the problems of flood control and erosion. Slopes in excess of 12 degrees are not recommended for cultivation by the Soil Conservation Service. The same source suggests that for reasons of erosion, these lands are unsuitable for development. The recommendations of the Soil Conservation Service are that steep slopes should be in forest and that cultivation of such slopes be abandoned.

In relation to its role in the water regimen, steepness is a matter not only of degree, but also of vegetation and porosity. Two ranges of slopes are identified in our study of the PSMSA: 15 to 25 percent, and greater than 25 percent. The first category of 15 percent is identified as those slopes for which major site-engineering begins to be necessary to accommodate development. Roads should be equally parallel to the slope rather than perpendicular. Coverage by houses and roads should be compensated by measures to slow down runoff. Examination of a number of examples suggests 15 percent as the danger point for any development at all, but further empiric research is necessary. Above 25 percent, however, there appears widespread agreement that no development should occur and land should be treated to decrease runoff as much as possible.[7]

In summary, erosion control and diminution of velocity of runoff are the principal water problems of steep slopes. Land uses compatible with minimizing these problems would be mainly forestry, recreation, and low-density development on the less-steep slopes. Since such slopes also tend to dominate landscapes, their planting in forests would provide great amenity.

Forests and Woodlands (588,816 acres; 32.7 percent)

The natural vegetative cover for most of this region is forest. Where present, this exerts an ameliorative effect upon microclimate; it exercises a major balancing effect upon the water regimen, diminishing erosion, sedimentation, flood, and drought. The scenic role of woodlands is apparent, as is the provision of a habitat for game. The recreational potential of forests is among the highest of all categories. In addition, the forest is a low maintenance, self-perpetuating landscape, a resource in which accrual of timber inventory is continuous.

Forests can be employed for timber production, water management, wildlife habitats, as airsheds, recreation, or for any combination of these uses. In addition, forests can absorb development in concentrations which will be determined by the demands of natural process which they are required to satisfy. Where scenic considerations alone are operative, mature forests could absorb housing up to a density of one house per acre without loss of their forest aspect.

Land uses for forests should be determined by the natural process roles which the forest is required to play in the water regimen.

As a result of analyzing the eight significant physiographic phenomena and their roles in the region, several land uses can be recommended. These land uses are summarized in table 2.

Table 2. Limited Development Areas and Recommended Land Uses

Limited Development Areas	Recommended Land Uses
1. Surface water and riparian lands	Ports, harbors, marinas, water treatment plants, water-related industry, open space for institutional and housing use, agriculture, forestry, and recreation
2. Marshes	Recreation
3. 50-year flood plains	Ports, harbors, marinas, water treatment plants, water-related and water-using industry, agriculture, forestry, recreation, institutional open space, open space of housing
4. Aquifers	Agriculture, forestry, recreation, industries which do not produce toxic or offensive effluents, all land uses within limits set by percolation

(continues)

Table 2. (continued)

5. Aquifer recharge areas	As aquifers
6. Prime agricultural lands	Agriculture, forestry, recreation, open space for institutions, housing at 1 house per 25 acres
7. Steep lands	Forestry, recreation, housing at maximum density of 1 house per 3 acres, where wooded
8. Forests and woodlands	Forestry, recreation, housing at densities not higher than 1 house per acre

Open Space and Airsheds

The atmosphere of a metropolitan area has a capacity to diffuse air pollution based upon temperature, air composition, and movement. Concentration of pollution is associated with cities and industries, replacement of polluted air and its diffusion depend upon air movements over pollution free areas. These will be related to wind movements, and must be substantially free of pollution sources if relief is to be afforded to air pollution over cities. One can use the analogy of the watershed and describe the pollution free areas, tributary to the city, as the airsheds.

The central phase of air pollution is linked to temperature inversion during which the air near the ground does not rise to be replaced by in-moving air. Under inversion, characterized by clear nights with little wind, the earth is cooled by long-wave radiation and the air near the ground is cooled by the ground. During such temperature inversions with stable surface air layers, air movement is limited; in cities, pollution becomes increasingly concentrated. In Philadelphia "significant" inversions occur one night in three. Parallel and related to inversion is the incidence of "high" pollution levels, which occurred on twenty-four "episodes" from two to five days in duration between 1957 and 1959. Inversions then are common as are "high" levels of pollution. The danger attends their conjunction and persistence. Relief other than elimination of pollution sources is a function of wind movement to disperse pollution over cities, and secondly, the necessity that in-moving air be cleaner than the air it replaces.

The windrose during inversions can establish the percentage direction of winds which might relieve pollution; the wind speed, combined with wind direction, will indicate these tributary areas over which the wind will pass to relieve pollution. These areas should be substantially, free of pollution sources.

The concentration of pollution sources in Philadelphia covers an area fifteen miles by ten miles with the long axis running approximately northeast.

Let us assume sulfur dioxide to be the indicator of pollution (830 tons per day produced), an air height of 500 feet as the effective dimension, an air volume to be replaced of approximately 15 cubic miles, a wind speed of four miles per hour, selected as a critical speed. Then one cubic mile of ventilation is provided per mile of windspeed and it is seen to require three and three-quarter hours for wind movement to ventilate the long axis, two and one-half hours to ventilate the cross axis. Thus, the tributary to ensure clean air on the long axis is 15 miles beyond the pollution area, ten miles beyond for the cross axis. The windrose for Philadelphia during inversions shows that wind movements are preponderantly northwest, west, and southwest, contributing 51.2 percent of wind movements, the other five cardinal points represent the remainder.

This very approximate examination suggests that airsheds should extend from 10 to 15 miles beyond the urban air pollution sources in those wind directions to be anticipated during inversion.[8] The width of these belts should correspond to the dimension of the pollution core and, in very approximate terms, would probably be from three to five miles. Such areas, described as airsheds, should be prohibited to pollution source industries.

Should this concept be realized, broad belts of land, free of industry, would penetrate radially toward the city center.

Under the heading of atmosphere the subject of climate and microclimate was raised. In the study area the major problem is summer heat and humidity. Relief of this condition responds to wind movements. Thus, a hinterland with more equable temperatures, particularly a lower summer temperature, is of importance to climate amelioration for the city. As we have seen, areas which are in vegetative cover, notably forests, are distinctly cooler than cities in summer, a margin of 10°F is not uncommon. Air movements over such areas moving into the city will bring cooler air. Relief from humidity results mainly from air movement. These correspond to the directions important for relief of inversion. We can then say that the areas selected as urban airsheds are likely to be those selected as appropriate for amelioration of the urban microclimate. However, in the case of the former, it is important only that pollution sources be prohibited or limited. In the case of microclimate control, it is essential that the airsheds be substantially in vegetative cover, preferably forested.

The satisfaction of these two requirements, the creation of urban airsheds as responses to atmospheric pollution control and microclimate control, would create fingers of open space penetrating from the rural hinterland, radially into the city. This is perhaps the broadest conception of natural process in metropolitan growth and metropolitan open space distribution. Clearly, this proposal directs growth into the interstices between the airshed corridors and suggests that metropolitan open space exists within them.

Conclusions

In summary, it is proposed that the form of metropolitan growth and the distribution of metropolitan open space should respond to natural process. The phenomenal world is a process which operates within laws and responds to these laws. Interdependence is characteristic of this process, the seamless web of nature. Man is natural, as is the phenomenal world he inhabits, yet with greater power, mobility, and fewer genetic restraints; his impact upon this world exceeds that of any creature. The transformations he creates are often deleterious to other biological systems, but in this he is no different from many other creatures. However, these transformations are often needlessly destructive to other organisms and systems, and even more important, by conscious choice and inadvertance, also deleterious to man.

A generalized effect of human intervention is the tendency toward simplification of the ecosystems, which is equated with instability. Thus, the increased violence of climate and microclimate, oscillation between flood and drought, erosion and siltation, are all primary evidence of induced instability.

Human adaptations contain both benefits and costs, but natural processes are generally not attributed values, nor is there a generalized accounting system which reflects total costs and benefits. Natural processes are unitary whereas human interventions tend to be fragmentary and incremental. The effect of filling the estuarine marshes or of felling the upland forests is not perceived as related to the water regimen, to flood or drought; nor are both activities seen to be similar in their effect. The construction of outlying suburbs and siltation of river channels are not normally understood to be related as cause and effect; nor is waste disposal into rivers perceived to be connected with the pollution of distant wells.

Several factors can be observed. Normal growth tends to be incremental and unrelated to natural processes on the site. But the aggregate consequences of such development are not calculated nor are they allocated as costs to the individual incremental developments. While benefits do accrue to certain developments, which are deleterious to natural processes at large (for example, clear felling of forests or conversion of farmland into subdivisions), these benefits are *particular* (related in these examples to that landowner who chooses to fell trees or sterilize soil), while the results and costs are *general* in effect. Thus, costs and benefits are likely to be attributed to large numbers of different and unrelated persons, corporations, and levels of government. It is unprovable and unlikely that substantial benefits accrue from disdain of natural process; it is quite certain and provable that substantial costs do result from this disdain. Finally, in general, any benefits which do occur—usually economic—tend to accrue to the private sector, while remedies and long-range costs are usually the responsibility of the public domain.

The purpose of this study is to show that natural process, unitary in character, must be so considered in the planning process that changes to parts of the system affect the entire system, that natural processes do represent values, and that these values should be incorporated into a single accounting system. It is unfortunate that there is inadequate information on cost-benefit ratios of specific interventions to natural process. However, certain generalized relationships have been shown and presumptions advanced as the basis for judgment. It seems clear that laws pertaining to land use and development need to be elaborated to reflect the public costs and consequences of private action. Present land-use regulations neither recognize natural processes, the public good in terms of flood, drought, water quality, agriculture, amenity, or recreational potential, nor allocate responsibility to the acts of landowner or developer.

We have seen that land is abundant, even within a metropolitan region confronting accelerated growth. There is, then, at least hypothetically, the opportunity of choice as to the location of development and locations of open space.

The hypothesis, central to this study, is that the distribution of open space must respond to natural process. The conception should hold true for any metropolitan area, irrespective of location. In this particular case study, directed to the Philadelphia metropolitan region, an attempt has been made to select certain fundamental aspects of natural process, which show the greatest relevance to the problem of determining the form of metropolitan growth and open space.

The problem of metropolitan open space lies then, not in absolute area, but in distribution. We seek a concept which can provide an interfusion of open space and population. The low attributed value of open space ensures that it is transformed into urban use within the urban area and at the perimeter. Normal urbanization excludes interfusion and consumes peripheral open space.

Yet as the area of a circle follows the square of the radius, large open space increments can exist within the urban perimeter without major increase to the radius or to the time distance from city center to urban fringe.

The major recommendation of this study is that the aggregate value of land, water, and air resources does justify a land-use policy which reflects both the value and operation of natural processes. Further, that the identification of natural processes, the permissiveness and prohibitions which they exhibit, reveals a system of open space which can direct metropolitan growth and offers sites for metropolitan open space.

The characteristics of natural processes have been examined; an attempt has been made to identify their values, intrinsic value, work performed and protection afforded. Large-scale functions have been identified with the major divisions of upland, coastal plain, and piedmont; smaller scale functions of air and water corridors have been identified; and, finally, eight discrete parameters have been selected for examination.

For each of the discrete phenomena and for each successive generalization, approximate permissiveness to other land uses and specific prohibitions have been suggested. While all are permissive to a greater or lesser degree, all perform their natural process best in an unspoiled condition. Clearly, if land is abundant and land-use planning can reflect natural process, a fabric of substantially natural land will remain either in low intensity use or undeveloped, interfused throughout the metropolitan region. It is from this land that public metropolitan open space may best be selected.

This case study reveals the application of the ecological view to the problem of selecting open space in a metropolitan region. It reflects the assumption that nature performs work for man and that certain natural processes can best perform this work in a natural or mainly natural condition. Clearly, this is a partial problem; one would wish that simultaneously, consideration were also given to those lands which man would select for various purposes, for settlements, recreation, agriculture, and forestry. Such a study would be more complete than the isolation of a single demand. Yet, it is likely that the same proposition would hold although the larger study would better reveal the degree of conflict. For the moment, it is enough to observe that the ecological view does represent a perceptive method and could considerably enhance the present mode of planning which disregards natural processes, all but completely, and which in selecting open space, is motivated more by standards of acres per thousand for organized sweating, than for the place and face of nature in man's world.

Notes

1. Wallace-McHarg Associates (1964). William G. Grigsby was economic consultant, Ann Louise Strong, governmental and legal consultant, and William H. Roberts, design consultant in this first practical application of the new approach. [Wallace-McHarg Associates was later Wallace, McHarg, Roberts, and Todd and is now Wallace Roberts and Todd.]

2. Ecological model is a theoretical construct, either descriptive or mathematical, by which the energy flow of an organic system can be described.

3. 5,671 linear miles in the PSMSA; surface water has been identified as all permanent streams shown on USGS (U.S. Geological Survey) 1:24,000 Series.

4. Kates, William, and White, suggest classification of flood zones into prohibitive, restrictive, and warning zones, based on physiographic analysis. The prohibitive zone would protect structures and fill to preserve the channel capacity in flood conditions; the restrictive zone would simply alert users they were

within the flood plain and the decision to accommodate would be theirs (Kates et al. 1962).

5. See Kates and William (1962) for thorough discussion of the conditions and value judgments concerning occupancy of flood plains. It is evident from this analysis that flood controls are most easily established where the certainty of flood occurrence is high.

6. See Burton (1962) for a more detailed consideration of agricultural occupancy of flood plains.

7. E.g., in Pittsburgh, 25 percent and greater slopes are now subject to an ordinance prohibiting further development.

8. Study on the Philadelphia airshed conducted under direction of the writer by Hideki Shimizu, Department of Landscape Architecture, University of Pennsylvania, 1963, unpublished.

References

Burton, Ian. 1962. *Types of Agricultural Occupancy of Flood Plains in the U.S.A.* Chicago: Department of Geography, University of Chicago.

Gottman, Jean. 1961. *Megalopolis.* New York: The Twentieth Century Fund.

Kates, C., and Robert William. 1962. *Hazard and Choice Perception in Flood Plain Management.* Chicago: Department of Geography, University of Chicago.

Kates, C., Robert William, and Gilbert F. White. 1962. "Flood Hazard Evaluation." In Gilbert F. White, ed., *Papers on Flood Problems.* Chicago: Department of Geography, University of Chicago, pp. 135–147.

McHarg, Ian. 1969. "Processes as Values." In *Design with Nature.* Garden City, N.Y.: Doubleday, Natural History Press.

MacKaye, Benton. 1928. *The New Exploration: A Philosophy of Regional Planning.* New York: Harcourt Brace.

Odum, Eugene. 1959. *The Fundamentals of Ecology.* Philadelphia: Saunders.

State of Wisconsin. 1962. *Recreation in Wisconsin.* Madison: Department of Resource Development.

Wallace-McHarg Associates. 1964. *Plan for the Valleys.* Towson, Md.: Green Spring and Worthington Valley Planning Council.

Wallace, McHarg, Roberts, and Todd. 1969. *An Ecological Study for the Twin Cities Metropolitan Region, Minnesota.* Prepared for Metropolitan Council of the Twin Cities Area. Philadelphia: U.S. Department of Commerce, National Technical Information Series.

Witala, S. W. 1961. *Some Aspects of the Effect of Urban and Suburban Development on Runoff.* Lansing, Mich.: U.S. Department of Interior, Geological Survey.

6

Ecological Planning: The Planner as Catalyst (1978)

Although McHarg challenged orthodox planning theory, especially the economic-social science deterministic approach of theorists such as John Friedmann and Britton Harris, he embraced the notion of the planner as catalyst for positive change. One role model was his partner David Wallace, who had helped transform Baltimore's downtown through his activism. In many ways, McHarg favored an activist place-making approach to environmental planning over more bureaucratic rule making, although he certainly recognized rules that are necessary to prevent environmental pollution, destruction, and degradation.

This paper was written for Robert Burchell and George Sternlieb for a conference at Rutgers University on planning theory. Other contributors to the conference and the later book included the crème of the orthodox planning theory crop, including Friedmann, Harris, Robert Beauregard, David Harvey, William Grigsby, and the most notable change agent-catalyst from the planning community, Paul Davidoff.

By and large the virtues of the planning I was taught were orderliness and convenience, efficiency and economy. The first set contains minor virtues, and the second set contains less than noble ones. These virtues have little to do with survival or success of plants, animals, and men in evolutionary time.

A fallacy is that planners plan for people. Actually this is not an assumption at all; it is a presumption. The planner who comes from out of town and is prepared to solve problems is a menace.

I prefer to think of planners as catalysts. The planner suppresses his own ego and becomes an agent for outlining available options. He offers predictability that science gives him about the consequences of different courses of action. He helps the community make its values explicit. He identifies alternative solutions with attendant costs and benefits. These vary with different constituencies, as do their needs and values.

This sort of planning might be called ecological. It is based on an understanding of both biophysical and social systems. Ecological planners operate within the framework of a biophysical culture.

Ecological planning addresses itself to the selection of environments. Ecological planners help institutions and individuals adapt these and themselves to achieve fitness.

For example, when I prepare a planning study, I insist that scientists of the environment study the region in terms of the processes which produce the phenomena constituting the region. They describe the phenomena of the region as an interacting biophysical model. Such a model can then be seen to have intrinsic opportunities and constraints to all existing and prospective users. Fitness is defined as the presence of all or most propitious attributes with none or few detrimental areas.

This notion of planning stems from two fundamental characteristics of natural processes: creativity and fitness. Creativity provides the dynamics that govern the universe. There is a tendency for all matter to degrade to entropy, but in certain energetic transactions there is a process by which some matter is transformed to a higher level or order. All of biology subscribes to this law: entropy increases but a local syntropy can be achieved. It is seen in both energetic transactions, in the evolution of matter, life, and man. This biological "creativity" enables us to explain the rich and diverse world of life today, as opposed to the sterile world of yesterday.

The second concept—fitness—stems partially from Darwinian notions about how organisms adapt and survive. Equally important is the thought that the surviving organisms are fit for the environment. The world provides an abundance of environmental opportunity. This teaches us that the world is environmentally variable, offering variable fitness. This results from the most basic elements—hydrogen, nitrogen, oxygen, and carbon—and the earth itself provides environmental opportunity.

All systems are required to seek out the environment that is most fit, to adapt these and themselves, continuously. This is a requirement for survival. This is called adaptation. It is an imperative of all life, it has been, and it always will be. Fitness can best be described as finding an environment—physical, biological, or social—in which the largest part of the work of survival is done by the environment itself. There is then an energetic imperative for evolutionary success. Systems which are "fit" are evolutionary successes; they are maximum success solutions to fitness.

Planning, of course, is more than understanding environments and explaining why they are what they are, and where they are going. It is also explaining why people are where they are, doing what they are doing. An ecological planner would look at this over time, through an ethnographic history: Where did the first people who occupied a given place come from? Why did they leave? Why did they choose the environment they did? What adaptive skills determined their location? What adaptive skills did they practice? What modifications did they make to the environment? What institutions did they develop? What plans?

The social value of a given environment is an amalgam of the place, the people, and their technology. People in a given place with opportunities afforded by the environment for practicing a means of production, will develop characteristic perceptions and institutions. These institutions will have perceptions and values that feed back to an understanding of the environment—both national and social—and that have a modification of technology. Thus, I believe, we have a continuous model, which emanates from the physical and biological, and extends to the cultural.

The most critical factor is the value system, for it determines the planning solution. I strongly object to much of the current planning philosophy as it is emerging in both teaching and practice, for it assumes that the planner imposes values and exercises for the "good of the people." I resist this. Given a set of data, the planning solutions will vary, not with respect to the set, but with respect to the value systems of the people who seek to solve the problem. Most of the important values are particular and there is no substitute for eliciting them from the constituents themselves. These values themselves become the data, whether it be for describing rocks, soils, animals, people, or institutions. Planners must elicit these data from their client if they are going to help solve the problems posed by the particular system within which the client functions. This, in fact, is the planner's most important role. After he has done it, he should step aside, and the resolution of the problem of the explicit system will be found through the political process, and ultimately, in some cases, through the courts.

In sum, the planner is a catalyst and a resource. He determines what skills and branches of knowledge are appropriate to solutions, and what institutions. He helps to describe the interactions of systems. He describes probable alternative courses of action and assists his constituents in making their value system explicit. The planner then helps his clients understand what the consequences of applying that value system are in terms of their costs and benefits. He participates with them in negotiations among different constituencies over the relaxation or change of values in order to come to some agreement about the allocation of resources.

If the process is successful the constituencies will select the fittest environments, adapting these and themselves to achieve a creative fitting. As health can be described as the ability of persons, families, or institutions to seek and solve problems, so planning is not only a measure of the health of a group or institution, but, is health-giving to such agents.

It could make planning more fitting, perhaps even healthier.

7

Human Ecological Planning at Pennsylvania (1981)

In 1981 Arthur Johnson, a faculty member at Penn, edited a special issue of Landscape Planning *(now called* Landscape and Urban Planning, *published by* Elsevier). *The special issue was devoted to the Penn Department of Landscape Architecture and Regional Planning. McHarg's article described the human ecological approach. He incorporates an understanding of the ecologies of people to the natural-resource approach, described in* Design with Nature. *To that end, he had encouraged colleagues such as Dan Rose, Jon Berger, and Setha Low, as well as graduate students, to pursue such an approach.*

Abstract

A theory of human ecological planning is presented which is based on the premise that all social and natural systems aspire to success. Such a state can be described as "syntropic-fitness-health." Understanding the process of interaction between the landscape and the people who inhabit it provides a basis for assessing the opportunities and constraints afforded by the environment, and the needs and desires of the population which can be combined to present alternative futures. Such a model allows examination of the impact of any plan upon the health of the inhabitants and the well-being of the social and natural systems.

Introduction

It is first necessary to define terms. The simplest term is the last in the title of this paper. Pennsylvania is a contraction for the Department of Landscape

Architecture and Regional Planning at the University of Pennsylvania (also called Penn). Here a faculty described in *Science* (Holden 1977) as one of the very few multi-disciplinary and interdisciplinary faculties in the United States, is committed to the development and teaching of human ecological planning. The faculty comprises physical, biological, and social scientists, architects, landscape architects, and city and regional planners.

It is next necessary to define human ecological planning. The central word in this compound noun has primacy: ecology has been defined as the study of the interactions of organisms and environment (which includes other organisms). The word human is adequately defined in standard dictionaries but human ecology is not. While ecology has traditionally sought to learn the laws which obtain for ecosystems, it has done so by investigating environments unaffected or little affected man; it has emphasized biophysical systems. Yet clearly no systems are unaffected by man, indeed studies of the interactions of organisms and environment are likely to reveal human dominance. Hence, ecology simply must be extended to include man. Human ecology can then be defined as the study of the interactions of organisms (including man), and the environment (including man among other organisms). However, if man is assumed to be implicit in both definitions of organisms and environment then the standard definition for ecology can apply to human ecology.

The possibilities for creating a human ecology seem to be afforded by a new extension and integration of existing scientific disciplines. Ecology has been used to integrate the sciences of the biophysical environment. If we extend ecology by adding ethology we introduce the subject of behavior as an adaptive strategy. If we extend further into ethnography and anthropology we can include the study of human behavior as adaptation. If, finally, we extend into medical anthropology and epidemiology we can close the cycle by examining the natural and human environment in terms of human health and well-being.

Planning cannot be defined succinctly. Planning consists of the formulation of hypothetical alternative futures. These are constituted into component actions comprising courses of action. These are subsequently measured in terms of costs and benefits (employing the value system of the initiator of the alternative futures). The least cost—maximum benefit solution selects the preferred hypothetical future.

When "planning" is linked to "ecological" the primacy of goals is modified. Goals are derived from the region. Ecological planning is an instrument for revealing regions as interacting and dynamic natural systems having intrinsic opportunities and constraints for all human uses. Preferred hypothetical futures will be proffered by locations where all or most propitious factors exist with none or few detrimental ones for any and all prospective uses. What constitutes detrimental or propitious is derived from the prospective use and the value system of the initiating person or group.

When the term is compounded into "human ecological planning" the region is expanded into a physical, biological, and cultural region wherein opportunities and constraints are represented in every realm. Geophysical and ecological regions are identified as cultural regions in which characteristic people pursue means of production, develop characteristic settlement patterns, have characteristic perceptions, needs and desires and institutions for realizing their objectives. Hypothetical future alternatives are derived from expressed needs and desires of groups. These are matched against the physical, biological, and cultural resources. Preferred hypothetical futures can be derived for each group with its associated value system.

Human ecological planning is a cumbersome and graceless title. Remedy, however, while possible, is distant. When it becomes accepted that no ecosystem can be studied without reference to man then we may abandon the "human" descriptor and revert to "ecological planning." Better still, when planning always considers interacting biophysical and cultural processes, then we can dispense with the distinction of "ecological" and simply employ the word "planning." However, that state is far in the future, as most planning today excludes physical and biological sciences, ecology, ethnography, anthropology, epidemiology, and concentrates upon economics and sociology. It remains necessary, not only to advance planning to become ecological, but even more, to develop a human ecological planning.

Theory

Having defined terms it is next necessary to describe the theory which impels human ecological planning. Clearly, as it incorporates the physical, biological, and social sciences it can also employ the theory of these sciences. Planning is not rich in theory, and no statement on a theory of human ecological planning has yet been propounded. In order to initiate this quest I offer the following as a tentative beginning.

It would appear that all living systems tend to oscillate between two extreme states. These can be described as: (1) syntropic-fitness-health; and (2), entropic-misfitness-morbidity. Entropy is the tendency for energy and matter to degrade from higher to lower levels of order in any energetic transaction. All energetic transactions result in an increase in entropy. However, while the preceding is true, certain energetic transactions produce a product of matter and energy at a higher level of order than at the onset. This process is described by Buckminster Fuller as syntropic. The explosion of super novae in a primeval universe composed of hydrogen resulted in an increase in entropy but there was a residuum, not only of hydrogen but also helium, lithium, beryllium, boron, on up the periodic table of elements, each more ordered than hydrogen. The evolution of matter in the universe is syntropic. In life forms, all of which constitute energetic transactions, photosynthesis is the most notable example of syntropy. Given continuous energy, in the presence of carbon dioxide and water, the chloroplast creates glucose, a higher level of order than the ingredients. The evolution of life forms itself is syntropic whereby successive forms represent increased capability, a higher level of ordered energy and matter in their beings.

Fitness has two definitions, each complementary. Charles Darwin (1859) stated that "the surviving organism is fit for the environment." Much later Lawrence Henderson (1913) augmented this proposition by showing that the actual world consists of an infinitude of environments, all exhibiting fitness for appropriate organisms. These two propositions can be linked into an evolutionary imperative. Every organism, system, or institution, is required to find the fittest environment, adapt that environment and itself in order to survive. This imperative is linked to the syntrophy-entropy criteria. An environment is defined as fit for an organism by the degree to which the environment, as found, provides the largest amount of needs for that organism. The corollary, then, is that the organism is required to import and employ the least amount of energy and time to modify the environment and itself to make it more fitting. Thus there is a condition of syntropic fitness. Entropic misfitness would be represented by an organism unable to find a fit environment and/or unable to adapt that environment and/or unable to adapt itself. Its fate would be non-survival, death, and extinction.

All creatures as individuals, species, or ecosystems, aspire to survival and success. The mechanism for achieving this state is adaptation. This has three modes: physiological adaptation by mutation and natural selection used by all life forms; innate behavior, shared by animals and man; and, the unique human instrumentality, cultural adaptation. Until recombinant DNA is employed, physiological adaptation will remain beyond voluntary control; innate behavior is similarly resistant to manipulation. Adaptation through modification of culture is the most plastic instrument for voluntary action leading to survival and success.

While the verb, "to fit," applies to the active selection of environments, adapting those and the self, the noun "fitness" has another meaning. It implies health. From another direction, the definition of a healthy person is one who solves and seeks problems. Yet a second definition of health is the ability to recover from insult or assault. Both definitions accord with evolutionary biology; they could be subsumed by adaptation, particularly the latter. It appears that fitness and health are states linked in a more profound way than is suggested by common usage. Fitness is defined as problem solving, i.e., finding fit environments, adapting these and the self. Health is similarly

defined as seeking and solving problems. It would appear that not only is fitness syntropic, but so is health. There seems to be a state of syntropic-fitness-
health. The antithesis confirms this assumption. Morbidity reveals a process
moving from higher to lower levels of order, decomposition after death is its
most complete expression. Morbidity is also a failure in adaptation: the environment is not fit for the cells, tissue, organ or organism; or the system
is unable to make it or itself fit, and finally, the system is unable to recover
from insult or assault, unable to solve problems resulting in entropic-misfit-
morbidity. There is one further observation of significance. Health, it would
appear, not only reveals evidence of the presence of syntropic fitness, but, if
health is defined as problem seeking and solving, then the quest for fitness is
also health-giving. This long preamble finally reaches planning. Of all the
instrumentalities available through cultural adaptation (language, religion,
symbol, art, philosophy, etc.), it would seem that one above all is most directly connected to the evolutionary imperative of finding fit environments and
adapting these, of accomplishing syntropic-fitness-health. This instrument is
planning, in particular human ecological planning, or planning for human
health and well-being.

The theory of human ecological planning can now be summarized: all
systems aspire to survival and success. This state can be described as syntropic-fitness-health. Its antithesis is entropic-misfitness-morbidity. To achieve
the first state requires systems to find the fittest environment, adapt it and
themselves. Fitness of an environment for a system is defined as that requiring the minimum work of adaptation. Fitness and fitting are indication of
health and the process of fitting is health giving. The quest for fitness is entitled adaptation. Of all of the instrumentalities available to man for successful
adaptation, cultural adaptation in general and planning in particular, appear
to be the most direct and efficacious for maintaining and enhancing human
health and well-being.

Method

Theory produces an objective which requires a method to achieve it. We are
required to promote human health and well-being by planning, specifically to
select fit environments for all users; to participate in the adaptation of that
environment and the user. We must be able to describe regions as interacting
physio-bio-cultural systems, reconstitute them as resources and hence as
social values, array these attributes as either costs or benefits for prospective
consumers, and select the maximum benefit—least cost solution. Thus, we
must be able to model regions, insofar as science permits, at least descriptive-
ly, at best quantitatively; we must employ all of the predictive skill which science provides to forecast the consequences of contemplated actions on the
interacting systems.

Before describing the method employed there is one important observation to be made. Human ecological planning incorporates the physical, biological, and social sciences and in so doing it utilizes the universal laws which those sciences employ. However, the distinction of ecological planning, unlike economic, transportation, or orthodox city planning, is that this planning theory and method emphasize locality. As with ecosystems and bioclimatic zones, it is believed that each region or locality is spatially determined. While responding to universal laws, each region is believed to comprise unique attributes of place–folk–work, as first identified by Patrick Geddes, and these will determine the capabilities, opportunities, and constraints of the region and thus the potential hypothetical futures.

The first objective of the method is to create a model of the region under study. As all of the sciences of the environment agree that things, creatures, places, and people are only comprehensible through the operation of laws and time, it is appropriate that the modeling exercise should employ evolution and history. Matter preceded life which preceded man. We should begin the construction of the model with its physical evolution, continue with biophysical evolution, and conclude with the addition of cultural history. This method selects the participants. Physical evolution is the province of meteorology, geology, hydrology, soil science, and where applicable, physical oceanography. Biophysical evolution adds botanists and marine biologists where appropriate. Human evolution requires anthropologists—physical, cultural and medical ethnographers, and such economists, sociologists, and political scientists as are compatible with the ecological view. The final participant is the planner, the person willing to undertake synthesis, oriented towards problem solving.

As science has divided this "one world" into discrete areas of concern, we are required to accept this situation, although the objective is to unite all of the discrete perceptions into a description of a single interacting system. While we must employ all disciplines which describe the environment we can collect and array their data in a way which employs history and causality to assist in the portrayal of reality. Let us build a layer-cake representation of the region with the oldest evidence on the bottom and new, consequential layers superimposed in place and in time.

We can properly begin with the oldest evidence, bedrock geology, as the basement and superimpose meteorology above. We ask that the geologist, mindful of meteorological history, reconstruct geological history to explain the phenomena of the region and its dynamics. Upon bedrock geology surficial geology is added with meteorology remaining on top. We ask a geomorphologist to add his more recent data and explain physiography in terms of bedrock and surficial geology. The next scientist, a groundwater hydrologist, interprets the previous data to explain historic and contemporary phenomena. A surface water hydrologist follows. Together they describe hydrological processes, contemporary phenomena, and tendencies. The next layer is the domain of the soils scientist. He, as with others, is required to invoke the data of all prior sciences to explain the processes and phenomena within his realm. However, he must also invoke the effect of life forms historically. The plant ecologist follows. He describes plants in terms of communities occupying habitats. The descriptions of these employ geology, meteorology, hydrology, and soils. He recapitulates vegetational history to explain the existing flora and its dynamics; the limnologist populates aquatic systems using a similar method, and finally, the animal ecologist, depending most upon plant ecology, constructs a history of wildlife and explains the contemporary populations and their environments. Arrayed as a cross-section, the layer cake is complete—bedrock geology, surficial geology, groundwater hydrology, physiography, surface-water hydrology, soils, plants, wildlife, micro-, meso- and macro-climate. The layer cake has evolved over time and continues to do so. The entire formulation of the ecological model has emphasized interacting processes and time. All phenomena have been, are now, and are in the process of becoming. The layer cake is an expression of historical causality. It is possible to peer from the surface to the bottom and explain process, reality, and form. We have, at once, a discipline and (to the degree science provides it) a predictive model.

The study of the evolutionary history of the region has revealed that all processes are interacting with each other: geological and meteorological history are expressed in surficial geology which, in turn, are expressed in hydrology and soils. The sum of these is reflected in environments populated by appropriate plant communities while these last are occupied and utilized by consonant animals. It becomes clear that physical processes are synthesized in physiography while biophysical processes are synthesized by ecosystems.

The next task is to populate the region with its inhabitants. Here we confront the threshold between ecological and human ecological planning. The physical and biological sciences assume the operation of order. While there is randomness in systems, randomness cannot explain them. In short, we accept that nature is systematic. Can we also assume that man and nature are systematic, or is man random with respect to a systematic nature? It seems more reasonable to believe that man and nature are systematic and to continue to employ the evolutionary method to explain folk–work–place. We wish to know who the people are, why they inhabit the region, why they are where they are, doing what they are doing.

In order to explain people, place, and work, using an evolutionary method, we need to undertake the study of ethnographic history. We can begin with the biophysical representation of the region before the advent of Western man. The primeval environment is then occupied by its aboriginal people. However, it is necessary to explain the anthropological model which underlies the ethnographic history before we proceed. This construct affirms that, while a region may be described as an interacting biophysical system, it is simultaneously, a social value system, i.e., it contains resources. However, what constitutes a resource is determined by the perception of the inhabitants or observers, and the available technology and capital. Given certain perceptions, technology, and capital, certain natural phenomena will be perceived as resources and exploited. These resources, e.g., minerals, lumber, wildlife, will be locationally determined by the natural history of the region. Thus the means of production, utilizing resource or resources, will also be locationally determined. The means of production implies labor selection, generally persons skilled in the appropriate kinds of employment, e.g., fishing, mining, lumbering, farming. In American history the exploitation of resources, in selecting accomplished practitioners, often attracted ethnic groups who had practiced similar skills in Europe. So we see Scots miners, Portuguese fishermen, Italian masons, Basque shepherds, Russian and Swedish farmers in the northern Great Plains, Spanish farmers in the arid Southwest, French Canadian and Swedish lumbermen, and others. People sharing an occupation tend to have similar perceptions of themselves, particularly when this is accompanied by shared ethnicity and religion. Each occupational type is likely to have characteristic land uses and settlement patterns, and, finally, groups associated with a particular means of production are likely to develop characteristic institutions to promote and enhance their success and well-being, both in the private and public domain.

Thus, we can anticipate that changes in land-use and settlement patterns respond to two causes: the first is technological change and the second includes massive social events, e.g., wars, immigration, and the like.

The method can proceed. It begins with the layer cake occupied by its aboriginal inhabitants, plants, animals and people, their settlement patterns, land uses, transportation corridors. The next land-use map should portray colonial settlement responsive to then-current perceptions and technology, and should explain the differences from the original map in terms of resource, technology, and social events. For example, in the age of sail, the colonizers of the eastern seaboard of the United States sought safe harbors and estuarine and river systems permitting penetration of the interior. The Hudson, Delaware, Christiana, Susquehanna, Potomac, and James rivers provided safe harbors, but penetration of the interior posed serious problems—waterfalls on the main rivers and their tributaries. All of the waterfalls occurred on the same geological phenomenon, the interface between the crystalline piedmont and the coastal plain. At this point, settlement occurred on each of the rivers Albany, Trenton, Philadelphia, Wilmington, Baltimore, Washington, D.C., and Richmond, Virginia. New York City was a special case of a granite island located in a drowned tidal estuary.

At the time of the American Revolution, iron for cannon and cannon balls was important. Iron was obtained from bogs, which were abundant in the coastal plain of New Jersey, but scarce elsewhere. This is comprehensible from natural history: the bogs located the bog iron which located the foundries which located settlement and which located operators. So with the grist and saw mills, ports, harbors, fisheries, and farming. Each successive map shows changes responsive to new options presented by technological innovation and/or impelled by social events, revolutions, war, immigration being the most notable. Throughout the ethnographic history, attention is also paid to nonphysical instruments of adaptation, e.g., laws, ordinances, and mores, the evolution of institutions, public and private. Finally, the last product is one of current land use, a document gravid with meaning, as ordered as a map of rocks, soils, or vegetation.

It transpires that people are who they are, where they are, doing what they are doing for good and sufficient reasons. Moreover, they are not reticent to describe themselves, in economic, ethnic, occupational, religious, and spatial terms. They have no doubt about the territory they occupy. They can define themselves, their territory, and their neighbors. The process of eliciting this people-place description is called "consensual mapping." When regions defined by inhabitants are compared to "natural" regions and features, a great conformity becomes apparent. In many cases there are physiographic-social regions and subregions. This applies not only to rural and metropolitan areas but also to urban neighborhoods in the City of Philadelphia. The discovery that people, far from being random with respect to the natural environment, are highly ordered, simplifies the next task. We wish to ascertain the needs and desires of the population. The theory presumes that health and well-being attend the task of finding fit environments, adapting these and the self. In order to ascertain what values constitute "fitness" and "misfitness" we must elicit those values because they are not objective; they cannot be attributed, but only elicited. But as it transpires that populations reveal discrete self-defined groups and locations, it is not necessary to interview large numbers to obtain this information. Key informant interviews with a small-sample questionnaire for each group will suffice. We wish to know what perceptions groups have of themselves and their environment. What are their needs and desires? In order to ascertain the values they apply, subjects are asked to reveal their positions on certain contemporary issues. This method proves more efficacious than direct questions on values.

When groups have been identified, it becomes necessary to ascertain their values and the instruments through which they seek to attain their objectives. Obviously, the formal political arena receives investigation, but informal institutions receive even greater attention. Voluntary associations, e.g., conservation groups, fraternal organizations, voluntary fire companies, parent-teacher associations, the League of Women Voters, the Grange, Mushroom Institute, Shell Fisherman's Association, each reveals its values, its position on issues, its membership, its financial capabilities, its strategies in its publications and public statements. This analysis, combined with one on kinship, reveals the social system as a complex network with a mosaic of overlapping constituencies, each having characteristic needs and desires, with varying capabilities of realizing them through the market, private and public institutions. However, there is a danger that the social data can become so complex as to be unusable. The ordering principle employs land use. Using matrices and maps, discrete social groups, e.g., Italian Catholic mushroom farmers, are located. Next, issues are identified and positions on these issues are also represented on matrices and maps. A conformity becomes apparent between land uses, occupants, locations and positions on issues. All of the preceding data are mapped on a single four-way matrix entitled Community Interaction. One ordinate enumerates the inhabitants as self-described constituencies. At right angles are shown the issues. Opposite constituencies are listed all land uses. The final quadrant identifies all agencies, private and public, through which the constituencies operate to achieve their ends. This matrix can also be employed to show which constituencies suffer or benefit from different reactions to any issue. The data are now ordered and comprehensible. As human ecological planning is future-oriented, it cannot be content with the existing population as the client group. It must make either assumptions or predictions about its size and composition at future times. This is the area of growth modeling and market analysis dominated by economists. The economy of the region is reviewed historically and, in conjunction with assumptions made for the national and regional economy, predictions of growth or decline are made for population, employment categories, and public facilities. This analysis includes the levels of private investment which can be anticipated in different sections of private enterprise and fiscal expenditures on the various levels of government.

We have come to the point where the elements of the Darwin-Henderson imperative can be resolved. We have modeled the natural region as an interacting system in which values repose. We have asked the occupants and users to describe their needs and desires, their conception of benefits (which also reveals dislikes, aversions, and costs). We can now search for fit environments for all users, present and prospective. Fitness remains unchanged—a fit environment requires the least work of adaptation. In other words, where all or most propitious factors co-exist with none or few detrimental ones, is, by definition, "most fitting." This requires a two-part process. First, we must interpret the data maps for their opportunities and constraints for all prospective land uses. For example, the geology map might be interpreted for seismic activity, landslide hazard, fault zones, economic minerals, subsidence, compressive strength, and more. The physiography map will be interpreted to show physiographic regions and features, elevation categories, slope categories, and so on, for each map. The sum of all of the legends on all maps constitutes the sum of attributes to be employed in the allocation process. Obviously, any single phenomenon can be an opportunity for one user and a constraint to another. The users must now be defined, either in terms of self-identified social groups, e.g., Italian mushroom farmers, or more broadly, agricultural types. The appropriate user-category will be determined from the anthropological study. When known, all of the relevant attributes in every data set are compiled in terms of opportunities and constraints for that land use. The region is then shown as a gradient of maximum to minimum suitability (fitness) for each and every land use, i.e., agriculture, industry, commerce, recreation, and housing all by type. In addition, one further map is generally prepared, entitled "Protection." This identifies and delimits all hazards to life and health from physical phenomena in flood plains, hurricane zones, seismic areas, and the like. It also identifies areas which can be made hazardous by human use, e.g., by induced subsidence by withdrawal of water, gas, oil, or by mining. It also locates all rare, endangered, scarce, or valuable species of plants and animals, and all buildings, places, and spaces deemed to be of historic, scenic, or scientific value. At this point, it is possible to synthesize all of the optima for all prospective land uses showing the intrinsic suitability (fitness) of the region for all existing and prospective uses. This should show locations where more than one land use can coexist compatibly in a single area. It should also show where co-existing uses would be in conflict. The preceding procedure is appropriate for government planning as an objective statement on intrinsic fitness of the region. However, planning decisions are not made on objective criteria alone. It is also possible to allocate resources using the value system of the discrete constituencies which constitute the region. The major variable in any allocation process in planning is the value system of the problem solver. Hence, there can be as many plans as there are groups. Moreover, for every allocation one can analyze who suffers and who benefits. The availability of such data would allow groups to see the consequences of the employment of their value system in terms of resource allocation. It would permit groups to see where values would have to be modified to achieve objectives which they sought. In short, it provides the opportunity for an overt, explicit and replicatable planning process, and indeed for planning as a truly informed democratic process.

Ecological planning seeks to fit consumer and environment. This problem-solving and problem-seeking quest conforms to the definition of health. Ecological planning should be health giving. Success in such planning or fitting should be revealed in the existence of healthy communities, physical, biological, and social systems in dynamic equilibrium. However, many persons and institutions may satisfy the definition of health by seeking and solving problems but still succumb to disease and death from causes of which they were ignorant or causes beyond their control. As a result a specialization in health planning has been developed within the realm of human ecological planning. This subscribes to the ecological theory and method which has been described but uses as its viewpoint the degree to which actions by persons, groups, or institutions enhance or diminish human health and well-being.

The first category of such actions comprises natural phenomena and processes which constitute a hazard to life and health. This would include areas susceptible to volcanism and earthquakes, floods, tsunamis, avalanches, landslides, fire, subsidence, and the like. It would also include vectors of disease inducing malaria, yellow fever, schistosomiasis, river blindness, sleeping sickness, cholera, amoebic dysentery, etc.

The subsequent category would comprise those situations where certain human actions would transform a benign situation into a hazardous one, e.g., where earthquakes may be induced by injecting wastes into faults, or subsidence induced by underground mining or the withdrawal of water, natural gas, and oil, the exacerbation of flood or drought, disposal of toxins into the environment, or contemplated inhabitation of environments wherever hazards existed.

A third category would include the hazards to life and health related to resources and occupations. This would include uranium, lead, mercury, zinc, asbestos, and beryllium, among others. It would include occupations which extracted these minerals, processed, and used them. This category of occupational diseases associated with resources would include the effect of pesticides and herbicides both upon farm workers and consumers.

A further realm of investigation would focus upon regions impacted by hazardous processes, e.g., a population subtended by a plume of air pollution from one or more sources, a population utilizing contaminated water sources, or one served by an unsanitary food distribution facility, etc.

The final area is social epidemiology, where populations are analyzed to discern their degree of health/morbidity attributable to multiple factors with an emphasis on behavior.

In all of these cases the human ecological presumption holds. Individuals and society can achieve health and well-being by seeking and solving problems. In the special case of health planning, the connection is visible and incontrovertible. Persons are assisted in identifying problems to which they would otherwise be oblivious and are therefore enabled to confront and resolve them.

As one reviews the amount of work to be undertaken to accomplish human ecological planning, the first response is that it is beyond the financial or human resources of most communities. Indeed, given present priorities it probably is. Yet, if the quest for health and well-being necessarily involves planning as the agent for accomplishing syntropic-fitness-health, is this not the single most important activity of persons, families, institutions and, not least, government? All units of government are enjoined by the U.S. Constitution to promote the health and well-being of citizens. Indeed, if this is the most powerful agency available to man, can he avoid employing it? It has multiple benefits. It requires that all activities, public and private, be reviewed in terms of the degree to which they promote and enhance well-being. The acquisition of both the natural inventory and the ethnographic history, if assimilated, provides the basis for an informed citizenry capable of exercising good judgment. In addition, access to the ecological model gives the opportunity for predicting the consequence of contemplated actions, both in the public and private realm. In terms of costs the initial cost of undertaking an ecological inventory and interpretation, an ethnographic history supplemented by interviews, would be high, but they would only have to be done once. The task of keeping the inventory current and enriched would not be demanding.

I have elsewhere (Wallace, McHarg, Roberts, and Todd, 1973) described a process whereby this conception could be employed as national policy. It was recommended that a National Environmental Laboratory be created to model the ecosystem of the United States and provide a depository of integrated and interpreted data available to all, either in published form, mapped form, or through a display terminal facility, located in all public libraries. In addition there would be thirty-four Regional Environmental Laboratories, one for each of the homogenous physiographic regions comprising the United States. These would provide data at scales appropriate to the nation and its regions. Those data should also be available at scales appropriate to states, countries, and finally, cities and towns.

Of course, university departments do not engage in national policy. While this subject is of intense interest to planners, the purpose of the Penn Department of Landscape Architecture and Regional Planning is to engage in research and instruction to train professional landscape architects and regional planners. The faculty have concluded that it is presumptuous to plan without knowledge of place and people and that planning involves fitting them together, mindful of the thermodynamic imperative of fitness and the supervening criterion of enhancing human health and well-being.

The evolution of the department at Penn over the past quarter century has been from a preoccupation with design in the absence of any scientific prerequisites or training to a continuous increase in the content of both physical and biological science, integrated by ecology. The present phase aspires to extend ecological planning and design into an applied human ecology. It is the hope of this author that this issue will help bring together others engaged in this and similar quests in order that there will be mutual benefit.

References

Darwin, C. 1859. *On the Origin of Species by Means of Natural Selection, or the Preservation of Favoured Races in the Struggle for Life.* London: Murray.

Henderson, L.J. 1913. *The Fitness of the Environment.* New York: The Macmillan Company.

Holden, C. 1977. "Champion for Design with Nature." *Science,* 195:379–382.

Wallace, McHarg, Roberts, and Todd. 1973. *Towards a Comprehensive Plan for Environmental Quality.* Washington, D.C.: American Institute of Planners for the U.S. Environmental Protection Agency.

8

Landscape Architecture (1997)

In 1996–97, Ian McHarg undertook a speaking tour on behalf of the American Society of Landscape Architects (ASLA). Jim Dalton, then executive vice president of ASLA, sought to promote membership in the society but, even more, wanted to elevate the aspirations of the existing members. He selected McHarg for this task. As a result of the speaking tour, McHarg wrote this reflective essay for ASLA.

I know of no other profession which escalated as swiftly from oblivion to international significance nor one where so few persons have accomplished so much. Landscape architecture is unique in both respects. This should give us inspiration, confidence, and courage.

Law had its origins in courtiers selling access to power and spawned an army of lawyers; the master builders bequeathed us architecture, what a gift; artificers, sappers, and miners led to engineers; witch doctors, shamans, and in the West, barbers with leeches, led to medicine. Originally this was a mixed blessing. Until this century interventions were just as likely to be detrimental as beneficial. Medicine was no better than chance. Not until the Flexner Report, when medical schools were induced, perhaps better, bribed, to espouse biology, did medicine rise to its present august position. The medical experience contains a powerful lesson. Do we wish our efforts to be random, inconsequential, or indeed malevolent, or should we follow medicine and espouse science, biology, perhaps ecology and anthropology, and justify a more central and consequential role? I hope so.

The precise date when landscape architecture emerged is clouded. There were transitions. But in sixteenth-century Italy there appeared a singular expression. Popes and cardinals chose to leave Rome in summer and reside in Frascati and other nearby towns, where they built villas. These were not remarkable, but their gardens and outdoor spaces certainly were, particularly Villa D'Este and Villa Lante, works of excruciating beauty, a major threshold.

Were Pirro Ligorio, Jacopo Barozzi da Vignola, or Donato Bramante members of a new breed, or were they simply green architects? I think not, the originality and the dominance of the gardens demands a new signature. How proud we can be to have these illustrious founders as our own antecedents. Landscape architecture would seem to have developed in full bloom.

The locus of power, invention and art moved to France where a single figure, André Le Nôtre, dominated the next century. First with Vaux-le-Vicômte for Nicolas Fouquet, later for Louis XIV at Versailles, Le Nôtre designed the largest exercise of garden art in history. It still excites our astonishment. Masses of tractable, docile, and colorful plants, with clay, sand, and gravel, were assembled into a great symmetrical composition. Its purpose was to portray the sovereignty and power of Le Roi Soleil, king by divine right, demonstrating his dominion over all men and nature, his power to subjugate them. The composition was an enormous genuflection to his majesty and power, it consumed half of the royal treasury. Would that other monarchs and princes had emulated him with the creation of gardens, or, even better, protecting and cherishing nature. But that was not the message of Versailles which sought to demonstrate man's dominion over nature. This constitutes the worst possible admonition to those explorers who were then about to discover and colonize the earth. Anthropomorphism, dominion, and subjugation are better suited to suicide, genocide, and biocide than survival and success.

Was Le Nôtre a green architect? I think not, the sheer dominance of the garden suggests a different scope of concerns, interests, and interventions. The fact that the palace was simply an exclamation point in the composition, suggests a new role and profession. Le Nôtre was truly a landscape architect. His works were the zenith of art on the seventeenth century. Consider his accomplishments or of the Italian trio of Ligorio, Vignola, and Bramante.

The English landscape movement began as Versailles was being finished. The handful of men who would proceed to transform an entire nation were dedicated to the expression of a harmony of man and nature. Of them there is no doubt. A new view was born in the eighteenth century. Whence its antecedents? I have not been able to discover. But here was Walpole saying of Kent, "he leap't the wall and discovered all nature to be a garden" and again "he found in nature a new creation." In my opinion, these are most powerful statements, evidence of a new view, indeed the emergence of the modern view.

William Kent, Capability Brown, Humphry Repton, Uvedale Price, Richard Payne Knight, and William Shenstone accomplished a total transformation of what was then an impoverished agriculture, deforested landscape, attenuated fields, and created the fairest, most productive, and beautiful landscape in Europe in less than a century. This, I suggest, is the finest

accomplishment of art in the Western tradition. It deserves our most profound admiration. It should be revered as an important precursor.

These six men led England to accept and display the unity of man and
nature and in so doing, transformed a nation. Persuasive and effective as was
this new view, it was unable to withstand the power of its successor which led
to the industrial revolution. Coal, iron, steel, mines, factories, railways, canals,
industrial cities assumed ascendancy. No longer was nature to be cherished,
nurtured, and emulated but rather to be exploited. The world was now seen
as a storehouse inviting plunder.

But the landscape ideal survived, absorbed by the father of the profession,
that great American, Frederick Law Olmsted, who visited England, observed
the first public park at Birkenhead by Joseph Paxton, and proceeded to
apply and expand the eighteenth-century principles into nineteenth-century
America. Certainly the creation of a system of national parks was an original
conception—the identification, protection, management of regions equiva-
lent to nation-states. The invention of the urban park was comparable—Central Park remains unmatched; Riverside and the American subdivision, Stan-
ford and the college campus, even the highway overpass falls within the
inventions of Olmsted who single-handedly equaled the entire production of
the professions of architecture, planning, and engineering during the nineteenth century.

This extraordinary paragon, in addition to his other virtues, had the wit
to identify his successor—Charles Eliot, son of Harvard's president. In 1880
Eliot determined to spend a productive summer. A student at Harvard, he
enlisted six classmates who entitled themselves the Champlain Society and
proceeded to undertake an inventory of Mount Desert Island in Maine. Over
six years they performed what was the first ecological inventory ever done. It
produced two products, "Outline of the Geology of Mt. Desert Island" and
"Flora of Mt. Desert, Maine."

But Eliot expanded this purpose to invent the first ecological planning study
in the United States or the world, for the Boston metropolitan region, the 1893
study which, to date, has neither been equaled nor surpassed. It included the
entire region from Blue Mountains to the sea, it included rivers, forests, marshes, the offshore islands. Eliot and his invention—regional planning—could not
have arrived at a better time. Here was the appropriate attitude to lead the colonization of the country, here was a visionary plan for the land, and the world.
But, it was not to be, for Eliot died of cerebrospinal meningitis prematurely at
37, to the loss of the nation, the world, and to nature.

The eighteenth-century view envisaged an ideal landscape, first expressed
by the painters Salvator Rosa, Nicolas Poussin, and Claude Lorraine, observed
in the *campagna*. This effort of restoration required and received massive energies. This was not necessary in America. Here the pioneers had discovered a

virgin continent. The task was not to represent harmony that existed in the systems which were being discovered. Here the task was to recognize, cherish, and protect first and also to develop with discrimination, employ art in accomplishing felicitous adaptations. This was a simpler task, but it was at odds with the explorer mentality, the extraction morality, be it of gold or silver, beavers and bison, timber or wheat, exploitation was its name.

Olmsted and Eliot had presented a better view, but Eliot had died even before Olmsted, and to our astonishment and loss, these extraordinary paragons did not reproduce themselves. The concept died in England at the end of the eighteenth century. Eliot died in 1897, Olmsted in 1903, and their movement stalled. It should have been enthroned at Harvard, spread to other leading institutions, and permeated the new profession of landscape architecture. To my continued chagrin, it did not. Indeed it declined from the elevated status achieved by Olmsted, promised by Eliot.

The time has come to rediscover and celebrate the accomplishments of our predecessors, not least Olmsted and Eliot. They should be enthroned at Harvard, represented by bronze statues, studied, admired, and emulated worldwide.

The traditions continued into this century. First in the person of the Brazilian polymath, painter, naturalist, designer of jewelry, floral decorations for state ceremonies in Brasilia, architect but, most of all, designer of gardens: Roberto Burle Marx. He was a man of such fame as to be known to cab drivers in Rio. He was also renowned as a belly dancer and singer of bawdy songs, and in several languages. Not least, he was a successful plant collector and created an elaborate arboretum.

Yet another is Lawrence Halprin, very much alive at 78, productive, notably in the United States and Israel. His reputation began with modern gardens, catapulted after the Portland Fountain, expanded with Sea Ranch, and had a fitting climax with the FDR Memorial in Washington, D.C., just completed and resoundingly appreciated. Halprin deserves inclusion in this pantheon.

These are emergents, hints of successors to this great lineage. First are the partners of Andropogon, Carol and Colin Franklin, Leslie Jones and Rolf Sauer; Jones & Jones of Seattle; Edward Stone of Florida; EDAW in San Francisco, Atlanta, and elsewhere; Jon Coe, Gary Lee, and their partners in Philadelphia; Design Workshop of Aspen, Tempe, and elsewhere; and, of course, there is A. E. Bye who disclaims scientific ecology, but whose works are of great beauty and very appropriate ecology. There is another figure, Jack Dangermond, President of ESRI in Redlands, California, who is the leader in spatial computation. Dangermond has drawn on his multidisciplinary academic training in landscape architecture, planning, and geography to create a new industry and lead it.

The giants who led the profession, Ligorio, Vignola, and Bramante, Le Nôtre, the English Six, Olmsted and Eliot, Burle Marx and Halprin have been augmented not by practitioners, but by science and technology. Concern for nature in the Renaissance was limited mainly to princes and pontiffs. In England it was the province of the landed aristocracy, artists, and scholars. The audience widened in the nineteenth century but exploded at the end of the twentieth. Newspapers, magazines, film, but mainly television, contributed to this effervescence. PBS, *National Geographic, The Planet Earth, Nature,* the Discovery and Learning Channels, brought rich, sophisticated, and persuasive insights into nature to a rapt public attention.

Science, long immured in subatomic particles and molecular biology, emerged into the sensate world with plate tectonics, atmospheric physics, chemosynthesis, and a new understanding of microbes and of the importance of environment. Surely the greatest benefit from the diminution of the nuclear threat was the recognition of the environment as having primacy on the global agenda. In this evolution emerged new technological marvels, sensors, satellite imagery, geo-positioning systems, computers, and geographic information systems. We can feel the world's pulse. We can undertake not only national, but also global inventories. We can monitor the planet.

Who would have thought that the Christian church would address man's relation to nature through the garden at D'Este?

Who would have expected that the major energies of the most powerful monarch in Europe would be employed to create a metaphysical symbol of his rank and role as at Versailles?

Was there reason to expect that the most compelling philosophical investigation would be a new and benign view of the relationship of man and nature in eighteenth-century England?

Who could have expected that the environment would emerge as the most compelling subject confronting the world at the end of this century?

The profession of landscape architecture has a client, the earth and its creatures. In order to meet this challenge, to respond to our client in a sustainable manner, the profession must ensure that it forms an alliance with the environmental sciences and that we come to be seen by them and the public as their agents for achieving felicitous, ecological adaptations.

Professional education must recognize this relationship and incorporate environmental science. The American Society of Landscape Architects must become a spokesman for the environment and appropriate adaptations. We must become leaders, not only in understanding the environment, but also in planning ecological restoration, management, and design, that is, in sustainable development.

To this day, neither architects nor city planners have been required to study environmental science and thus bring only innocence and ignorance to bear. Engineers traditionally study physical environmental sciences, notably geology and hydrology, but learn nothing of life or people. Landscape architects have a long association with botany, horticulture, and, more recently, ecology.

There is a vacuum of environmental competence which the profession should fill. Success is contingent upon landscape architects learning enough environmental science to be unerringly selected to answer all questions relating to its planning and design. When this comes to pass the profession will receive the appreciation, adulation, and rewards befitting to the descendants of our illustrious ancestors. We have increased our numbers a thousandfold. We have inherited an unimaginable expansion of capabilities. While problems have escalated with population, our scientific understanding and technological competence have more than kept pace. The canvas has expanded from site to region, to nation to now embrace oceans, atmosphere, and the planet earth.

The only necessary elements are confidence and conviction. I have long ago concluded that knowledge is the essential ingredient. Given this, then confidence will follow. Consider the example of Frederick Law Olmsted. Has anyone ever equaled his conviction of the salubrious effect of nature, particularly necessary for urban man?

What an extraordinary lineage we have inherited. It gives us example, confidence, and courage. Let us follow their example and proceed into the twenty-first century.

9

Natural Factors in Planning (1997)

The idea for this essay came from Lloyd Wright, then director of conservation and ecosystem assistance for the U.S. Natural Resources Conservation Service (NRCS). A dedicated member of the federal bureaucracy, Lloyd Wright believed other government employees needed inspiration and challenge in light of the harsh criticism that had been leveled against them beginning with the Ronald Reagan administration and perhaps culminating in the bombing of the Alfred P. Murrah Federal Office Building in Oklahoma City.

Wright identified McHarg as the best person for such inspiration and challenge. McHarg's charge was to provide a theoretical framework for using natural resource information in planning. The NRCS provided support through a cooperative agreement with the Arizona State University School of Planning and Landscape Architecture to commission McHarg to write this essay. It was subsequently published in the Journal of Soil and Water Conservation, *which is widely read by NRCS staff and other governmental natural resource managers. The paper was also translated into Italian by Danilo Palazzo and published in* Urbanistica, *an Italian planning journal.*

In earlier times, in predominantly agricultural societies, conventional wisdom and folklore included an understanding of the region, its phenomena, processes, and calendar—time to plow, farrow, seed, harvest, first and last frosts, the probability of precipitation. Cultural memories recalled past events, flood and drought, pestilence, earthquakes, hurricanes, tornadoes. Given the crucial importance of this knowledge, essential to survival and success, it seems pointless to restate the obvious, but, sadly, it is increasingly necessary, more so than in earlier, simpler times. The phenomenal increase in urban concentrations, combined with exponential population growth and the reduction of the agricultural component in society and economy, have produced asphalt people who know little of nature and care less. To such people, knowledge of nature is apparently irrelevant to their success or future.

This view is not merely wrong. It is diametrically opposed to need. The greater the population and the greater the urban concentration, the greater the need to understand nature and to act prudently, using the best available knowledge.

The world population is growing exponentially; five billion now, doubling how soon? This enlargement is increasingly concentrated; megacities of 30 million, unknown only decades ago, are commonplace now. Mexico City, São Paulo, Calcutta, Tokyo are the most conspicuous examples and more will follow. The presence of such mammoth populations, of unprecedented size and concentration, is a recipe for disaster.

Surely the combination of massive populations in such urban concentrations should be warning enough but the situation is exacerbated by location—the annual flooding in the Gangetic flood plain takes an enormous toll now; the view of the circle of volcanoes, surrounding Mexico City, is not reassuring.

But this is not enough; it appears that the future includes increased frequency and violence in climatic events. Warm a pot of water, see activity increase with temperature until boiling occurs. So too with the earth. Whether or not from the accumulation of greenhouse gases, world temperatures rise and with them climatic violence. This is thought to include not only flood and drought, hurricanes, tsunamis, and tornadoes but earthquakes and volcanoes too. So we have actively increased the threat of death, disaster, pain, and loss by those concurrent processes, population increase, concentration, and now climatic violence.

The consequences of national disasters are awesome now. What of the future? A flood in Bangladesh and an earthquake in the Crimea accounted for half a million deaths. Two hundred thousand lives were lost from twenty events in the last forty years. There are also damages. In 1989, Hurricane Hugo incurred over $6 billion in damages and 80 lives were lost. In the same year, the Loma Prieta earthquake caused $10 billion in damages. Hurricane Andrew caused another $25 billion in 1992, approximately seven percent of Florida's Gross State Budget. The 1994 Midwest floods in the Mississippi River basin and the Northbridge earthquake the same year together resulted in over $50 billion in destruction. Insurance claims for the first three years of this decade exceeded claims for the entire earlier one. These are significant costs, only exceeded by the U.S. Department of Defense budget and the national debt. These costs can be reduced significantly.

In the face of this massive indictment, it would seem impossible to disregard natural calamities in the planning process. The burden of discussion paper is that natural factors have for too long been either excluded or inadequately incorporated in planning. Surely, you say, this is a restatement of the obvious. How can effective planning proceed without the inclusion of this crucial realm? It has, can, and does, and the absence of such data causes planning to be either irrelevant, exclusionary, or inconsequential. How did this paradoxical situation come to be? How can it be corrected?

There are many reasons. The first reposes in the historic disinterest of leading scientists and institutions in the environment. Fashions tend to vary, but for half a century particle physics has dominated the physical sciences, molecular biology has preempted attention in the biological sciences. As recently as the 1950s, the environment was barely an accepted term. I recall when in the 1950s the Audubon Society was preoccupied with birds, the Sierra Club concentrated on preserving the scenic American West. Then the only organization concerned with the national environment was the Conservation Foundation, housed in a one-room office in New York City. In the 1960s, there were few writers or speakers prepared to discuss the environment: Rachel Carson, Ralph Nader, Paul Ehrlich, Barry Commoner, René Dubos, and me.

Rachel Carson was the first spokesperson for the environment: Her message was that we were poisoning natural systems and ourselves; Ralph Nader brought the subject of the environment to national attention and illustrated the impact of the issue on the consumer; Paul Ehrlich gave vivid attention to the population problem; Barry Commoner emphasized chemical pollutants; René Dubos, pathologist, the most humane of the group, insisted that the way the French peasant lived with the environment provided the appropriate answer; my theme was design with nature.

The Fragmentation of Knowledge

Science itself was fragmented. Reductionism held sway. Integration requires bridging between separate sciences, an attitude resisted by universities and governmental institutions. Meteorologists study climate, geologists rocks, hydrologists address water, pedologists focus on soils. Vegetation is addressed by ecologists, limnologists, and marine biologists; animals and wildlife have their appropriate investigators: animal ecologists, ethnologists, fish and wildlife scientists. For almost every discipline there will be an associated institution. National Oceanic and Atmospheric Adminstration (NOAA) links to climate, the U.S. Geological Survey controls rocks and water, soils repose in USDA Natural Resources Conservation Service, fish and wildlife are located in the National Biological Survey and in the U.S. Fish and Wildlife Service. The U.S. Environmental Protection Agency (EPA) limits itself to regulation while natural vegetation alone has no institutional sponsor. The Smithsonian Institution seems to have no niche.

Each of these elements, either in universities or in government, is like a piece of a jigsaw puzzle which has never been assembled. Is there anyone with the wit, capability, and energy to do this? Unlikely.

Humpty Dumpty sat on a wall;
Humpty Dumpty had a great fall;
All the king's horses and all the king's men;
Couldn't put Humpty together again.

The environment is like a pile of eggshell fragments. Not only has the environment been disdained by all but a handful of our leading scientists but inevitably by the most prestigious institutions. There the mandarins scorned the workmen of the environment with their black rimmed fingernails, soiled shirt collars, inhabiting land-grant colleges in declining programs in agriculture and forestry. And moreover, the single integrative science, ecology, absent or little represented in the Ivy League, was housed in broom closets in the land-grant and state colleges.

The Fragmentation of Government

In addition, of course, there are redundant and often conflicting policies, evidence of cross purposes. The U.S. National Park Service is charged with the preservation and interpretation of national scenic wonders but the U.S. Forest Service is charged with exploiting our national forests, the U.S. Bureau of Land Management (BLM) fills a comparable role for rangeland. While the U.S. Geological Survey (USGS) studies geological and hydrological systems, the U.S. Army Corps of Engineers concentrates on intervention in riverine systems, as does the BLM. Regulation mainly reposes in the EPA, but the Army Corps of Engineers is charged with managing wetlands; the agent which supervised the filling of wetlands is now charged with protecting them! The study of climate by NOAA is very impressive. Satellites, sensors, and computers have advanced meteorology. This advance is not paralleled in hydrology. The massive midwestern floods of 1994 may well have been enhanced by public actions—floods as a public gift at great public cost.

As molecular biology assumed dominance, biology became a crucial component of medicine. Organismic and community biology was abandoned. Generalists were cytologists, preoccupied with the cell. Organismic biology declined with the retirement or death of the nineteenth-century naturalists in biology—never to be replaced. In geology this same interest focused physical sciences on carbon dating and planetary physics. It was only the discovery of plate tectonics which brought geology back to spatial studies. But here the disdain of geologists for hydrologists or soil scientists remains an important obstruction to integration.

Natural Processes Affect Our Health and Safety

If science has been indifferent to the environment, victims of natural calamities certainly have not been. These natural disasters—flood, drought, hurricanes, tsunamis, tornadoes, volcanoes, and earthquakes—have caused enormous loss of life, plus considerable damage, suffering and pain, and promise more. Indeed, it would appear that the sum of global behavior is to increase this damage, pain, suffering, and loss of life.

This is particularly poignant because so much of it could be avoided. Surely it is neither wise nor necessary to locate populations in areas prone to natural disasters. Nor is it necessary to exacerbate them. One example might suffice.

The 1994 Mississippi flooding was exacerbated by failure to understand the role of river ecologies in mitigating flooding and by years of engineering practices that neutralized much natural protection.

The explanation for the lack of interest in natural processes in planning began with the long-term rejection of the environment as a fitting subject of research by both prestigious academic institutions and governmental agencies. The commitment to reductionism and the fragmentation of science provide other reasons. The passion for obtaining data as a commonplace obsession is paralleled by a disinterest in integration. A widespread public belief that natural calamities are acts of God and must be endured is also a culprit. Yet management of natural disaster is one area where profound advances have been made. The understanding of tectonic and meteorological processes, improved monitoring and prediction, and better communication have reduced the consequences of natural calamities.

The Inadequacies of Planning to Respond to the Environmental Challenge

Yet another explanation lies in the composition of those engaged in city and regional planning. In the postwar years planning was described as an "applied social science," certainly in the dominant planning schools, such as the University of Pennsylvania, the University of North Carolina, the Massachusetts Institute of Technology, the University of California-Berkeley, and Harvard University. Such a description had a profound effect on the planning operation.

Go into a local city or county planning office, anywhere in the United States. Establish that you have been commissioned to write an article on the importance of natural factors in the processes of planning and community design. Speak to the staff. You will find that their training has been predominantly in the applied social sciences. They are likely to have studied economics, sociology, computation, statistics, perhaps (hopefully) land-use and zoning law. Only the planners with an education in geography are likely to have received any training in physical and biological science. So your investigation will not assure you of the central importance of natural science in planning and community design. Indeed, the absence of planners trained in the natural sciences is an explanation for the exclusion of environmental science.

The Emergence of the Environment in Public Policy

Since the 1970s, the environment has emerged as a significant subject. However, the science departments of most prestigious universities still focus on molecular biology and subatomic physics. While the environment may have emerged from oblivion in the public consciousness it is still not prominent. Agencies continue in their ad hoc, reductionist ways, although there are timid efforts of integration—the National Science Foundation-Environmental Protection Agency combined focus on watersheds is a welcome and belated innovation; the creation of the National Biological Survey (NBS) in the U.S. Department of Interior is an attempt at integration. The U.S. Fish and Wildlife Service Gap Analysis Program and the Clinton administration's Interagency Ecosystem Management Task Force are other hopeful efforts.

But in sum, it is a lugubrious review. What is the remedy? Well, clearly there must be widespread recognition of the necessity for all of the sciences to address the problems of the environment. In this fragmented and reductionist world it is necessary to recognize and to acknowledge that the greatest progress can be accomplished, not by providing additional data (we already have quantities beyond our ability to use them). No, the greatest advance will occur when it is recognized that integration and synthesis constitute the greatest challenge and provide the greatest promise of success.

On the positive side the increase in scientific knowledge, the availability of sensors, not the least global positioning systems (GPS), offer great opportunities for ecological planning. As important are computers, their ability to digitize massive data sets, retrieve data, analyze them, and undertake automatic analytic procedures and finally perform complex planning syntheses.

Human Ecological Planning

I have called such a process human ecological planning. It includes data and precepts from the relevant physical, biological, and social sciences. In the 1970s, the Ford Foundation made grants to support ecology at Princeton

University, the University of Georgia, and the University of Pennsylvania. At Penn, we designed a new curriculum in ecologically based regional planning, recruiting persons with undergraduate qualifications in the natural sciences. An integrated, ecology-based curriculum was developed, a natural scientist faculty was hired, including such luminaries as Ruth Patrick, a 1996 recipient of the National Medal of Science. This program prospered for twenty years. It produced 15 deans, 38 chairmen and directors, and 150 professors world-wide. From this cadre came 15 new programs emphasizing ecological planning and design. The Penn program ultimately shrank in parallel with the opposition to planning and the environment initiated by former Presidents Ronald Reagan and George Bush and continued by the current U.S. Congress.

Ecological planning, developed at Penn and employed in instruction and research, produced over a thousand graduates who employ ecological planning in many academic institutions and government agencies in North America and around the world. This initiative should receive massive support. It represents an unmatched degree of integration, the incorporation of all of the environmental sciences—physical, biological, and social—combined with advanced computational capability. Descriptions of human ecological planning have been published elsewhere but can be presented in synopsis here. First, it requires that all of the environmental sciences be included and unified by chronology and depicted as a "layer cake." These would include meteorology, geology, physical oceanography, surficial geology, geomorphology, groundwater and surficial hydrology, soils, vegetation, wildlife (including marine biology), and limnology. The social sciences should be included in ecological inventories too with ethology, ethnography, cultural anthropology, economics, sociology, and geography, particularly computational science.

Our faculty teams undertook numerous studies with the landscape architecture and regional planning students at Penn. From that work, we identified the baseline natural resource data necessary for a layer-cake inventory of a place (table 1).

In addition to being comprehensive and inclusive, the integrating device recommended is chronology. That is, all studies should involve a historic recapitulation ordered by time. Information from the sciences should be organized in a "layer cake" fashion, with older components including rocks at the bottom of the cake and younger layers, such as soil and vegetation above. The completion of such a human ecological study presents an understanding of how the region came to be, what it is, how it works, and where it tends to go. A human perspective is essential—how people relate to their environments both historically and today. The ethnographic history should describe the populations, structured in constituencies, having characteristic values, settlement patterns, resource utilization, and specific issues and attitudes to them. When the inventory is complete, and the data accumulated

Table 1. Baseline Natural Resource Data Necessary for Ecological Planning

The following natural resource factors are likely to be of significance in planning. Clearly the region under study will determine the relevant factors but many are likely to occur in all studies.

Climate. Temperature, humidity, precipitation, wind velocity, direction, duration, first and last frosts, snow, frost, fog, inversions, hurricanes, tornadoes, tsunamis, typhoons, Chinook winds

Geology. Rocks, ages, formations, plans, sections, properties, seismic activity, earthquakes, rock slides, mud slides, subsidence

Surficial geology. Kames, kettles, eskers, moraines, drift and till

Groundwater hydrology. Geological formations interpreted as aquifer with well locations, well logs, water quantity and quality, water table.

Physiography. Physiographic regions, subregions and features, contours, sections, slopes, aspect, insolation, digital terrain model(s)

Surficial hydrology. Oceans, lakes, deltas, rivers, streams, creeks, marshes, swamps, wetlands, stream orders, density, discharges, gauges, water quality, flood plains

Soils. Soil associations, soils series, properties, depth to seasonal high water table, depth to bedrock, shrink-swell, compressive strength, cation and anion exchange, acidity-alkalinity

Vegetation. Associations, communities, species, composition, distribution, age and conditions, visual quality, species number, rare and endangered species, fire history, successional history

Wildlife. Habitats, animal populations, census data, rare and endangered species, scientific and educational value

Human. Ethnographic history, settlement patterns, existing land use, existing infrastructure, population characteristics

chronologically, and thus meaningfully, the history of the region under study, its constituent processes, its past, its current form, and its tendencies for the future will become apparent. The product should be an interacting biophysical model on which a human population is causally located.

Determining Suitability

This database is now available for queries. One realm of such queries will involve correlation. Where are hurricane-prone zones? Where is landslide susceptibility? Tornado zones? What aspects of elevation, geology, climate, soil, slope are associated with vegetation types? What environmental aspects combine to proffer a habitat for, let us say, an endangered species? One can say that the richer the data set, the better the answers.

There is a process which I have called suitability analysis. This requires that prospective land uses be identified. Normally this would include forestry, agriculture, extractive minerals, recreation, and urbanization. Each of these can be further subdivided, urbanization might include housing of various densities, commerce, and industry. When the consumers have been identified, the inventory is reviewed to identify all factors on the legends of all maps and to determine those which are propitious, neutral, or detrimental for each prospective land use. Maps, either manually or computer produced, will depict all propitious factors for each land use. They will also depict all detrimental attributes. Finally, the computer will solve the command "show me those locations where all or most propitious factors are located, and where all or most detrimental factors are absent" by superimposing the propitious and detrimental factors. A reasonable convention is to colour all propitious factors in shades of green, all detrimental ones in oranges and reds. Dominant green shows the intrinsically suitable locations.

Of course, the method can be enhanced by weighting and scaling each of the factors. I have generally produced a map entitled "protection" which depicts all factors and regions wherein exist hazards to life and health. These environmentally sensitive areas will vary from location to location but are likely to include the following: flood plains, ocean surges, hurricane zones, tornadoes, tsunamis, earthquakes, vulcanism, wildfires, and subsidence. This protection map and associated text should identify the degrees of hazard represented by these processes and recommend a prudent response. As a result, suitability analysis suggests both constraints and opportunities for future land uses.

Reasons for Optimism

There are reasons for optimism. The subject of the environment has been embraced by the media, surely more for vicarious thrill than for science and understanding. Children's books and television carry much superior information about the environment than they did in your or my childhood. Indeed, I have an excellent sample: my older two sons, in their thirties and forties now, are sympathetic to the environment and lived in a household where ecology was a common word, but their stepbrothers, fourteen and eight, have experienced richer insights into the environment from *Nova*, *National Geographic* specials, *The Planet Earth*, and more. There is an emerging generation, well informed on the environment, indignant at pollution and destruction. They may follow the lead of the 1970s which gave us the flood of environmental legislation. The environmental groups—the World Wildlife Fund, Audubon, Sierra Club, Friends of the Earth, The Nature Conservancy, the National Resources Defense Fund, the Soil and Water Conservation Society—should all constitute youth clubs to embrace these young potential soldiers for the environment.

Scientific knowledge of the environment has grown. The study of plate tectonics alone have advanced our knowledge of the environment; the world warming hypothesis and accompanying research have expanded our knowledge of the atmosphere and meteorology. The development of sensors has added to our ability to monitor the environment, not least GPS which has so simplified surveys and thus landscape inventories. The continuing advances in computation may be the greatest reason for optimism. More data can be ingested, evaluated, synthesized faster, more accurately than ever before.

There are also some sinister reasons for optimism. I would assert that the greatest impetus to improved ecological planning is the last disaster. A disaster amplifies awareness. The succession of alphabetic hurricanes, Edward, Fran, added to Hugo, Agnes, and Andrew have sensitized coastal communities to incipient disaster. Increased population, increased concentration combined with greater climatic violence guarantees more and bigger disasters. If the assertion is true, then each increment of pain and suffering should lead to the greater application of knowledge and wisdom to the planning process.

Can we use our massive brain, augmented by the great prosthesis of sensors and computers, to diminish such pain? Let us hope so.

The last and most important steps begin with resolve. Let us applaud the benefits of analysis and reductionism. They have contributed much to modern science which because of its fragmented nature clearly is not enough. It need not be superseded, but certainly it must be augmented to include synthesis and holism. The environment is now subdivided by science and language. We must direct our energies toward synthesis. There is a vital role here for all scientific institutions, all government departments and agencies. There should be a serious effort to reorganize contradictory views, programs at cross purposes, above all exclusionary myopia, and initiate cooperative procedures. Can we study watersheds, physiographic regions, oceans, tectonic plates, ecosystems? There is a new instrument which does not insist upon scientific disciplines or boundaries, which can accomplish synthesis. It is GIS, geographic information systems, capable of handling immense quantities of data, describing processes and undertaking planning. Not only can GIS undertake the most complex of planning studies undertaken manually it is possible to do studies which cannot be manually done.

Moreover, the computer and the GIS fraternity are already constituencies with magazines, conferences, vendors of hardware and software, oriented to the computer world, irrespective of university, agency, or country. Can this new constituency accomplish the integration which orthodox science has so resolutely rejected? Will GIS provide the belated integration required for planning? Will it spur an integration of inter- and intradisciplinary research and application? Will it lead to integration and synthesis?

The availability of GIS makes inventories a necessity. These should be extensive. A few years ago, I wrote a report with John Radke, Jonathan Berger, and Kathleen Wallace for the EPA entitled "A Prototype Database for a National Ecological Inventory." Our proposal includes a demonstration 40-km^2 sample, the Washington Crossing Hexagon. We chose this to examine two states, with different counties each with distinct nomenclature of geology, soils, vegetation, land use, and zoning. We mapped geology, produced sections, a digital terrain model, digitized aquifers, wells, well logs, discharge gauges, rivers, streams, marshes, wetlands, flood plains, and soils. We digitized 1929 and 1992 vegetation. We mapped all properties, land uses, and zones. It should be noted that making inventories is also an integrative process, particularly if extensive, employing the layer-cake method and using chronology as the underlying principle for organization.

In sum the opportunities for integration, organization of rich data, its analysis and planning using GIS are true, they are available. Will they be used to fulfill their promise, meet society's needs, and give government a larger role in understanding, planning, and regulating the environment and by so doing diminish death, damage, pain, and enhance human health and well-being? Let us hope so—even more, resolve to make it so.

Conclusion

Newt Gingrich, speaker of the house, archcritic of bureaucracy, insists upon across-the-board reductions of 33 percent for USGS, NBS, EPA, and many more agencies. This approach is unable to distinguish excellence from indolence; it mutilates, rather than accomplishes remedial surgery. Yet there are bums, fools, incompetents, failed programs galore, many in competition. Can we not dispose of surplus, failures, incompetence and, above all, eliminate cross-purposes and ensure integration? But can programs be seen as complementary, contributing to our national purpose?

A White House Task Force should be convened to investigate the integration of scientific perceptions of the environment by accomplishing the following:

- Propose a uniform ecological planning method to be employed by all agencies
- Propose a process to develop and monitor the sets of environmental data that must be employed by all agencies
- Create a master agency devoted to assembling, updating, and inter-

preting all digital environmental data; it should develop a national GIS
- Produce a uniform policy to handle "greenhouse gases" and plan for carbon fixing
- Develop government-wide strategies to improve biodiversity
- Develop plans to minimize the losses from environmental disasters
- Produce a plan to construct a national ecological inventory

The White House Task Force should design a training process to be offered by selected institutions to instruct senior officials from all agencies on the ecological planning process. A further training program should be designed as a prerequisite for existing junior staff and for all new employees on all environmental agencies.

So, the natural sciences have either been excluded or lightly incorporated in the planning process. As we have seen, natural calamities cost thousands of lives annually, billions of costs, and enormous insurance claims. There is a mood for economy present in Congress but economies in environmental protection are not popular, so why not achieve economies by diminishing the pain and cost of hurricanes, floods, tornadoes, fires, and other catastrophes? To accomplish such real economies, we should undertake a national ecological inventory, monitor the environment and improve both understanding and prediction of natural phenomena, employ these data in ecological planning processes. Announce the intention to convene a White House Task Force to address the subjects of the environment, reorganization of government, a commitment to integration, address the problems of world warming, biodiversity, greater climatic violence, the increased threats from megacities and the necessity of bringing the environmental sciences into an improved planning process.

Let us plan to save lives, to protect the environment, to achieve savings from appropriate ecological planning, to improve prediction and placement, and to improve the human condition.

10

Ecology and Design (1997)

In 1992 Arizona State University (ASU) initiated a new degree in landscape architecture. In the process a Department of Planning became the School of Planning and Landscape Architecture. To celebrate the event George Thompson of the Center for American Places and Frederick Steiner organized a symposium and a book on landscape architecture theory. They received a grant from the National Endowment for the Arts for the symposium and the book.

The concept was to pull together the senior and junior theorists in the discipline around the theme of ecological design and planning. The senior figures had pioneered the use of ecology in landscape architecture. Several younger theorists had been critical of this use and noted that ecology had drained some of the creative juices from design.

Ian McHarg was the central figure at the symposium. Each of the other theorists referred to his influence in some way or the other. McHarg responded to the criticisms of ecology with this spirited essay. It appears in the book Ecological Planning and Design, *edited by Thompson and Steiner and published by John Wiley & Sons.*

I am unabashedly committed to the imperative *design with nature*, or ecological design and planning. Indeed, I conceive of nonecological design as either capricious, arbitrary, or idiosyncratic, and it is certainly irrelevant. Ecology, the study of environments and organisms, among them people, is totally inclusive. What falls outside this definition? Not content, perhaps only attitude. Nonecological design and planning disdains reason and emphasizes intuition. It is antiscientific by assertion.

There is no doubt about my attitude toward this topic. I invented *ecological planning* during the early 1960s and became an advocate of *ecological design* thereafter. This was explicit in *Design with Nature*; it was not only an explanation, but also a command.[1]

Ecological planning is that approach whereby a region is understood as a biophysical and social process comprehensible through the operation of laws and time. This can be reinterpreted as having explicit opportunities and constraints for any particular human use. A survey will reveal the most fit locations and processes.

Ecological design follows planning and introduces the subject of form. There should be an intrinsically suitable location, processes with appropriate materials, and forms. Design requires an informed designer with a visual imagination, as well as graphic and creative skills. It selects for creative fitting revealed in intrinsic and expressive form.

The deterioration of the global environment, at every scale, has reinforced my advocacy of ecological design and planning. Degradation has reached such proportions that I now conclude that nonecological design and planning is likely to be trivial and irrelevant and a desperate deprivation. I suggest that to ignore natural processes is to be ignorant, to exclude life-threatening hazards—volcanism, earthquakes, floods, and pervasive environmental destruction—is either idiocy or criminal negligence. Avoiding ecological considerations will not enhance the profession of landscape architecture. In contrast, it will erode the modest but significant advances that ecology has contributed to landscape architecture and planning since the 1960s.

Yet, you ask: What of art? I have no doubt on this subject either. The giving of meaningful form is crucial; indeed, this might well be the most precious skill of all. It is rare in society, yet it is clearly identifiable where it exists. Art is indispensable for society and culture.

Does art exclude science? Does art reject knowledge? Would a lobotomy improve human competence, or is the brain the indispensable organ?

There is a new tendency by some landscape architects to reject ecology, to emphasize art exclusively. This I deplore and reject. Such an approach is tragically ironic when so many world leaders are calling for sustainable development, when architects are issuing green manifestos, and professional associations in architecture and engineering are refocusing their attention on the environment.

We have been at this impasse before; it was not beneficial, and the result was calamitous. We have only to remember that, by the end of World War I, landscape architecture was firmly established at Harvard University. It was the world center for this subject. It had inherited the concepts and accomplishments of Frederick Law Olmsted and Charles Eliot, but all was not well: There was dissension.

It transpired that there were opposing camps within landscape architecture. The Olmsted disciples wished to emphasize conservation and regional and town planning. They included Henry Hubbard and Theodora Kimball, Harland Bartholomew, John Nolen, Warren Manning, and, later, Howard

Mennhenick. The remainder were oriented to Beaux Arts; they were self-proclaimed aesthetes, interested in designing estates for the rich and famous: Bremer Whidden Pond, James Sturgis Pray, Steven Hamblin, and Robert Wheelwright. The aesthetes defined landscape architecture design between the world wars at Harvard and elsewhere. Meanwhile the Olmsted disciples founded the field of planning during the 1920s, and inadvertently created a schism between design and planning that persists to this day.[2] Brains and knowledge abandoned landscape architecture, which experienced a massive decline from the peaks of Olmsted and Eliot to an abyss with little intelligence, skill, or passion.

This antagonism between art and science, as well as between design and planning, has lasted too long. It is now a serious obstruction to education and the earth's well-being. Both art and science have their antique, prepared positions, their mandarin advocates, their lines of competence defined, and their proprietary jargons. Yet, when stripped of pomp and pretensions, at root art merely means skill and science means knowledge. Can we imagine, in the challenging environment we occupy, the rejection of either art or science? Surely knowledge needs skill to give form and significance to our landscapes and our adaptations. Surely skill needs knowledge just as a solver needs a problem. Surely, once and for all time, art and science, skill and knowledge, ecology and design and planning should unite.

What the world needs from landscape architecture is an enlarged vision, greater knowledge, and commensurate skill. Landscape architects are engaged in the challenge of adaptation. They must acquire the accomplishments that can make a significant contribution to preserving, managing, planning, and restoring the biosphere, to designing human environments.

And, thanks to Charles Darwin and Lawrence Henderson, we have a theory. Darwin said: "The surviving organism is fit for the environment." Henderson, another biologist and author of *The Fitness of the Environment* (1913), wrote that Darwin's assertion was insufficient. He concluded that, as there are infinite environments and organisms, the evolutionary challenge for every participant is to seek and find the fittest available environment, to adapt that environment and the self to accomplish a better fit. Moreover, Henderson's writing defined a fit environment as one in which most of a consumer's needs exist in the environment as found, requiring less work for adaptation than for any competitor. The thermodynamic challenge implies that successful adaptation is creative.[3]

What are the instruments for adaptation? The universal adaptations—mutation and natural selection—while manipulated extensively for food, plants, and animals, are not widely applied to human breeding (thank goodness). Mutation and natural selection are slow processes. And innate behavior in living organisms is similarly difficult to manipulate. Cultural adaptation is the more pliant and useful. Language, philosophy, science, art, and technology are such instruments. If one is to ask which aspect of cultural adaptation most clearly meets the Darwin-Henderson challenge—to find the fittest environment and then to engage in adaptation—surely the most direct response is landscape planning and design.

But we need an appropriate criterion for guiding and evaluating landscape architecture in the twenty-first century. Art critics evaluate the contribution of painting, sculpture, dance, photography, and other art forms. Can their appreciation extend from the product to the source of creation, the painter, his or her brain, eye, hand, bones, sinews, arteries, and veins? Beauty alone is an inappropriate criterion for evaluating art or the organs that create it, so why should beauty be used exclusively to evaluate a landscape? Fitness, as explained by Henderson, for me is a thoroughly suitable criterion. We have, then, not only a theory, but also criteria for performance and fitness.

If one is fit, then one is healthy, and this applies equally to a landscape. Furthermore, if being healthy enables one to seek and solve problems, or provides the ability to recover from insult or assault, then fitness confers health. Therefore, fitness is an index of health. Extending this thought to landscape architectural theory and practice, do we have a method for accomplishing creative planning and design and, more simply, an ecological method for adaptation?

We live in a physical world, a biological world, and a social world, and our investigations must include them all. As matter preceded life and the human species was late in biological evolution, we can employ chronology as a unifying force. We can recapitulate events and retrace time. Thus, when we design and plan, we should begin with the geological history of a landscape, working in concert with an understanding of climate. Bedrock and surficial geology as well as climatic processes can be reinterpreted to explain geomorphology and hydrology. These processes set the stage for soil formation. Now, the relationships among the constituent parts of a landscape become clear: The past informs the present, and each feature is only comprehensible from understanding its earlier layers. After we learn about a landscape's geology, climate, hydrology, and soils, then vegetation patterns become more apparent, as does the resultant wildlife. At which point we can ask the human occupants who they are, how they distinguish themselves from others, how they view the environment and its occupants, and what are their needs and desires, their preferences and aversions.

I wish to emphasize my belief that ecological study includes natural and cultural processes. We will find that discrete value systems are associated with distinct human constituencies, and we can associate these groups with their needs and values. This approach allows landscape architects to interpret all phenomena in the light of these systems. With such vision and knowledge, we can plan, because we have developed the context for planning and design.

This is the biophysical model I developed more than three decades ago for ecological design and planning. This is the model I live by. It can be reinterpreted to explain social values, technological competence, an ethnographic history of human settlements—urban as well as rural. We then are able to see the primeval landscape successively modified, through history, in order to arrive at the present.

Ecological study is indispensable to planning, but it also produces a context for a regional design vocabulary. The settlements of Dogon, the Berbers in Morocco, the settlement of the Greek islands, Italian hill villages, and pueblo communities in New Mexico and the Colorado Plateau are fitting examples of ecological responses in planning and design. Contemporary examples of ecological designers are too few. I am able, however, to select three firms.

The first is Andropogon in Philadelphia, whose principals are Carol and Colin Franklin, Leslie Jones, and Rolf Sauer. These landscape architects possess unchallenged primacy in ecological design and restoration. Their science is impeccable, their applications cross the threshold of art, and their realizations of design and planning are wonderfully effective, fitting, and, even for the uninitiated, beautiful.[4] Coe Lee Robinson Roesch in Philadelphia is the second example; the third is Jones & Jones in Seattle. Both firms have built sterling reputations designing and building appropriate exhibits for zoos. Their science, too, is elegant, employing inventories of the native environments of animals, replicating these environments with consummate skill. Their creations include ecological and psychological factors never before employed, to my knowledge, for human habitations. It is more difficult to find other examples. These three exceptions simply prove the rule. Ecological design is still an aspiration, not yet a practice, within landscape architecture.

A major obstruction to ecological design is the architecturally derived mode of representation drawings. This is paper-oriented, two-dimensional, and orthogonal. In contrast nature is multi-dimensional, living, growing, moving with forms that tend to be amorphous or amoebic. They can grow, expand, interact, and alternate. Field design would be a marvelous improvement over designing on paper removed from the site. Yet new representations must be developed to supersede the limitations of paper-oriented, orthogonal investigations with their limited formal solutions. We should be committed in our work to designing living landscapes in urban, rural, and wild settings. Yet there are infinite opportunities afforded to those who would study natural systems, their components, rules, succession, and, not least, their forms. This should be the basis for an emerging ecological design.

This system does not need invention. Forms, materials, and processes have evolved by trial and error over eons of time and represent the finest solutions of materials and form that nature could invent. Such ecosystems are exquisitely adapted and provide an example for people to design and plan.

Strangely, the area where art and science have been most successfully employed is neither architecture nor landscape architecture. It is in the creation of prostheses. Here biological knowledge is indispensable, but skill produces the adaptation. The purposes are to amplify the performance of a biological function—to see small and far, we have the microscope and the telescope; to speak far, we have the telephone and the microphone; to move far and fast, we have the plane and the rocket. Our major prosthesis is the expansion of power from muscle to tools, mechanical equipment to atom bomb.

Consider the steps to improve sight—spectacles, bifocals, magnifying glasses, laser operations for cataracts and glaucoma, and soft contact lenses—a miracle of adaptive design. Or walking—first a shoe, then a crutch, a walker, the wheelchair, now titanium hips and Teflon knees. The computer may be the prosthesis for the brain.

Should we pursue this track we would reconsider membranes. The giant clam and nudibranch have incorporated chloroplasts; those animals can now photosynthesize. Why not build membranes, walls, and roofs? Could they do so? Consider vegetation on walls and roofs to add carbon, fixing and minimizing carbon dioxide. Consider creating calcium carbonate, with electric charges in seawater.

Membranes modulate freshwater and saltwater. They facilitate the transport of nutrients. Consider the adaptations to cold in plants, reduction in water content, hairy surfaces, corrugations, and color. Wastes in nature are often nutrients, not problems. The route that Andropogon, Coe Lee Robinson Roesch, and Jones & Jones have developed is superb but needs to be augmented. The example of prosthetic development is a fitting analog. It is indisputably ecological, without caprice.

Of course, the best example of successful adaptation is the coral. The ocean floor is generally sterile. Coral transforms such areas into some of the most fertile and beautiful environments on earth. Would that landscape architects could equal this.

When the training of landscape architects includes at least an introduction to all of the relevant natural and social sciences, as well as design proficiency, then a new proposal can provide them with an exceptional opportunity to design and plan ecologically and artfully.

There are moves afoot to initiate a National Biological Survey. I recommended this in 1974 to Russell Train, then of the U.S. Environmental Protection Agency (EPA). When William Reilly became EPA administrator in 1990, he asked me to advise him on the reorganization of the EPA, and the conduct of the Environmental Monitoring and Assessment Program (EMAP), the proposed inventory. EMAP was proposed to be a broadly conceived ecosystem inventory integrating regional and national scales, allowing for monitoring and assessment, and designed to influence decision making. With my colleagues John Radke, Jonathan Berger, and Kathleen Wallace, I produced a document, "A Prototype Database for a National Ecological Inventory" (1992). This recommended a three-part process, a national inventory at 1:2,000,000 with all natural and social regions delineated; a regional scale inventory at 1:250,000; and, finally, samples at the scale of 1:24,000.

Our first assertion was that the resolve to undertake a National Ecological Inventory should be recognized as the most important governmental action ever taken in the history of the American environment. This resolve contains implicit resolutions: That inventory, monitoring, and modeling are indispensable to the EPA and essential to the fulfillment of its regulatory roles.

This first requires the reconstitution of the EPA to include leadership from all environmental sciences. To provide such leadership, we recommended the creation of an executive committee composed of leading officers in all of the scientific societies. Regional groups of environmental scientists and planners would be assembled to undertake regional inventories. And landscape architects, being among the most competent professionals to decide on the appropriate data to be incorporated and its contribution to planning and design, would participate in the content of these inventories. For the crystalline piedmont and adjacent coastal plain in Pennsylvania and New Jersey, for example, we would assume that landscape architects and regional planners at the University of Pennsylvania, Rutgers University, and Pennsylvania State University would be part of a central group to that association of regional scientists. This model would be replicated throughout the country with other university landscape architecture faculties, professional designers, and planners contributing to the regional groups. By such an involvement the landscape architecture profession would vastly enhance its social contribution and academic reputation.

It is then necessary to produce a plan for the process to undertake the inventory as well as to monitor its progress. This would involve the recommended scientific committee, an expanded staff representing all of the environmental sciences, and an appropriate organizational structure. When the plan is completed, we advocate a massive public relations and advertising campaign to inform the general public, conservation groups, the scientific community, and government officials at all levels of the significance of the enterprise.[5]

Our proposed inventory must include physical, biological, and social systems. The last is indispensable for understanding human environments. We suggested a demonstration ethnographic survey to illustrate that these are crucial for understanding human ecology. In our recommendation to the

EPA, we observed that the greatest problem lies not in data collection, but rather with integration, synthesis, and evaluation.

Now, there is a new development. Secretary of the Interior Bruce Babbitt announced, shortly after his appointment by President Clinton in 1992, his intention to undertake a National Biological Survey (NBS). This may supersede EMAP. There is another possibility: NASA, the Defense Mapping Agency, and the federal departments of defense and energy have collected global environmental data since the onset of the Nuclear Age, employing instrumentalism that is unavailable to civilians. There is discussion of declassifying these data, which, of course, could be included in a National Ecological Inventory or a National Biological Survey. There is, also, the possibility that this capability could be invested in the United Nations as the U.S. arm of the U.N. Environmental Program and employed for a global inventory. Others are recommending the creation of a National Institute of the Environment in which the inventorying and modeling might be invested.

Clearly massive data will soon become available, ultimately in digital form, globally and locally. Whoever has access to this cornucopia will have immense power. Landscape architects should become advocates for such ecological inventories and become primary users of these data for planning and design. Landscape architects must learn to lead.

In 1992 I received a signal honor from President George Bush, the National Medal of Art. The noteworthy aspect of this act was the inclusion of landscape architecture as a category eligible for this high honor. As preface to the award President Bush stated, "It is my hope that the art of the twenty-first century will be devoted to restoring the earth."

This will require a fusion of science and art. There can be no finer challenge. Will the profession of landscape architecture elevate itself to contribute to this incredible opportunity? Let us hope so. The future of our planet—and the quest for a better life—may depend on it. So let us resolve to green the earth, to restore the earth, to heal the earth with the greatest expression of science and art we can muster. We are running out of time and opportunities.

Notes

1. Ian L. McHarg. *Design with Nature*. Garden City, N.Y.: Doubleday, Natural History Press, 1969. Second edition, New York: Wiley, 1992.
2. Frederick Law Olmsted was an amateur farmer, familiar with science, and Charles Eliot consorted with the leading scientists of his time, but their influence was bred out of city planning, which became the applied social science department that I encountered as a student at Harvard University in 1946. The natural sciences were banished. It is barely credible that the accomplish-

ments of that giant, Olmsted, and the opportunities presented by Eliot were disregarded—first, by landscape architecture and, then, by city planning at Harvard. Nor were either replaced by a superior doctrine. We have yet to rediscover their significance.

3. I use the word *consumer* because the roots of *ecology* and *economics* both lie in the Greek word, *oikos*, or "a dwelling place." Henderson used terms such as *consumer* close to this root meaning.

4. See Carol Franklin, "Fostering Living Landscapes," in George F. Thompson and Frederick R. Steiner, eds., *Ecological Design and Planning*. New York: Wiley, 1997, pp. 263–92, as well as Leslie Jones Sauer, *The Once and Future Forest*. Washington, D.C.: Island Press, 1998.

5. It is worthwhile to remember that Charles E. Little and David Brower, among other leading conservationists, have for decades advocated the necessity of employing advertising and public relations techniques in the cause to inform the public, industry, government, and university officials about environmental matters. Also of note is Richard Beamish's important book, *Getting the Word Out in the Fight to Save the Earth*. Baltimore: Johns Hopkins University Press, 1995. Beamish is one of the unsung heroes of the modern environmental movement, especially for his work on saving the Adirondacks.

Complete Bibliography
of Ian L. McHarg

Publications

Books

Lynn Margulis, James Corner, and Brian Holt Hawthore, eds. 2006 *Ian McHarg: Dwelling in Nature, Conversations with Students*. New York: Princeton Architectural Press.

Ian L. McHarg. 2001. *Some Songs to the Stars*. Easton, Pennsylvania: The Knossus Project with Chelsea Green Publishers.

Ian L. McHarg and Frederick R. Steiner, eds. 1998. *To Heal the Earth: Selected Writings of Ian McHarg*. Washington, D.C.: Island Press.

Ian L. McHarg. 1996. *A Quest for Life*. New York: Wiley.

Ian L. McHarg. 1969. *Design with Nature*. Garden City, New York: Natural History Press. (Paperback edition, 1970, Garden City, New York: Natural History Press/Doubleday; 2nd ed., 1992, New York: Wiley; 25th anniversary paperback edition, 1994.) National Book Award Finalist. Translated into French (*Composer avec la nature*, with original French contribution, edited by Max Falque, Cahiers de L'IAURIF, vol. 58–59, 1980), Italian (*Progetto con la natura*, Franco Muzzio, ed., 1989, Padova, Italy), Japanese (1994, Shubunsha), and Spanish (*Proyectar con la Naturaleza*, Juan Luis de las Rivas and Ignacio San Martin, technical eds.; Fernández Nistal, Mar San Miguel Blanco, Alfonso Centeno González, and Raquel Fernández, translators, 2000, Barcelona: Editorial Gustavo Gili).

Chapters in Books

Ian L. McHarg. 1998. "Fitness, the Evolutionary Imperative." In Andrew Scott, ed. *Dimensions of Sustainability*. London: E&FN SPON, an imprint of Routledge, pp. 13–19.

Ian L. McHarg. 1997. "Ecology and Design." In George F. Thompson and Frederick R. Steiner, eds. *Ecological Design and Planning*. New York: Wiley, pp. 321–332. Translated into Chinese by Liu-Ho.

Ian L. McHarg. 1997. "Fuller's Contribution" (pp. 42–43), "Why Is Architecture Oblivious to the Environment" (pp. 54–61), "On the Origins of Ecological Design" (pp. 190–191), and "Teaching the Ecological World View" (pp. 302–304). In Chris Zelov, executive ed., Phil Cousineau, co-editor, and Brian Danitz, contributing ed. *Design Outlaws on the Ecological Frontier*. Cape May, New Jersey: Knossus.

Ian L. McHarg. 1996. "Nature in the Metropolis" (reprinted chapter from *Design with Nature*). In Richard T. LeGates and Frederic Stout, eds. *The City Reader*. London: Routledge, pp. 132–141.

Ian L. McHarg. 1990. "Nature Is More Than a Garden." In Mark Francis and Randolph T. Hester Jr., eds. *The Meaning of Gardens*. Cambridge, Massachusetts: MIT Press, pp. 34–37.

Ian L. McHarg. 1985. "Natural and Cultural Heritage Resources in Your Community." In J. Toby Tourbier, ed. *Taproots, Stewardship through Heritage Discovery: Description of a Program for Secondary Schools and Proceedings of the Conference "Knowing Home."* Newark: Water Resources Center, University of Delaware, pp. 113–118.

Ian L. McHarg. 1982. "Postscript: A Natural/Human Ecological Model of the United States." In Gregory A. Daneke, ed. *Energy, Economics, and the Environment: Toward a Comprehensive Perspective*. Lexington Massachusetts: D.C. Heath, pp. 277–280.

Ian L. McHarg. 1981. "Ecological Planning." In William J. Cairns and Patrick M. Rogers, eds. *Onshore Impacts of Offshore Oil*. London: Applied Science Publishers, pp. 139–143.

Ian L. McHarg. 1980. "Appropriate Stormwater Management." In J. Toby Tourbier and Richard Westmacott, eds. *Stormwater Management Alternatives*. Newark: Water Resources Center, University of Delaware, pp. 23–30.

Ian L. McHarg. 1980. "Three Essays on Urban Space." In ICA Staff, eds. *Urban Encounters*. Philadelphia: Institute of Contemporary Art, pp. 21–24.

Arthur H. Johnson, Jonathan Berger, and Ian L. McHarg. 1979. "A Case Study in Ecological Planning: The Woodlands, Texas." In Marvin T. Beatty, Gary W. Petersen, and Lester D. Swindale, eds. *Planning the Uses and Management of Land*. Madison, Wisconsin: American Society of Agronomy, Crop Science Society of America, and Soil Science Society of America, pp. 935–955.

Ian L. McHarg. 1978. "Ecological Planning: The Planner as Catalyst." In Robert W. Burchell and George Sternlieb, eds. *Planning Theory in the 1980s* (2nd ed., 1982). New Brunswick, New Jersey: Center for Urban Policy Research, pp. 13–15.

Ian L. McHarg. 1976. "Biological Alternatives to Water Pollution." In Joachim Tourbier and Robert W. Pierson Jr., eds. *Biological Control of Water Pollution*. Philadelphia: Center for Ecological Design and Planning, University of Pennsylvania, pp. 7–12.

Ian L. McHarg. 1976. "Il Bacino del Fiume." In Guido Ferrara, ed. *Risorse del Territorio e Politica di Piano*. Venice: Marsilo, pp. 77–98.

Ian L. McHarg. 1975. "Must We Sacrifice the West?" In Terrell J. Minger and Sherry D. Oaks, eds. *Growth Alternatives for the Rocky Mountain West*. Boulder, Colorado: Westview, pp. 203–211.

Ian L. McHarg. 1974. "The Place of Nature in the City of Man." In D. R. Coates, ed. *Urban Areas*. Stroudsburg, Pennsylvania: Dowden, Hutchinson & Ross, pp. 30–41.

Ian L. McHarg and Michael G. Clarke. 1973. "Skippack Watershed and the Evansburg Project: A Case Study for Water Resources Planning." In Charles R. Goodman, James McEroy III, and Peter J. Richerson, eds. *Environmental Quality and Water Development*. San Francisco: W.H. Freeman, pp. 299–330.

Ian L. McHarg. 1972. "Architecture in an Ecological View of the World." In Nicholas Pole, ed. *Environmental Solutions*. Cambridge, England: Cambridge University Conservation Society Eco-Publications, pp. 83–92.

Ian L. McHarg. 1971. "Values, Process and Form." In W. A. Johnson and J. Hardesty, eds. *Economic Growth vs. the Environment*. Belmont, California: Wadsworth, pp. 19–25.

Ian L. McHarg. 1970. "Ecological Planning for Evolutionary Success." In Angelo J. Cerchione, Victor E. Rothe, and James Vercellino, eds. *Master Planning the Aviation Environment*. Tucson: University of Arizona Press, pp. 7–10.

Ian L. McHarg. 1970. "Open Space from Natural Processes." In David A. Wallace, ed. *Metropolitan Open Space and Natural Process*. Philadelphia: University of Pennsylvania Press, pp. 10–52.

Ian L. McHarg. 1970. "The Place of Nature in the City of Man." In Pierre Dansereau and Virginia A. Weadock, eds. *Challenge for Survival: Land, Air, and Water for Man in Megalopolis*. New York: Columbia University Press, pp. 37–54.

Ian L. McHarg. 1970. "The Plight." In Harold W. Helfrich Jr., ed. *The Environmental Crisis: Man's Struggle to Live with Himself*. New Haven, Connecticut: Yale University Press, pp. 15–31.

Ian L. McHarg. 1970. "Values, Process and Form." In R. Disch, ed. *The Ecological Conscience: Values for Survival*. New York: Prentice Hall.

Ian L. McHarg. 1969. "An Ecological Method for Landscape Architecture." In Paul Shepard and Daniel McKinley, eds. *The Subversive Science: Essays Toward an Ecology of Man*. Boston: Houghton Mifflin, pp. 328–332.

Ian L. McHarg. 1969. "Man's Debt to Nature: Ecology and the Goals of Urban Development." In David Popenoe, ed. *The Urban Industrial Frontier: Essays on Social Trends and Institutional Goals in Modern Communities*. New Brunswick, New Jersey: Rutgers University Press, pp. 141–156.

Ian L. McHarg. 1968. "Values, Process and Form." In Smithsonian Institution staff, eds. *The Fitness of Man's Environment*. New York: Harper and Row, pp. 207–227. (Paperback edition, 1970, New York: Harper Colophon.)

Ian L. McHarg. 1967. "The Place of Man in Nature and Nature in the Environment of Man." In H. Wentworth Eldredge, ed. *Taming Megalopolis*. New York: Praeger, pp. 540–547.

Ian L. McHarg. 1966. "Ecological Determinism." In Frank Fraser Darling and John P. Milton, eds. *The Future Environments of North America*. Garden City, New York: Natural History Press, pp. 526–538.

Ian L. McHarg. 1963. "Man and Environment." In Leonard J. Duhl and John Powell, eds. *The Urban Condition*. New York: Basic Books, pp. 44–58.

Ian L. McHarg. 1963. "Regional Landscape Planning." In A. J. W. Scheffey, ed.

Resources, The Metropolis, and the Land-Grant University (Proceedings of the Conference on Natural Resources, No. 410). Amherst: University of Massachusetts, pp. 31–35. (Comments by others on McHarg's remarks continue through p. 37.)

Introductions and Forewords in Books

Ian L. McHarg. 2000. "Foreword." In Gerald McSheffrey. *Planning Derry, Planning and Politics in Northern Ireland.* Liverpool, England: Liverpool University Press.

Ian L. McHarg. 1998. "Foreword." In William M. Marsh. *Landscape Planning: Environmental Applications* (3rd ed.). New York: Wiley.

Ian L. McHarg. 1998. "Foreword." In Leslie Jones Sauer. *The Once and Future Forest.* Washington, D.C.: Island Press.

Ian L. McHarg. 1998. "Introduction." In Timothy W. Foresman, ed. *The History of Geographic Information Systems: Perspectives from the Pioneers.* Upper Saddle River, New Jersey: Prentice Hall.

Ian L. McHarg. 1994. "Introduction." In Tom J. Bartuska and Gerald L. Young, eds. *The Built Environment.* Menlo Park, California: Crisp Publications, pp. ix–xi.

Articles

Ian L. McHarg. 2001. "Some Songs to the Stars" (Poetry). *Landscape Journal* 20(1):1–3.

Ian L. McHarg. 1997. "I fattori naturali nella pianificazione." (Translated into Italian by Danilo Palazzo.) *Urbanistica* 108 (January–June):47–52.

Ian L. McHarg. 1997. "Natural Factors in Planning." *Journal of Soil and Water Conservation* 52(1, January–February):13–17.

Ian L. McHarg. 1992. "Green the Earth, Heal the Earth." *Journal of Soil and Water Conservation* 47(1):39–41.

Ian L. McHarg. 1992. "The House We Live In: Remembering a Meeting of Minds." *1991–1992 Almanac* (The Annual of the International Council of National Academy of Television Arts and Sciences): 47–50.

Ian L. McHarg. 1989. "The American Landscape into the 21st Century." *Renewable Resources Journal* (Summer):17–18.

Ian L. McHarg. 1981. "Human Ecological Planning at Pennsylvania." *Landscape Planning* 8:109–120.

Ian L. McHarg. 1980. "The Garden as a Metaphysical Symbol" (The Riding Reflection Lecture 1979). *Journal of Royal Society* 128(February):132–143.

Ian L. McHarg. 1979. "Human Ecological Planning." *Proceedings of Australian and New Zealand Academies of Science* (January).

Ian L. McHarg and Jonathan Sutton. 1975. "Ecological Plumbing for the Texas Coastal Plain." *Landscape Architecture* 65(1, January):78–89.

Ian L. McHarg. 1973. "Design with Nature" and "The Garden as a Metaphysical Symbol." *Ontario Naturalist* 13(1, March):20–39.

Ian L. McHarg. 1972. "Best Shore Protection: Nature's Own Dunes." *Civil Engineering/ASCE* 42(September):66–70.

Ian L. McHarg. 1972. "Values, Process and Form." *Options Meditéranées* 13 (June):19–25.

Ian L. McHarg. 1971. "Architecture: An Ecological View of the World." *The Structuralist* 11(August):83–89.

Ian L. McHarg. 1971. "Man and Nature: A Space Odyssey." *Consulting Engineer* 36(March):79–82.

Ian L. McHarg. 1971. "Man, Planetary Disease." *Vital Speeches of the Day* (August): 634–640.

Ian L. McHarg. 1970. "Architecture in an Ecological View of the World." *AIA Journal* 54(5, November):47–51.

Ian L. McHarg. 1970. "Design and Nature." *Cities 70* (Architecture and Engineering Forum). Los Angeles: Southern California Extension Company and Los Angeles Department of Water and Power. Section III.

Ian L. McHarg. 1970. "Ecological Values and Regional Planning." *Civil Engineering/ASCE* 40(August):40–44.

Ian L. McHarg. 1970. "Is Man a Planetary Disease?" (Annual Discourse: Ian McHarg). *RIBA Journal* 77(July):303–308.

Ian L. McHarg. 1969. "What Would You Do With, Say, Staten Island?" *Natural History* 78(4, April):27–37, with an introduction by Frances Low on p. 26.

Ian L. McHarg. 1968. "A Comprehensive Highway Route–Section Method." *Highway Research Record* 246:1–15.

Ian L. McHarg. 1968. "Ecology, for the Evolution of Planning and Design." *Via* 1:44–66.

Ian L. McHarg. 1967. "An Ecological Method for Landscape Architecture." *Landscape Architecture* 57(2):105–107.

Ian L. McHarg. 1967. "Where Should Highways Go?" *Landscape Architecture* 57(3):179–181.

Ian L. McHarg. 1966. "Architecture, Ecology and Form." *Perspective* 50–59 (published by the Students' Architectural Society, University of Manitoba).

Ian L. McHarg. 1966. "Blight or a Noble City?" *Audubon Magazine* 68(1, February):47–52.

Ian L. McHarg and David A. Wallace. 1965. "Plan for the Valleys vs. Spectre of Uncontrolled Growth." *Landscape Architecture* 55(3, March):179–181.

Ian L. McHarg. 1964. "The Place of Nature in the City of Man." *The Annals of the American Academy of Political and Social Sciences* (Urban Revival: Goals and Standards) 352(March):1–12.

Ian L. McHarg. 1964. "School News: A New Role for Landscape Architects." *Landscape Architecture* 54(3, April):227–228.

Ian L. McHarg. 1962. "The Ecology of the City." *AIA Journal* 38(5, November):101–103.

Ian L. McHarg. 1962. "The Ecology of the City." *Journal of Architectural Education* 17(2, November):101–103.

Ian L. McHarg. 1958. "The Humane City, Must the Man of Distinction Always Move to the Suburbs." *Landscape Architecture* 48(January):101–107.

Ian L. McHarg. 1957. "The Court House Concept." *Architectural Record* 122(September):193–200.

Ian L. McHarg. 1957. "The Court House Concept." *Architects' Year Book* 8:74–102.

Ian L. McHarg. 1957. "The Return to the City." *The General Magazine and Historical Chronicle* 59(Spring):1–6.

Ian L. McHarg. 1956. "Can We Afford Open Space? A Survey of Landscape Costs." *Architects' Journal* 123(March):260–273.

Ian L. McHarg. 1955. "Landscape Architecture." *Pennsylvania Triangle* 41(7, April):36, 42.

Ian L. McHarg. 1955. "Open Space and Housing." *Architects' Year Book* 6:75–82.

Ian L. McHarg. 1953. "Architecture in the Netherlands." *Quarterly Journal of the Royal Incorporation of Architects in Scotland* 94:41–46.

Reviews, Essays, and Published Symposia and Proceedings

Ian L. McHarg. 1998. "Human Ecological Planning at Pennsylvania." In *Regional Physical Planning: Practice and Challenges*, Proceedings of the International Conference on the Occasion of the 30th Anniversary of Nationally Organized Physical Planning in Slovenia. Bled, Slovenia, pp. 43–53.

Ian L. McHarg. 1997. "Natural Drainage." In David H. Merritt, ed. *Aesthetics in the Constructed Environment*, Proceedings of the 24th Annual Water Resources Planning and Management Conference. Houston, Texas: American Society of Civil Engineers, pp. 790–797.

Ian L. McHarg. 1996. "The DMZ in Korea." In *The International Symposium on Environmental Conversation and Development of DMZ (Demilitarized Zone) in Korean Peninsula*. Seoul: Korean Institute of Landscape Architecture & Joong-Ang Development, June 18–19.

Ian L. McHarg. 1995. "Ian McHarg, FASLA, Keynote Address." In Karen L. Niles, ed. *Renewing the American City*, Proceedings of the 1995 Annual Meeting & Expo. Washington, D.C.: American Society of Landscape Architects, p. 15.

Ian L. McHarg. 1993. "On Finding the Earth." *GSD News*. Cambridge, Massachusetts: Graduate School of Design, Harvard University, p. 31.

Ian L. McHarg. 1993. "This Bug's for You." *New York Times Book Review* (June 6):45–46.

Ian L. McHarg. 1992. "An Ecological Basis for Human Settlement." In *International Symposium on City Planning in Harmony with the Human Environment*. Japan: Ministry of Construction, pp. 7–25.

James F. Thorne, Ian L. McHarg, Jon Berger, and D. Andrew Pitz. 1990. "Issues for Landscape Ecology in Urban Park Planning." In Julius Fabos and Jack Ahern, eds. *Proceedings from Selected Educational Sessions of the 1990 American Society of Landscape Architect's Annual Meeting,* Landscape Land Use Planning Committee, October 27–30, San Diego, California, pp. 56–78.

Ian L. McHarg. 1989. "The Legislative Landscape, A Quarterly Update: Summer 1989." *Landscape Architecture News Digest* 30(7):7–8.

Ian L. McHarg. 1983. "A Model for Unity." *Penn in Ink* (Fall):2.

Ian L. McHarg. 1981. "Ecological Planning of Metropolitan Regions." A paper presented at Primer Congreso Internacional de Planificación de Grandes Ciudades (1st Congress of Planning of Major Cities). Mexico City: Departamento del Distrito Federal, Programa de Intercambio Científico y Capacitación Técnica del Departamento del Distrito Federal, pp. 248–249.

Ian L. McHarg. 1976. "Design with Nature." In University of Illinois at Chicago Circle, College of Architecture and Art, Department of Art. *On Human Dimensions* (excerpts from papers presented on May 20, 1975, at the John Walley Commemoration Design Conference). Champaign: Trustees of the University of Illinois, pp. 37–44.

Ian L. McHarg. 1974. "The Preconditions for Effective Comprehensive Planning for Environmental Quality." In *Proceedings of the Conference on Landuse Planning: Implications for Citizens and State and Local Governments,* March 26–27, Columbus, Ohio, pp. 19–50.

Ian L. McHarg. 1973. "Planning Procedures and Techniques for Environmental Conservation in the Natural Landscape." In *Planning for Environment Conberiata* (International Symposium). Pretoria, South Africa: Department of Planning and the Environment, Institute of Lands Architecture.

Ian L. McHarg. 1971. "The Consequences of Today." A record of papers given at the Royal Australian Institute of Architects Centenary Convention, May 22–28, Wentworth Hotel, Sydney. Supplement to *Architecture in Australia* (August):638–646.

Ian L. McHarg. 1971. "Man: Planetary Disease" (The 1971 B. Y. Morrison Memorial Lecture). Washington, D.C.: U.S. Department of Agriculture, Agricultural Research Service.

Ian L. McHarg. 1970. "The Plight." *Ecosphere, A News Bulletin of the International Ecology University* 1(1, November):10–16.

Ian L. McHarg. 1969. "The Metropolitan View." In *Transcript of the Proceedings of the Planning Seminar for Water Resources Development.* New York: Department of the Army Corps of Engineers.

Ian L. McHarg. 1966. "And in Leisure Time" (manuscript). *Urban America Conference Proceedings.* Washington, D.C.: Urban America, Inc., pp. 59–71.

Wayne N. Aspinall, Edward C. Crafts, Arthur Greeley, Henry M. Jackson, Philip Lewis, Ian McHarg, Max Nicholson, William H. Whyte, and William J. Lewis. 1965. "Landscape Action Program," Chapter 16 in *Beauty for America,* Proceedings of the White House Conference on Natural Beauty, May 24–25, Washington, D.C.: U.S. Government Printing Office, pp. 469–505 (Ian McHarg, specifically, pp. 481–484, see below).

Ian L. McHarg. 1965. "Landscape Action Program" (extract). In *Beauty for Amer-*

ica, Proceedings of the White House Conference on Natural Beauty, May 24–25, 1965. Washington, D.C.: U.S. Government Printing Office, pp. 481–484 (pages of his presentation, whole chapter, pp. 469–505).

Ian L. McHarg. 1964. "Natural Sciences and the Planning Process." Conference on Natural Resources, the Ford Foundation Discussion Papers. February 27, 28, 29, March 1.

Ian L. McHarg. 1962. "Ecology of the City: A Plea for Environmental Consciousness." In Marcus Whiffen, ed. *The Architect and the City* (Papers from the AIA-ACSA Teacher Seminar, Cranbrook Academy of Art, June 11–12). Washington, D.C.: AIA Department of Education, pp. 43–58.

Excerpts from A Quest for Life

Ian L. McHarg. 1996. *Harvard Graduate School of Design News* (Winter–Spring):44–47.

Ian L. McHarg. 1996. "In His Own Image." *The Pennsylvania Gazette* 94(5, March):38–43.

Ian L. McHarg. 1996. *Landscape Architecture* 86(3, March):88–93, 99–101.

Ian L. McHarg. 1996. "Mr. McHarg's Opus." *Planning* (May):12–13.

Professional Reports, Plans, and Designs

University of Pennsylvania Projects (1963–1992)

Ian L. McHarg, John Radke, Jonathan Berger, and Kathleen Wallace. 1992. A Prototype Database for a National Ecological Inventory. Washington, D.C.: U.S. Environmental Protection Agency.

Center for Ecological Research in Planning and Design. 1975. Guidelines for Land Resource and Analysis for Planning. Philadelphia: Department of Landscape Architecture and Regional Planning, University of Pennsylvania, and Harrisburg: Department of Environmental Resources, Commonwealth of Pennsylvania. The report was written by Ian L. McHarg, Narendra Juneja, E. Bruce Mac-Dougall, and Jonathan Berger.

Narendra Juneja. 1974. Medford: Performance Requirements for the Maintenance of Social Values Represented by the Natural Environment of Medford Township New Jersey. Philadelphia: Center for Ecological Research in Planning and Design, Department of Landscape Architecture and Regional Planning, University of Pennsylvania. Ian L. McHarg, principal investigator; Narendra Juneja, deputy principal investigator and report author; Arthur Sullivan, deputy principal investigator; W. Robinson Fisher, project director; Robert Giegengack; Ronald Hanawalt; Michael Levin; Seymour Subitsky; Ruth Patrick; Thomas Lloyd; Robert Snyder; Victor Yannacone; Arthur Palmer; and University of Pennsylvania graduate students.

Department of Landscape Architecture. 1963. Sea, Storm and Survival, A Study of the New Jersey Shore. Philadelphia: University of Pennsylvania. Ian L. McHarg, Roger D. Clemence, Ayre M. Dvir, Geoffrey A. Collins, Michael Laurie, William J. Oliphant, and Peter Ker Walker.

University of Pennsylvania. 1963. Metropolitan Open Space from Natural Processes. Philadelphia: Urban Renewal Administration and the States of Pennsylvania and New Jersey. Ian L. McHarg, principal investigator; David A. Wallace, project director; Ann Louise Strong; William Grigsby; Anthony Tomazinis; Nohad Toulan; William H. Roberts; Donald Phimister; and Frank Shaw.

Post-Wallace, McHarg, Roberts and Todd Professional Projects (1981–1994)

Ian L. McHarg, Cristian Basso, Elke Bilda, Ho-Shu Chou, Buzz Constable, Paul Cote, Iram Farooq, Karen Mans, Sarah Peskin, Girish Ramachandran, and Joel Young. 1994. Mount Desert Island, Maine. Cambridge, Massachusetts: Landscape Architecture Studio, Graduate School of Design, Harvard University.

Ian L. McHarg and Jonathan Berger. 1989. A Re-Examination of the Medford Master Plan. Medford, New Jersey.

Ian L. McHarg, John Radke, and Jonathan Berger. 1989. The Settlement Plan. Ann Arbor, Michigan: Domino Farms.

Ian L. McHarg, James Thorne, Jonathan Berger, John Radke, and Kate Deregibus. 1987–1990. Blue Heron Lake Park Plan. New York: Department of Parks and Recreation.

Ian L. McHarg, Joseph McBride, James Thorne, Steven Sitz, and Lan Shing Huang. 1986. White Oak Ranch Plan. Colusa County, California: Gerald Blakeley.

Ian L. McHarg. 1984. Report of Taroko Gorge: Planning a National Parks System for Taiwan. Taipei, Taiwan: Government of the Republic of China.

Ian L. McHarg, Carol A. Smyser, James Thorne, Dorothy Wurman, and Kim Sorvig. 1984–1989. Riverdale Park Plan. New York: Department of Parks and Recreation.

Ian L. McHarg. 1983. A Proposal to Undertake an Ecological Planning Study for Sedona, Arizona. Philadelphia, Pennsylvania.

Ian L. McHarg. 1981. Comprehensive Plan, Edith Macy National Training Center, Chappaqua, New York. Washington, D.C.: Girl Scouts of America National Council. Ian McHarg, project director; Jorge G. Sanchez-Flores; Robert Turner; Edward Hollander; Barbara Seymour; Robert Giegengack, geomorphologist; William Johnson, biochemist; and Michael Skaller, ecologist.

Ian L. McHarg and M. Paul Friedberg. 1981. Gateway National Park Plan. New York: U.S. National Park Service.

Marty Zeller, Don Walker, Russell Moore, Ian McHarg, and Michael Skaller. 1981. Stewards of the Valley Plan, Evans Ranch. Denver: Colorado Open Land Trust.

Wallace, McHarg, Roberts and Todd Projects (1965–1980)

Wallace, McHarg, Roberts and Todd. 1980. Environmental Assessment and Planning Strategies for Indian River Shores, Vero Beach, Florida. Amherst, Massachusetts: Otto Paparazzo. Ian L. McHarg, partner-in-charge; and John Keene. Additional planning and architecture by Callister Payne & Bischoff of Tiburon, California. The project was partially completed. Philadelphia, Pennsylvania.

International Planning Associates. 1979. The Master Plan for Abuja, The New Federal Capital of Nigeria. Lagos, Nigeria: The Federal Capital Development Authority. Archisystems; Planning Research Corporation; Wallace, McHarg, Roberts and Todd. Abraam Krushkhov, project director; Walter G. Hansen, associate project director; Thomas A. Todd, partner-in-charge for Wallace, McHarg, Roberts and Todd planning and design; Ian L. McHarg supervised the ecological study, and others contributed.

International Planning Associates. 1978. A New Federal Capital for Nigeria (Report No. 2. Site Evaluation and Site Selection). Lagos, Nigeria. Archisystems; Planning Research Corporation; Wallace, McHarg, Roberts and Todd. Abraam Krushkhov, project director; Walter G. Hansen, associate project director; Thomas A. Todd, partner-in-charge for Wallace, McHarg, Roberts and Todd planning and design; Ian L. McHarg, technical review; and others.

Wallace, McHarg, Roberts and Todd. 1978. "208" Study for Detroit Metropolitan Area. Detroit: Southwest Michigan Council of Governments. Ian L. McHarg, partner-in-charge; Michael Clarke; David Hamme; and Ronald Walters. Philadelphia, Pennsylvania.

Wallace, McHarg, Roberts and Todd. 1978. Ecological Study for Northwestern Colorado Council of Governments. Frisco: Northwestern Colorado Council of Governments. Ian L. McHarg, partner-in-charge; Michael Clarke, associate partner; Robert Giegengack; Arthur Johnson; and Richard Nalbandian. Philadelphia, Pennsylvania.

Wallace, McHarg, Roberts and Todd in association with Economic Research Associates and Alan M. Voorhees Associates, Inc. 1978. Denver Metropolitan Areawide Environmental Impact Statement (Volume I, Introduction, Summary, and Conclusions). Denver: Region VIII, U.S. Department of Housing and Urban Development. Ian L. McHarg, George Toop, John Beckman, and Anne Spirn. Philadelphia, Pennsylvania.

Wallace, McHarg, Roberts and Todd. Circa 1977. Laguna Creek Study. Sacramento, California: Laguna Creek. Ian L. McHarg, partner-in-charge; Michael Clarke; and Robert Grunewald. Philadelphia, Pennsylvania.

Wallace, McHarg, Roberts and Todd. 1977. "208" Study for Toledo, Ohio. Toledo: Toledo Metropolitan Area Council of Governments. Ian L. McHarg, partner-in-charge; and Michael Clarke. Philadelphia, Pennsylvania.

Wallace, McHarg, Roberts and Todd. 1977. Washington Metropolitan Transit Authority F Route Environmental Impact Study. Washington, D.C.: Washington Metropolitan Transit Authority. Ian L. McHarg, partner-in-charge; David

Hamme, associate; and Richard Nalbandian. The F Route is now known as the Green Line of the Washington D.C. Metro. Philadelphia, Pennsylvania.

Ian L. McHarg. 1976. Evaluation of Major 208 Facility Plans. Prepared for the Toledo Metropolitan Area Council of Governments. Philadelphia, Pennsylvania: Wallace, McHarg, Roberts and Todd. Ian L. McHarg, Michael Clarke, and others. Philadelphia, Pennsylvania.

Ian L. McHarg. 1976. Regional Goals for Planned Growth. Prepared for the Toledo Metropolitan Area Council for Governments. Philadelphia, Pennsylvania: Wallace, McHarg, Roberts and Todd. Ian L. McHarg, Michael Clarke, and others. Philadelphia, Pennsylvania.

Wallace, McHarg, Roberts and Todd. 1976. Environmental Resources of the Toronto Central Waterfront. Prepared for the Central Waterfront Planning Committee, City of Toronto. Philadelphia, Pennsylvania: Winchell Press. Ian McHarg, partner-in-charge; Narendra Juneja, senior associate partner; Anne Spirn, project director; Carol Reifsnyder; Clive Goodwin; Arthur Johnson; Marta Griffiths; Roger Smith; Beth Kitchen; William Robinson; John Czarnowski; Jane Laughlin; Margaret Dewey; John Purkess; and Rodney Robinson. Narendra Juneja was the project leader, with Anne Sprin playing a major role. Philadelphia, Pennsylvania.

Wallace, McHarg, Roberts and Todd. 1976. Lake Austin Growth Management Plan. Austin, Texas: City of Austin, Department of Planning. William H. Roberts, partner-in-charge; Ian L. McHarg, partner; Michael G. Clarke, senior associate partner and project director; Narendra Juneja, senior associate partner; Susan Drew; Beth Kitchen; Anne Whiston Spirn; Mukund Lokhande; Carol Reifsnyder; Richard Nalbandian; Jane Laughlin; Espey, Huston and Associates, Incorporated, hydrologic studies; and Richard Lillie, director, Department of Planning, City of Austin. Philadelphia, Pennsylvania.

The Mandala Collaborative/Wallace, McHarg, Roberts and Todd. 1975. Pardisan, Plan for an Environmental Park in Tehran. Prepared for the Department of Environment, Imperial Government of Iran. Philadelphia, Pennsylvania: Winchell Press. The report was written by Ian L. McHarg, assisted by W. Robinson Fisher, Anne Spirn, and Narendra Juneja. Eskandar Firouz and Jahangir Sedaghatfar were responsible from the Iran Department of the Environment. Nadar Ardalan and others from the Mandala Collaborative of Tehran were involved in the planning. Many Wallace, McHarg, Roberts and Todd staff were involved including William Roberts; Colin Franklin, project director; Tom Atkins; Rob Turner; Richard Collier; Tim Van Epp; Carol Franklin; Leslie and Rolf Sauer; Ed Boyer; and Siddartha Thakar; in addition to those who assisted writing the report and others. Several Wallace, McHarg, Roberts and Todd project staff, including Neal Belanger and Vicki Steiger, lived and worked in Iran for periods of the project. Key consultants included Yehudi Cohen, Charles Eames, R. Buckminster Fuller, Glen Fleck, David R. Goddard, David Hancocks, Brian Spooner, Solomon Katz, Jones and Jones (especially Jon Coe of their staff), and Sven Svendsen. Hosein Nasr was an advisor to the project.

Wallace, McHarg, Roberts and Todd. 1974. Owl Creek. A Feasibility Study for Future Development. Houston, Texas: Mitchell Development Corporation of the Southwest. Ian L. McHarg, supervising partner; Narendra Juneja, senior associate partner; David C. Hamme, senior associate partner; Colin Franklin, project director; Mukund Lokhande; Faye Brandon; Hans Harald Grote; Carol Reifsnyder; Jane Laughlin; A. Allen Dyer and others from Colorado State University; Thomas Prather; F. Robert McGregor; Kenneth R. Wright; and Charles Wolcott.

Wallace, McHarg, Roberts and Todd. 1974. San Francisco Metropolitan Regional Environmental Impact Procedure Study, California. San Francisco: Bay Area Council of Governments. David Wallace, partner-in-charge; Ian L. McHarg, consulting partner; Richard Nalbandian; Ed Boyer; Carol Reifsnyder; Leslie Sauer; John Rogers; Frits Golden; Robert Pierson; and others. Philadelphia, Pennsylvania.

Wallace, McHarg, Roberts and Todd. 1974. Woodlands New Community, An Ecological Inventory. Houston, Texas: The Woodlands Development Corporation. Ian L. McHarg, partner-in-charge; Narendra Juneja, associate-in-charge; James Veltman, project manager; Richard Nalbandian; Dennis McGlade; Doris Zorensky Cheng; Jonathan Sutton; Colin Franklin; Leslie Sauer; and others. Philadelphia, Pennsylvania.

Wallace, McHarg, Roberts and Todd. 1974. Woodlands New Community, An Ecological Plan. Houston, Texas: The Woodlands Development Corporation. Ian L. McHarg, partner-in-charge; Jonathan S. Sutton; Narendra Juneja; Richard Nalbandian; Dennis McGlade; Doris Zorensky Cheng; Mukund Lokhande; Anne Whiston Spirn; Colin Franklin; Leslie Sauer; William P. Lowry, and others. Philadelphia, Pennsylvania.

Wallace, McHarg, Roberts and Todd. 1974. Woodlands New Community, Phase One: Land Planning and Design Principles. Houston, Texas: The Woodlands Development Corporation. Ian L. McHarg, partner-in-charge; Jonathan S. Sutton; Narendra Juneja; Richard Nalbandian; Dennis McGlade; Anne Whiston Spirn; Doris Zorensky Cheng; Mukund Lokhande; Colin Franklin; Leslie Sauer; William P. Lowry; and others. Philadelphia, Pennsylvania.

Wallace, McHarg, Roberts and Todd. 1973. Hugh Moore Parkway. Easton, Pennsylvania: The Hugh Moore Parkway Commission. Ian L. McHarg, partner-in-charge; Thomas Todd, contributing partner; Michael Clarke, associate partner-in-charge; Narendra Juneja, contributing associate partner; Doris Cheng; Colin Franklin; Dennis McGlade; Carolyn Jones; Leslie Sauer; Edward Boyer; Margaret Dewey; Caren Glotfelty; Carol Reifsnyder; Donald Phoenix; Frank Gill and Rick Mullen of the Academy of Natural Sciences; J. C. Fisher Motz; Carol Franklin; Liz Colley; and James Reilly, executive director, Hugh Moore Parkway. Philadelphia, Pennsylvania.

Wallace, McHarg, Roberts and Todd. 1973. Outer Wilmington Beltway Corridor Study. Dover: Delaware Department of Highways and Transportation, Division of Highways. Ian L. McHarg, partner-in-charge; Narendra Juneja; David

Hamme; E. Bruce MacDougall; Lewis D. Hopkins; Ed Boyer; Meir Gross; and Dennis McGlade. Philadelphia, Pennsylvania.

Wallace, McHarg, Roberts and Todd. 1973. Pardisan, A Feasibility Study for an Environmental Park in Tehran, Iran, for the Imperial Government of Iran. William H. Roberts, partner-in-charge; Ian L. McHarg, participating partner; Colin Franklin, project captain; Leslie Sauer; Ross Bateup; Charles Fleisher; Richard Nalbandian; William Becker; Dennis McGlade; Sven Svendsen; Nader Ardalan; Jack McCormick; Theodore Reed; Brian Spooner; R. Buckminster Fuller; and others.

Wallace, McHarg, Roberts and Todd. 1973. Progress Report: Evolution of Land Planning and Design Guidelines for Eaton's Neck Point, Asherochen, Long Island, New York. Amherst Fields, Amherst, Massachusetts: Otto Paparazzo. Ian L. McHarg, partner-in-charge; Jonathan S. Sutton, project director; Leslie Jones Sauer; Oscar R. Martinez-Conill; Mihran R. Nalbandian; Edward Boyer; Mark Weglarz; Charles Watson; Anne Spirn; Carol Reifsnyder; Charles Barnett; Orville Terry; and John Burger. In collaboration with Callister Payne & Bischoff of Tiburon, California, master planners and architects. The project was not completed. Philadelphia, Pennsylvania.

Wallace, McHarg, Roberts and Todd. 1973. Towards a Comprehensive Plan for Environmental Quality. Washington, D.C.: American Institute of Planners for the U.S. Environmental Protection Agency. Ian L. McHarg, partner-in-charge; Gerald R. Mylroie was the American Institute of Planners (AIP) project director. An AIP advisory group was formed that included Robert C. Einsweiler, chairman; Alan Kreditor; James C. Park; Robert Paternoster; E. Jack Schoop; Paul H. Sedway; and Harold F. Wise. Philadelphia, Pennsylvania.

Wallace, McHarg, Roberts and Todd. 1973. Woodlands New Community, Guidelines for Site Planning. Houston, Texas: The Woodlands Development Corporation. Ian L. McHarg, partner-in-charge; Jonathan Sutton, associate partner-in-charge; Richard Nalbandian; Anne Whiston Spirn, project director; and others. Philadelphia, Pennsylvania.

Wallace, McHarg, Roberts and Todd in association with Tippetts, Abbett, McCarthy, Stratton and Gladstone Associates. 1973. Pontchartrain New-Town-in-Town, New Orleans, Louisiana. Dallas, Texas: Murchison Brothers, Pontchartrain Land Corporation. David A. Wallace, managing partner; Ian L. McHarg, partner; William H. Roberts, partner; Thomas A. Todd, partner; Richard W. Huffman; Narendra Juneja; Donald H. Brackenbush; David C. Hamme; Michael G. Clarke; Robert Gladstone; Dennis McGlade; and others. Philadelphia, Pennsylvania.

Wallace, McHarg, Roberts and Todd. Circa 1972. Comprehensive Planning Study of the Piedmont District, New Castle County, Delaware. Ian L. McHarg, partner-in-charge; David C. Hamme, project director; and others. Philadelphia, Pennsylvania.

Development Research Associates and Wallace, McHarg, Roberts and Todd. 1972. Ecology: Natural Suitabilities for Regional Growth. Denver: Regional Transportation District. William H. Roberts, partner-in-charge; Ian L. McHarg, consulting partner; Ross Whaley, reconnaissance coordinator, and others from Colorado State University; F. A. Branson; R. F. Miller; R. S. Aro; Dennis McGlade; Ed Boyer; and others. Philadelphia, Pennsylvania.

Development Research Associates and Wallace, McHarg, Roberts and Todd. 1972. Regional Growth 1971–2000. Denver: Regional Transportation District. William H. Roberts, partner-in-charge; Ian L. McHarg, consulting partner; Dennis McGlade; Ed Boyer; and others. Philadelphia, Pennsylvania.

Wallace, McHarg, Roberts and Todd. 1972. An Ecological Planning Study for Wilmington and Dover, Vermont. Brattleboro, Vermont: Windham Regional Planning and Development Commission and the Vermont State Planning Office. Ian McHarg, project director; Michael Clarke, project manager; David Hamme; Narendra Juneja; and others. Philadelphia, Pennsylvania.

Wallace, McHarg, Roberts and Todd. 1972. Study of the Integrity of Chesapeake Bay. Annapolis: Maryland Department of State Planning and Chesapeake Bay Interagency Planning Committee. David Wallace, partner-in-charge. (Ian McHarg had a minor consulting role.) Philadelphia, Pennsylvania.

Development Research Associates and Wallace, McHarg, Roberts and Todd. 1971. Ecological Studies of the Regional Transportation District, Denver, Colorado (Interim Technical Memorandum, Task 5 of the Joint Venture). Denver: Regional Transportation District. William H. Roberts, partner-in-charge; Ian L. McHarg, consulting partner; Ross Whaley, reconnaissance coordinator; William Marlatt; Stanley Schumm; Robert Longenbaugh; Robert Heil; Dale Romine; William Moir; and Harold Steinhoff.

Wallace, McHarg, Roberts and Todd. 1971. Amelia Island, Florida, A Report on the Master Planning Process for a Recreational New Community. Hilton Head Island, South Carolina: The Sea Pines Company. William H. Roberts, partner-in-charge; Jonathan Sutton, project director; Ian L. McHarg, consulting partner; Jack McCormick, vegetation studies and coordinator of the work of natural scientists; Dennis McGlade; and others. Philadelphia, Pennsylvania.

Wallace, McHarg, Roberts and Todd. 1971. Ecological Planning Study for the New Community. Houston, Texas: George Mitchell Development Corporation. Ian L. McHarg, partner-in-charge. Philadelphia, Pennsylvania.

Wallace, McHarg, Roberts and Todd. 1970. Skippack Creek Ecological Study, Montgomery County, Pennsylvania. Norristown, Pennsylvania: Commissioners of Montgomery County and the Supervisor of Lower Providence Township. Ian L. McHarg, partner-in-charge; Michael Clarke; Ruth Patrick; and others. Philadelphia, Pennsylvania.

Wallace, McHarg, Roberts and Todd. Late 1960s. Sunstein Garden. Philadelphia, Pennsylvania: Lee and Emily Sunstein. Ian L. McHarg, landscape architect. Philadelphia, Pennsylvania.

Wallace, McHarg, Roberts and Todd. 1969. An Ecological Study for the Future Public Improvement of the Borough of Richmond (Staten Island). New York: City of New York Office of Staten Island Development, Borough President of

Richmond and Park, Recreation and Cultural Affairs Administration. Ian L. McHarg, partner-in-charge; Narendra Juneja; Charles Meyers; Derik Sutphin; Robert Drummond; Richard Ragan; Ravindra Bhan; Archibald Reid; and Howard M. Higbee. Philadelphia, Pennsylvania.

Wallace, McHarg, Roberts and Todd. 1969. An Ecological Study for Twin Cities Metropolitan Region, Minnesota. Prepared for Metropolitan Council of the Twin Cities Area. Philadelphia: U.S. Department of Commerce, National Technical Information Series. Ian L. McHarg, partner-in-charge; Narendra Juneja; Ravindra Bhan; Charles Meyers; Derik Sutphin; James Veltman; Michael Clarke; Thomas Dickert; Robert Drummond; Keith Grey; Anthony Neville; Richard Ragan; and Mark Turnbull. Philadelphia, Pennsylvania.

Wallace, McHarg, Roberts and Todd. 1968. Least Social Cost Corridor Study for Richmond Parkway, New York City. New York: New York City Department of Parks and Recreation. Ian L. McHarg, partner-in-charge; Narendra Juneja, project supervisor; Derik Sutphin; Lindsay Robertson; and Charles Meyers. Philadelphia, Pennsylvania.

Wallace, McHarg, Roberts and Todd. 1967. Toward a Comprehensive Landscape Plan for Washington, D.C. Prepared for the National Capital Planning Commission. Washington, D.C.: U.S. Government Printing Office. Ian L. McHarg, partner-in-charge; Narendra Juneja; Derik Sutphin; Charles R. Meyers Jr.; Karen Meyers; Lindsay Robertson; and Robert Drummond. Philadelphia, Pennsylvania.

Wallace, McHarg, Roberts and Todd. 1966. The Lower Manhattan Plan. New York: New York City Planning Commission. David Wallace, partner-in-charge; and Ian L. McHarg, William Roberts, and Thomas Todd, consulting partners. Philadelphia, Pennsylvania.

Wallace, McHarg, Roberts and Todd. 1966. The Lower Manhattan Plan, Summary Report. New York: New York City Planning Commission. David Wallace, partner-in-charge; and Ian L. McHarg, William Roberts, and Thomas Todd, consulting partners. Philadelphia, Pennsylvania.

Wallace, McHarg, Roberts and Todd. Mid-1960s. Red Clay Creek Reservation Study, New Castle County, Delaware. Red Clay Creek Association. Ian L. McHarg, partner-in-charge. Philadelphia, Pennsylvania.

Wallace, McHarg, Roberts and Todd. Mid-1960s. West Point Area Study, Hudson River Valley, New York. Tarrytown, New York: Hudson River Valley Commission. Ian L. McHarg, partner-in-charge. Philadelphia, Pennsylvania.

American Institute of Architects Task Force on the Potomac; Wallace, McHarg, Roberts and Todd; and the University of Pennsylvania. 1965–1966. The Potomac. Washington, D.C.: U.S. Government Printing Office. David Wallace, partner-in-charge; Ian McHarg; Narendra Juneja; Nicholas Muhlenberg; D. Bradford; S. Manwell Bradford; John Chitty; Barry Christie; Marjorie Dawson; Gary Felgemaker; Richard Galantowicz; Louise Kao Leach; Charles Meyers; John Murphy; William Rosenberg; James Sinatra; Griet Terpstra; Joachim Tourbier; Richard Westmacott; and Mary Wolfe.

Wallace, McHarg, Roberts and Todd. 1965. A Comprehensive Highway Route Selection Method Applied to I-95 between the Delaware and Raritan Rivers. Princeton, New Jersey: Princeton Committee on I-95. Ian L. McHarg, partner-in-charge; Narendra Juneja; and Lindsay Robertson. Philadelphia, Pennsylvania.

Wallace–McHarg Associates Projects (1963–1964)

Wallace–McHarg Associates. 1964. Inner Harbor Master Plan. Baltimore, Maryland: City of Baltimore. David Wallace, partner-in-charge; Ian McHarg, consulting partner; with Thomas Todd, William Roberts, Narendra Juneja, and Lindsay Robertson. Philadelphia, Pennsylvania.

Wallace–McHarg Associates. 1964. Plan for the Valleys. Towson, Maryland: Green Spring and Worthington Valley Planning Council. David A. Wallace, Ian L. McHarg, Thomas A. Todd, William H. Roberts, Ann Louise Strong, William G. Grigsby, Nohad Toulan, Anthony Tomazinas, and others. Philadelphia, Pennsylvania.

Wallace–McHarg Associates. 1963. Lauer Farm. Wyomissing, Pennsylvania: Wyomissing Foundation. Ian L. McHarg, partner-in-charge; William Roberts; and Nicholas Muhlenberg. Philadelphia, Pennsylvania.

Wallace–McHarg Associates. 1963. May's Chapel Village, Greenspring Valley, Maryland. Baltimore County, Maryland: Keelty Realty Corporation. Ian L. McHarg, partner-in-charge; and William Roberts, project director. Philadelphia, Pennsylvania.

As Ian L. McHarg, Landscape Architect (1945–1962), Landscape Plans and Designs

PARKS AND PLAZAS

Delaware River Park, Philadelphia, Pennsylvania
Fables Memorial Park, Cranford, New Jersey
Farragut Square, Washington, D.C.
Maple Shade Park, Maple Shade, New Jersey
Pennsylvania State Office Building, Philadelphia, Pennsylvania (1955)
Southwest Washington Town Center Park, Washington, D.C. (1962)
Springfield Township, Philadelphia, Pennsylvania
Swiss Pines, Phoenixville, Pennsylvania
York Memorial Park, York, Pennsylvania

UNIVERSITIES, SCHOOLS, AND COLLEGES

Botany Building, University of Pennsylvania, Philadelphia, Pennsylvania (with Anthony Walmsley, 1960)
Campus, University of Pennsylvania, Philadelphia, Pennsylvania (with Anthony J. Walmsley, 1959–1960)
Germantown Friends School, Philadelphia, Pennsylvania (with Anthony J. Walmsley and Michael Langlay-Smith, 1960–1961)

Medical Research Building, University of Pennsylvania, Philadelphia, Pennsylvania (Louis I. Kahn, Architect, with Anthony J. Walmsley, 1960)
Plattsburg Junior College, Plattsburg, New York
Stamford Nursery School, Stamford, Connecticut
Woodland Avenue Gardens, University of Pennsylvania, Philadelphia, Pennsylvania (1955)

HOUSING
Eastwick, Area #1, Philadelphia, Pennsylvania
Eastwick New House Study, Philadelphia, Pennsylvania
Henry Meigs Development, Philadelphia, Pennsylvania
Jenkintown Apartments, Jenkintown, Pennsylvania
Red Rock Heights, San Francisco, California
Southwark Public Housing, Society Hill, Philadelphia, Pennsylvania (Oscar Stonarov and Frank Haws, architects, 1959)

SHOPPING AND TOWN CENTERS
Cheltenham Shopping Center, Philadelphia, Pennsylvania (Solomon Kaplan, Architect, and with contributions by Anthony J. Walmsley and Michael Langlay-Smith, 1959–1960)
Newtongrange Town Center, Newtongrange, Scotland

GARDENS
Mrs. Albert M. Greenfield, Philadelphia, Pennsylvania (with Anthony J. Walmsley, 1959–1960)
Lawrence K. Meltzer, Philadelphia, Pennsylvania
Miller House, Norristown, Pennsylvania
Lloyd Wells, Whitemarsh, Pennsylvania

CEMETERY
Design of Cemetery for British Soldiers Killed in Action in Greece, Athens: British Army War Graves Commission (1945)

Miscellaneous Professional Report
Lt. McHarg, editor and collator, and Major McNeil, translator. 1943. *Report on Destruction and Repairs to Apulian Aqueduct.* Bari, Italy: Allied Army Command (September–October).

Films, Television, and Videos
Charlie Rose. 1997. *The Charlie Rose Show.* New York: PBS (April 14).
Chris Zelov, Producer. 1994. *Ecological Design: Inventing the Future.* Cape May, New Jersey: Ecological Design Project. Ian McHarg appears in this film about design and planning projects influenced by R. Buckminster Fuller.

Joan Saffa, Producer. 1991. *Lawrence and Anna Halprin: Inner Landscapes.* San Francisco: KQED-TV. Ian McHarg appeared in the documentary.

Frederick Steiner, Bob Curry, and Bill Wagner. 1979. *The Only Essential Industry: Farmlands Preservation in Whitman County, Washington.* Pullman, Washington: KWSU-TV Film Documentary. Ian McHarg was interviewed in the documentary.

Glen Fleck, Producer. 1977. *Pardisan.* Venice, California: Charles Eames Studio.

Austin Hoyt, Producer; Ian McHarg, organizer and on-screen host. 1969. *Multiply and Subdue the Earth.* Boston: WGBH.

Ian L. McHarg. 1960–1961. *The House We Live In* (TV Series). New York: CBS; Philadelphia: WCAU-TV. Guests included Harlow Shapley, David Goddard, Carleton Coon, Margaret Mead, Abraham Heschel, Gustave Weigel, Paul Tillich, Swami Nikhilananda, Alan Watts, Erich Fromm, Julian Huxley, Loren Eiseley, Lewis Mumford, Arnold Toynbee, Alexander Leighton, Kenneth Rexroth, Frank Frazer Darling, Luna Leopold, and others.

Profiles, Critical Reviews, and Obituaries

William John Cohen. (Forthcoming) *The Ecological Imperative: Ian McHarg's Legacy on Environmental Planning and Education.* Santa Fe, New Mexico: Center for American Places.

Frederick Steiner. Forthcoming. "Ian McHarg." In Charles A. Birnbaum and Stephanie Foell, eds. *Pioneers of American Landscape Design: II.* Charlottesville: University of Virginia Press.

Frederick Steiner. 2004. "Healing the Earth: The Relevance of Ian McHarg's Work for the Future." *Philosophy & Geography* 7(1):141–149.

Ann Forsyth. 2002. "Planning Lessons from Three U.S. New Towns of the 1960s and 1970s: Irvine, Columbia, and The Woodlands." *Journal of the American Planning Association* 68(4):387–417.

William J. Cohen. 2001. "Ian McHarg's Triumph." *Planning* 67(5, May):10–13.

James M. O'Neill. 2001. "Ian McHarg, 80, Penn Professor, Innovative Environmental Thinker." *The Philadelphia Inquirer* (March 7):B05.

Andrew C. Revkin. 2001. "Ian McHarg, 80, Architect Who Valued a Site's Natural Features." *New York Times* (March 12):A17.

Frederick Steiner. 2001. "Following Nature's Lead." *Landscape Architecture* 91(7, July):60–65, 96, 97.

Frederick Steiner. 2001. "Ian L. McHarg, 1920–2001." *Landscape Journal* 20(1):vi.

Kan Shulman. 2000. "The Gospel According to Ian McHarg." *Metropolis* (August–September):86–89, 103, 105.

Kan Shulman. 2000. "McHarg to Receive Japan Prize." *Gazette* 98(4):19.

Laughlin Fawcett. 1999. "Book Review of *To Heal the Earth.*" *Landscape Architecture* 89(1, January):83.

Herbert Gottfried. 1999. "Book Review of *To Heal the Earth.*" *Environmental History* 4(2):288–289.

Wendy A. Kellogg. 1999. "Book Review of *To Heal the Earth.*" *Journal of the American Planning Association* 65(3, Summer):335–336.

Marie McCullough. 1999. "Ecology Pioneer Is Honored." *The Philadelphia Inquirer* (December 18):A20.

Grady Clay. 1998. "The Woodlands." *Landscape Architecture* 88(9, September):131–132.

Karen Auerbach. 1997. "His Work Continues, Naturally." *The Philadelphia Inquirer* (April 20):B1, B6.

Jan Beyea. 1997. "Straight Talk: Reminiscences from the Father of Landscape Ecology." *Audubon Magazine* (May–June):113–116.

Gillian Darley. 1997. "Life in the Limelight." (Review of *A Quest for Life.*) *The Architectural Review* 202(1207, September):96.

Ruth Knack. 1997. "Utopia!" AICP Awards, Planning Landmarks and Pioneers. *Planning* (April):22–24.

E. Bruce MacDougall. 1997. "Book Review of *A Quest for Life.*" *Journal of the American Planning Association* 63(Spring, 2):301–302.

Michael Maynard. 1997. "McHarg's Visit Energizes Landscape Architects, Planners in Alaska." *Land* 37(7, July–August):1–2.

John Stuart-Murray. 1997. "Book Review of *A Quest for Life.*" *Landscape Design* 262(July–August):43.

Robert Yaro. 1997. "Book Review of *A Quest for Life: An Autobiography.*" *Urban Design Update*, Newsletter of the Institute for Urban Design 13(2, March–April):2–3.

Robert Campbell. 1996. "Book Review of *A Quest for Life.*" *Publishers Weekly* (March 25):75–76.

Robert Campbell. 1996. "Whose Dominion?" *New York Times* (May 5):20.

Julius G. Fabos. 1996. "Book Review of *A Quest for Life.*" *Landscape and Urban Planning* 36:79–83.

Françoise Fromonot. 1996. "Correction écologique." (Book review of 25th anniversary edition of *Design with Nature.*) *L'Architecture d'Aujourd'hui* 303 (February):24.

Lawrence Halprin. 1996. "Book Review of *A Quest for Life: An Autobiography.*" *The Quarterly Review of Landscape Architecture and Garden Design Publications. Land Books* (Winter):8.

Robert Hsin. 1996. "Review of *A Quest for Life.*" *edesign* 3(3, June):6.

Akiko Ishii. 1996. "Ian McHarg: Ecological Planning" (in Japanese). *BIO-City* (8, Spring):2–17.

Ruth Knack. 1996. "Book Review of *A Quest for Life: An Autobiography.*" *The Washington Post Book World* 26 (27, 7 July):13.

Ruth Knack. 1996. "An Optimist Views the World." *Planning* (May):13.

Sir Peter Shepheard. 1996. "Book Review of *A Quest for Life: An Autobiography.*" *The Quarterly Review of Landscape Architecture and Garden Design Publications. Land Books* (Winter):9.

Cynthia L. Girling. 1994. "The Marketing of Recreation and Nature: The Woodlands, Texas Revisited." In Robert G. Ribe, Robert Z. Melnick, and Kerry Ken Cairn, eds. *CELA 1993 Public Lands/scapes Proceedings of the 1993 Conference of the Council of Educators in Landscape Architecture.* Washington, D.C.: Landscape Architecture Foundation, pp. 43–56.

Richard Ingersoll. 1994. "L'Orizzonte perduto delle città nuove: The Woodlands e Almere nella vastità megalopolitana" ["The lost horizon of new towns: The Woodlands and Almere in the megalopolitan sprawl"]. *Casabella* 614:22–35. (English summary pages 70–71.)

David Salvesen. 1994. "The Woodlands, Special Award, The 1994 ULI Awards for Excellence." *Urban Land* 53(12):24.

Amedeo Petrilli. 1993. "Design with Nature [by] Ian L. McHarg" (book review). *Spazio e Società* 16(64, October–December):127–128.

Daniel S. Smith. 1993. "The Woodlands, Texas." In Daniel S. Smith and Paul Cawood Hellmund, eds. *Ecology of Greenways.* Minneapolis: University of Minnesota Press, pp. 196–202.

William Thompson. 1991. "A Natural Legacy: Ian McHarg and His Followers." *Planning* 57(11):14–19.

Laura Biondi. 1990. "Progettare con la Natura." *Casabella* 54(574, December):29.

Heidi Landecker. 1990. "In Search of an Arbiter." *Landscape Architecture* 80(1):86–90.

John Gilbert Widrick. 1990. "Ian McHarg." In Ann L. Strong and George E. Thomas, eds. *The Book of the School.* Philadelphia: Graduate School of Fine Arts, University of Pennsylvania, pp. 178–179.

Marshall Ledger. 1987. "On Getting the Lay of the Land." *The Pennsylvania Gazette* 85(4):30–36.

Joseph C. Dunstan. 1983. "*Design with Nature,* 14 Years Later." *Landscape Architecture* 73(1, January):59, 61.

Keith Croes. 1982. "Profile: Ian McHarg." *County Lines* 5(10, June):18–25.

Brenda J. Lee. 1982. "An Ecological Comparison of the McHarg Method with Other Planning Initiatives in the Great Lakes Basin." *Landscape Planning* 9:147–169.

Harvey Shapiro. 1979. "The Introduction of the McHargian Method to Japan." *Landscape Architecture* 69(6, November):575–577.

Constance Holden. 1977. "Ian McHarg: Champion for Design with Nature." *Science* 195(4276, 28 January):379–382.

Constance Holden. 1977. "Ian McHarg: Champion for Design with Nature." *Landscape Architecture* 67(2, March):154–156, 180.

Lewis D. Hopkins. 1977. "Methods for Generating Land Suitability Maps: A Comparative Evaluation." *Journal of the American Institute of Planners* 43(4): 386–400.

Yukihisa Isobe and Harvey A. Shapiro. 1977. "Ecological Planning: Its Method and Application, Part II, The Implications of Ecological Planning Regions for Land Use Policy Making and Planning in Japan" (special issue). *Kenchiku Bunka* 32(367, May):29–152 (in Japanese).

Yukihisa Isobe, Harvey A. Shapiro, and Teiji Ito. 1975. "Ecological Planning: Its Method and Application, Part I" (special issue). *Kenchiku Bunka* 30(344, June):47–136 (in Japanese).

Dennis Farney. 1974. "Land Politics." *The Atlantic Monthly* 233(1, January):10–17.

Andrew J. Gold. 1974. "Design with Nature: A Critique." *Journal of the American Institute of Planners* 40(4):284–286.

Andrew J. Gold. 1974. "Planner McHarg on Cities, Cars and Chicken Dung." *People Weekly* (April):48–51.

Irene Kiefer. 1972. "An Angry Advocate for Nature's Plans." *Smithsonian* 2(10, January):54–57.

David Streatfield. 1972. "Ideas into Landscape: Leaders Do Not Wait to Be Called." *Landscape Architecture* 62(2):148–151.

Jean-Paul Viguiar. 1972. "L'évaluation d'impact des décisions sur l'environnement: Trois approaches Américaines." *Urbanisme: Revue Française* 41(129):11–14.

Dennis Farney. 1971. "Father Nature." *The Wall Street Journal* 178(42, August):1.

Edmund Fuller. 1971. "McHarg: Seeking a Humane City." *The Wall Street Journal* (December 27):6.

Y. Isobe. 1971. "Leaders for Tomorrow's America: Ian L. McHarg, *Design with Nature.*" *Kenchiku Bunka* 26(291, January):149–166 (in Japanese).

Michael Laurie. 1971. "Notes on Professor Ian McHarg." *Edinburgh Architectural Association Yearbook* 15:97–103.

Michael Laurie. 1971. "Scoring McHarg: Low on Method, High on Values." *Landscape Architecture* 61:206, 248.

R. Burton Litton Jr. and Martin Kieieger. 1971. "Book Review of *Design with Nature.*" *Journal of the American Institute of Planners* 37(1):50–52.

Robert McClintock. 1971. "Book Review of *Design with Nature.*" *Main Currents in Modern Thought* 7:133–135.

Roger Barnard. 1970. "Man in Nature: On Ian McHarg." *Journal of the Royal Institute of Architects* 77(May):211–212.

Ursula Cliff. 1970. "Ian McHarg: The Designer as Ecologist." *Design and Environment* 1(2):28–32, 65.

Max Ways. 1970. "How to Think About the Environment." *Fortune* 81(2):98.

Ursula Cliff. 1969. "Environment—The Land: How to Design with Nature." *Time* 94(15, October 10):70–71.

Ursula Cliff. 1969. "Ian L. McHarg." *Parks & Recreation* 4(7, July):27–29.

Ursula Cliff. 1969. "Ian McHarg vs. Us Anthropocentric Clods." *Life* 67(7, August 15):48B–48D.

Raymond K. Belknap and John G. Furtado. 1968. "The Natural Land Unit as a Planning Base." *Landscape Architecture* 58(2):145–147.

Raymond K. Belknap and John G. Furtado. 1967. *Three Approaches to Environmental Resource Analysis.* Washington, D.C.: The Conservation Foundation.

Elizabeth B. Kassler. 1964. "Ian McHarg: Project for Town Center Park, South

West Washington, D.C. 1962." *Modern Gardens and the Landscape.* New York: The Museum of Modern Art.

Edward J. Milne. 1950. "Providence Tomorrow?" *The Rhode Islander Magazine (Providence Sunday Journal)* (June 11):1–6. (A review of Harvard graduate student plan for downtown Providence, Rhode Island. The team included Robert L. Geddes, William J. Conklin, Ian L. McHarg, and Marvin Sevely.)

Published Interviews and Panel Discussions

Kim A. O'Connell, ed. 1999. "The Profession in Memory." *Landscape Architecture* 89(11):164–169.

GIS World Interview. 1995. "Ian McHarg Reflects on the Past, Present and Future of GIS, 1995 GIS World Lifetime Achievement Award Winner." *GIS World* (October):46–48.

Louise Mozingo. 1995. "Ecologically Informed Designers, An Interview with Ian McHarg." *On the Ground* 1(2):1–4.

E. Lynn Miller and Sidónio Pardal. 1992. *The Classic McHarg, An Interview.* Lisbon, Portugal: CESUR, Technical University of Lisbon.

Michael Leccese. 1990. "At the Beginning, Looking Back." *Landscape Architecture* 80(10, October):92–97.

Cliff Ellis, ed. 1987–1988. "Ian McHarg on City Planning." *Berkeley Planning Journal* 3(2):34–55.

Larry Paul Fuller, ed. 1985. "The Land: America the Beautiful" (panel discussion including Ian McHarg). In *The Land, the City and the Human Spirit.* Austin: University of Texas, pp. 18–20.

Ed Hollander, ed. 1982. "An Interview with Ian McHarg." *Penn in Ink* (Spring):41–43.

Charles Blessing, Edmund N. Bacon, Oscar Newman, Ian McHarg, and George Ramsey. 1978. "Five Experts Describe Their Concept of the Ideal City." *Planning* 44(11, December):30–33.

MY (pseudonym, author's full name unknown). 1976. "What Do We Use for Lifeboats When the Ship Goes Down? Conversations with Robert Reiner, John Todd, Ian McHarg, Paolo Soleri, and Richard Saul Wurman." New York: Harper Colophone. Copyright held by "Observations from the Treadmill, RFD 1, Union, Maine 04862." Interview with McHarg is referred to as Lifeboat #3, pp. 99–120.

Urban Design Jury (Charles A. Blessing, M. Paul Friedberg, and Ian L. McHarg). 1972. "No Awards, No Citations." *Progressive Architecture* 53(January): 102–109.

Ian L. McHarg and Athelstan Spilhaus. 1970. "Two Views of the Environmental–Ecological Problems" (excerpts from talks at the Sixth Annual Architects and Engineers Forum in Los Angeles, April 14th, on "Cities in the 70s"). *Environmental Design: West* 1(4, August–September).

James Nathan Miller. 1970. "A Sensible Plan for Future Development." *Reader's*

Digest 97(580):77–81. Translated into Italian: "Evitiamo che il progresso distrugga l'ambiente." *Selezione del Reader's Digest* (October):35–39.

Ian L. McHarg and Athelstan Spilhaus. 1957. *Proceedings of the National Conference on Instruction in Landscape Architecture.* Asilomar, Pacific Grove, California (July 5–7).

Slide–Tape Presentation

Monica Pidgeon. 1984. *Ian McHarg, Ecological Planning.* London, England: Pidgeon Audio Visual.

Miscellaneous

Ann Forsyth. 2005. *Reforming Suburbia: The Planned Communities of Irvine, Columbia, and The Woodlands.* Berkeley: University of California Press.

Roger Galatas with Jim Barlow. 2004. *The Woodlands: The Inside Story of Creating a Better Hometown.* Washington, D.C.: The Urban Land Institute.

Mark Mao, Becky Ziebro, and Ann Patton. 2004. "Tulsa Turnaround: From Disaster to Sustainability." *Natural Hazards Review* 5(1, February):1–9.

Gerald F. Vaughn. 2004. "Sheffield's Richard P. Wakefield: Advocate for Human Values, World Futures, and the Environment." *Historical Journal of Massachusetts* 32(2):198–213.

David A. Wallace. 2004. *Urban Planning/My Way.* Chicago: APA Planners Press.

William John Cohen. 2003. *A Critical Assessment of Ian McHarg's Human Ecological Planning Curriculum at the University of Pennsylvania* (Ph.D. dissertation). Philadelphia: Department of City and Regional Planning, University of Pennsylvania.

Ann Forsyth. 2003. "Ian McHarg's Woodlands: A Second Look." *Planning* (August):10–13.

Ann Forsyth. 2002. "Planning Lessons from Three U.S. New Towns of the 1960s and 1970s: Irvine, Columbia, and The Woodlands." *Journal of the American Planning Association* 68(4):387–415.

Forster Ndubisi. 2002. *Ecological Planning: A Historical and Comparative Synthesis.* Baltimore, Maryland: Johns Hopkins University Press.

Michael Leccese. 1997. "Ship Shape." *Landscape Architecture* 87(7, September):34–39.

Harvey A. Shapiro. 1997. *Ecological Planning in East Asia: Its Past, Present and Future* (Doctor of Agriculture dissertation). Kyoto, Japan: Faculty of Agriculture.

Russell Clive Claus. 1994. *The Woodlands, Texas: A Retrospective Critique of the Principles and Implementation of an Ecological Planned Development* (Master of City Planning thesis). Cambridge: Department of Urban Studies and Planning, Massachusetts Institute of Technology.

Cynthia L. Girling and Kenneth I. Helphand. 1994. *Yard.Street.Park.* New York: Wiley. (The authors describe the planning of the Woodlands and its contribution to new community design.)

Richard Ingersoll. 1994. "Utopia Limited: Houston's Ring Around the Beltway." *Cite* 31 (Winter–Spring):10–16.

Peter Wood. 1994. "37,000 Woodlanders Can't Be Wrong." *Cite* 31 (Winter–Spring):17.

Peter Walker and Melanie Simo. 1994. *Invisible Gardens: The Search for Modernism in the American Landscape.* Cambridge, Massachusetts: MIT Press. (The authors include a chapter, "The Environment: Science Overshadows Art," in which McHarg's work is featured, and contributions by other leading landscape architects are mentioned briefly.)

James Bischoff. 1991. "From Barn to Royal Cottage: The Planning of Old Farms Forest—Devonwood, USA." *Ekistics* 58(346–347):97–109.

Ann L. Strong and George E. Thomas. 1990. *The Book of the School: 100 Years.* Philadelphia: Graduate School of Fine Arts, University of Pennsylvania.

Frederick Steiner, Gerald Young, and Ervin Zube. 1988. "Ecological Planning: Retrospect and Prospect." *Landscape Journal* 7(1):31–39.

Nao Hauser. 1987. "New Year's Dinner from a Country Kitchen." *Bon Appetit* 32(1):76–84.

George T. Morgan Jr. and John O. King. 1987. *The Woodlands: New Community Development, 1964–1983.* College Station: Texas A&M Press.

Philip Bedient, Alejandro Flores, Steven Johnson, and Plato Pappas. 1985. "Floodplain Storage and Land Use Analysis at the Woodlands, Texas." *Water Resources Bulletin* 21(4):543–551.

Department of Landscape Architecture and Regional Planning. 1985. *501 Course Primer.* Philadelphia: University of Pennsylvania.

Anne Whiston Spirn. 1984. *The Granite Garden. Urban Nature and Human Design.* New York: Basic Books. (Professor Spirn includes discussion about the Woodlands New Town. She was a participant in the planning and design of the Woodlands.)

Thomas Todd. 1984. "The Master Plan for Abuja, The New Federal Capital of Nigeria." In F. R. Steiner and H. N. van Lier, eds. *Land Conservation and Development: Examples of Land-Use Planning Projects and Programs.* Amsterdam: Elsevier, pp. 115–144.

Grady Clay. 1982. "On Baltimore's Inner Harbor." *Landscape Architecture* 72(6, November–December):48–53.

Simpson Lawson. 1982. "Baltimore Re-Examined." *AIA Journal* 71(13, November):56–63.

Arthur E. Palmer. 1981. *Toward Eden.* Winterville, North Carolina: Creative Resource Systems, Inc.

Narendra Juneja and James Veltman. 1980. "Natural Drainage in the Woodlands." In J. Toby Tourbier and Richard Westmacott, eds. *Stormwater Management Alternatives.* Newark: Water Resources Center, University of Delaware, pp. 143–157.

Noel Moffett. 1980. "Abuja: The Pros and Cons." *West African Technical Review* (July):94–99.

Noel Moffett. 1980. "Abuja: The City of the Future." *West African Technical Review* (June):68–69.

Noel Moffett. 1980. "Abuja: The City Plan." *West African Technical Review* (May):76–78.

Noel Moffett. 1980. "Abuja: The Regional Plan." *West African Technical Review* (March):116–120.

Thomas A. Todd. 1980. "Nigeria Plans Its New Capital." *Urban Design International* 1(2, January–February):12–17.

Ajose-Adedgun and Abubakar Koko. 1979. "Nigeria Builds Abuja in the Shadow of Aso Hill." *Architectural Record* 165(June):37.

Noel Moffett. 1978. "The Federal Capital City, Part Two." *West African Technical Review* (May):107–111.

Noel Moffett. 1978. "Nigeria's New Federal Capital City." *West African Technical Review* (April):109–113.

Boyd Gibbons. 1977. *Wye Island*. Baltimore, Maryland: Johns Hopkins University Press. (Boyd Gibbons describes the planning process for a new community on Wye Island, Maryland. The Wallace, McHarg, Roberts and Todd physical plan was directed by William Roberts for James Rouse.)

John Clark. 1976. *The Sanibel Report: Formulation of a Comprehensive Plan Based on Natural Systems*. Washington, D.C.: The Conservation Foundation. (John Clark describes the planning process for the Wallace, McHarg, Roberts and Todd plan directed by William Roberts.)

Grady Clay. 1974. "Radicalism Revisited in Wilmington and Dover, Vermont." *Landscape Architecture* 64(3, April):132.

Philip Morris. 1973. "The Southern Seacoast: Keeping Its Balance." *Southern Living* (March): 76–83, 103–104.

William H. Roberts and Jonathan Sutton. 1973. "Seeking the Right Environmental Fit for a New Resort Community at Amelia Island, Florida." *Landscape Architecture* 63(3, April):239–250.

Paul Beaver and Bernard L. Krause, composers. 1970. *In a Wild Sanctuary* (WB 1850; album dedicated to Ian McHarg and others). Burbank, California: Warner Brothers Records.

Walter Sullivan. 1970. "Computers: Probing Questions Too Tough for a Mere Brain." *New York Times* IV(December 6):12.

David A. Wallace, ed. 1970. *Metropolitan Open Space and Natural Process*. Philadelphia: University of Pennsylvania Press.

Department of Landscape Architecture and Regional Planning. 1968. "An Ecological Approach to Regional Planning." Philadelphia: Graduate School of Fine Arts, University of Pennsylvania.

William H. Whyte. 1968. *The Last Landscape*. Garden City, New York: Doubleday.

P/A Staff. 1967. "Ecology: Man Shapes His Environment." *P/A News Report* (September):51–55.

G. Holmes Perkins. 1960. *University of Pennsylvania, Graduate School of Fine Arts* (exhibition catalog of work of the school on the occasion of the American Institute of Architects' 1960 Convention in Philadelphia). Philadelphia: University of Pennsylvania.

John D. Black and Ayers Brinser. 1952. *Planning One Town, Petersham, a Hill Town in Massachusetts*. Cambridge, Massachusetts: Harvard University Press. (Based on a Harvard student studio project by Robert Barre, William Barton, Sanford Farness, Roscoe Jones, Donald Kimmel, George Kolinsky, Charles Lettek, Blanche Lemco, Ian McHarg, Vincent Oredson, Harold Taubin, Caleb Warner, and J. E. Zemanek.)

Bibliography Acknowledgments

Ed Deegan of the University of Pennsylvania Library provided valuable information about specific citations. Graduate students Paul Langdon and Michael Skinner of Arizona State University School of Planning and Landscape Architecture assisted with checking the accuracy of several citations and identified additional works. William Roberts was extremely helpful in providing details for the Wallace, McHarg, Roberts and Todd projects. Dennis C. McGlade, Leslie Sauer, Anne W. Spirn, Ann L. Strong, Michael G. Clarke, William Cohen, John Keene, Anthony Walmsley, Danilo Palazzo, E. Bruce MacDougall, Richard Westmacott, and James Bischoff also helped with specific information for several of the citations. Chris Duplissa word processed the many drafts of this bibliography, and I am most grateful for her attention to detail.

Acknowledgement of Sources

"Man and Environment." In Leonard J. Duhl and John Powell, eds. *The Urban Condition*. New York: Basic Books, pp.44–58 (1963).

"The Place of Nature in the City of Man." *The Annals of the American Academy of Political Science* (Urban Revival: Goals and Standards) 325 (March): 1–12 (1964).

"Ecological Determinism." In F. Fraser Darling and John P. Milton, eds. *Future Environments of North America*. Garden City, N.Y.: The Natural History Press, pp. 526–38 (1966). From *Future Environments of North America* by Fraser Darling and John P. Milton. Copyright © 1966 by the Conservation Foundation. Used by permission of Doubleday, a division of Bantam Doubleday Dell Publishing Group, Inc.

"Values, Process and Form." In The Smithsonian Institution. *The Fitness of Man's Environment*. New York: Harper & Row, pp.207–27 (1968). Used by permission of the publisher.

"Natural Factors in Planning." *Journal of Soil & Water Conservation* 52 (1, January-February): 13–17 (1997).

"Open Space from Natural Processes." In David A. Wallace, ed. *Metropolitan Open Space and Natural Processes*. Philadelphia: University of Pennsylvania Press, pp. 10-52 (1970). From *Metropolitan Open Space and Natural Process*, edited by David A. Wallace. Copyright © by the University of Pennsylvania Press. Reprinted with permission of the publisher.

"Ecological Planning: The Planner as Catalyst." In Robert W. Burchell and George Sternlieb, eds. *Planning Theory in the 1980s* (2nd edition, 1982). New Brunswick, N.J.: The Center for Urban Policy Research, Rutgers University, pp. 13–15 (1978). Reprinted with permission of Rutgers University, Center for Urban Policy Research, from *Planning Theory in the 1980s: A Search for Future Directions*, edited by Robert W. Burchell and George Sternlieb. Copyright © 1978 Rutgers University.

"Human Ecological Planning at Pennsylvania" Landscape Planning 8:109–120 (1981).

"Ecology and Design." In George F. Thompson and Fredrick R. Steiner, eds. *Ecological Design and Planning*. New York: Wiley, pp.321–32 (1996). Copyright © 1996. Reprinted by permission of John Wiley & Sons, Inc.

"An Ecological Method for Landscape Architecture." *Landscape Architecture* 57 (2): 105–7 (1967).

Index